MOBILE
UNLEASHED

The Origin and Evolution of
ARM Processors in Our Devices

Daniel Nenni

Don Dingee

Foreword by Sir Robin Saxby

Published by SemiWiki LLC
Danville, CA

Although the authors and publisher have made every effort to ensure the accuracy and completeness of information contained in this book, we assume no responsibility for errors, inaccuracies, omissions, or any inconsistency herein.

ISBN: 1519547269

First printing: December 2015
Printed in the United States of America

Edited by: Shushana Nenni

Contents

Foreword

"If you're not making any mistakes, you're not trying hard enough." I've been quoted as saying that in an interview some years ago and when you find yourself defining a new industry, as we did, you try very hard and you make a lot of mistakes. The key is to make the mistakes only once, learn from them and move on.

ARM, in one way, originated from a failure of mine. While at Motorola, I tried to sell the 68000 to Acorn for their next generation of personal computer. I failed, as did several others, and the result was Acorn taking that bold decision to design their own processor. The story of what happened to Acorn, to that processor, and to the company that eventually took ownership of it is well told in "Mobile Unleashed".

In the early days, it often seemed that we were never very far from failure. We had great technology, which had already been proven, but which was not ready for the mass market. We worked very hard to build an open culture and assemble a talented team by hiring very carefully and extending equity ownership to every employee from the start. We also bet everything on assembling a worldwide customer base, creating a global standard with companies who traditionally competed with each other, molding them into a partnership, pulling in the same direction, and united around one architecture that evolved over time. This unique combination made us into a force much larger than the sum of the parts. It was thanks to all those involved that ARM succeeded including people at every level in partner companies, staff from ARM's global offices, and the end customers of our partners. Their efforts contributed as much to ARM's success as did the ARM founders and technology originating in Cambridge.

I may no longer work for ARM but I am still a shareholder and am delighted that people I hired, Warren East and his successor Simon Segars, have continued to lead the exciting journey we started. I take great interest in seeing the proliferation of ARM's technology in more and more of the products I use every day and expect that process to continue.

We have waited over two decades for someone to tell this story and reading this book reminds me of the sheer hard work that went into bringing it off. But it is also a tribute to the groundbreaking technology we designed, the group of incredibly talented people who made it happen, and the satisfaction of knowing that a small group in a barn just outside Cambridge dared to entertain a vision of becoming a world standard - and succeeded. I'm delighted to have made my contribution. We worked together in teams across multiple companies from different backgrounds and cultures very effectively. Part of that success comes from an ability to be brutally honest with each other.

ARM is still a young company and perhaps in 25 years' time one of my successors will write the foreword to the next chapter.

Sir Robin Saxby, November 2015

Prologue

How does a company go from a crazy idea a couple of engineers had for designing a processor from scratch to power a "business computer," to being the maker of the family of processor cores at the heart of roughly 95% of the world's mobile phones today?

At the dawn of the ARM architecture, the project was a tightly kept secret in a few technologist's hands at Acorn Computer Group. It was so secret that Olivetti, a firm at that time in the process of shifting its fortunes from typewriters to computers, was not aware of the existence of the chip design or its development team until after an investment stake in Acorn became final.[1]

What Acorn had was a processor quite unlike any other of the period – but that was far from all. They established a reduced instruction set for machine-level programming most users never see, software development tools for using it, and the concept of a customized processor core for independent fabrication.

Challenging the Mainstream

Given that breakthrough, one would think Acorn could have taken the world by storm right out of the gate. However, in the mid to late 1980s, the scene was far from ready for an alternative to the mainstream chips.

Intel was building its empire on the processors that throbbed inside nearly every personal computer. Semiconductors came from Silicon Valley, designed in big, expensive buildings – not in rustic barns near Cambridge, UK. Parts were typically complex, huge, costly, and hot. Being the fastest gun in town, and staying that way, was priority number one under Moore's Law.

The source of popular software was Redmond, Washington, and anything incompatible with Microsoft was unable to survive for long. A thriving flock of personal computer companies found out the hard way that PC compatibility was the only thing people cared about, or asked for. If a processor could not run MS-DOS, Lotus 1-2-3, Word Perfect, and Turbo Pascal, what good was it?

Those forces left even the now mighty Apple dangerously near bankruptcy at one point after initial success with the Apple II. The comeback was in progress; their latest innovation was the Macintosh, built on a Motorola processor and a graphical user interface (GUI) that introduced the mouse to millions of people. It was just different enough to hang on pitted against a wide row of function keys and never-ending combinations of ALT, CRTL, and SHIFT codes on the other side.

Coincidentally, those two companies – Apple and Motorola – running on separate tracks in the early 1990s paved the way for ARM to rise from the relative obscurity and limited volumes of Acorn.

Research on computing alternatives had been underway at Apple for some time, spawned in part by a leadership change from Steve Jobs rev 1.0 to John Sculley. The objective: break off from the desktop and into handheld platforms then known by the clunky category name of "personal digital assistant." The first Apple PDA project was Newton, and along the way, they reached out to Acorn for an ARM core.

Meanwhile, Motorola led the way to the height of the analog cellular telephone sensation. As phones evolved from analog to digital, one key to reducing size and bill of materials cost became digital signal processing (DSP). In a twist of fate, seeking to diversify business and not compete with customers for capacity, Motorola did not leverage their own semiconductor parts. Instead, as the digital handset revolution took shape they opted mostly for popular DSP chips from Texas Instruments – as had Ericsson, Nokia, and others.

More Than a Cool Idea

Those Apple and Motorola tracks may seem completely separate, but they collided head on in digital mobile devices. Microprocessors were too big and power hungry, and microcontrollers were too slow. Code such as multitasking operating systems, wireless communication stacks, and handwriting recognition – once thought to be the killer application for PDAs – sucked the life out of most CPU architectures.

A dire need was developing for a more optimized but fast processor core, and better integration with lower power DSP capability for handling wireless signals.

With a complex instruction set, or CISC, changing anything to improve performance risked mangling instructions, and breaking software. Motorola would enjoy early success in PDAs with their scaled-down part, the MC68328 DragonBall, winning designs such as the original Palm Pilot. Intel and their X86-compatible ecosystem had initial device wins at IBM, Research In Motion, and Nokia. Both CISC processors found themselves displaced as alternatives emerged.

Long before Steve Jobs rev 2.0 returned and eventually defined the post-PC era, Apple saw greater potential for the ARM architecture. With the Acorn development team and their fab partner VLSI Technology, Apple helped form a joint venture in 1990: Advanced RISC Machines, Ltd. One brand was born, and another remade, ushering in sweeping change in mobile device leadership.

If ARM had been just another company with a cool idea for an embedded processor core, there would not be much more to add to the history – one that others have visited numerous times. Covering ARM from its stealthy origins as a few determined, creative people inside Acorn to today with over 60 billion processor cores shipped and counting is inspiring, but not the whole story.[2]

In this book, we explore the origin story of ARM from an industry perspective, and the evolution of its processor technology that unleashed mobile devices.

Once the Acorn and Apple teams joined forces, sharing their early parallel experience that we open this book with, the bond between mobile devices and the ARM architecture formed. That bond is now nearly unassailable despite massive investments from competitors, mostly because its basis is more than a semiconductor company designing and selling parts to a segment of customers.

An entire ecosystem, in many ways more diverse and more powerful than the impressive PC community, has developed around the combination of mobile and ARM. It reaches across the entire supply chain, from EDA firms, foundries, semiconductor companies, software companies, mobile device manufacturers, carriers, application developers, and makers, who have rather recently joined in.

We will look at not just the processors and phones and tablets and other devices, but the business of mobile as it evolved along the lines drawn by each successive generation of ARM technology. We will have insights on the obvious names – Apple, Google, Qualcomm, and Samsung among them – and some not so prominent ones that played important roles building up to today. Perhaps most fun, we will wrap up with brief analysis on where we see this going in the future.

A journey of billions of processors and beyond begins with a single step. Now, we go back to the beginning of ARM, which on the surface had nothing to do with mobile but everything to do with creating a better processor core.

Part I: ORIGIN

Chapter 1: RISC-y Business

The year was 1983 and the economics of technology were booming.

In perhaps the second most important development of the year, commercial mobile devices were just materializing. After 10 years of incubation, Marty Cooper and his team obtained FCC approval for the Motorola DynaTAC 8000X. That behemoth weighed in at 794g, lasted an entire 30 minutes of talk time, and set users back almost $4K at launch. For now, mobile was for the rich and famous.[3]

Computers for Everyone

On a shorter trajectory, and grabbing more press and converts daily, was the personal computer. A gaggle of home-use machines had been out for a few years – with Acorn Computer, Apple, Atari, Commodore, Sinclair, Tandy, and Texas Instruments among the nameplates. IBM had hit both Wall Street and Main Street, with their revered brand and a machine powerful enough for business use.

The combination of Microsoft MS-DOS and the Intel 8088 had set the benchmark for the entire PC industry. In technology, if the first product is a home run, the expectations for the second at-bat become enormous. IBM was now looking beyond the 8088 microprocessor (with its 16-bit internal, 8-bit external architecture) cranked at 4.77 MHz, for its next launch.

Wintel, the informal software/hardware consortium that gathered around Intel and Microsoft, was not in control just yet. What was in place was a sweetheart deal between IBM and Intel. It granted favorable pricing on the processor and peripherals, a second source provision with AMD, and later would add a contingency for IBM to manufacture parts if necessary.[4]

Competitively, what everyone was seeing was the sort-of-32-bit but mostly 16-bit internal, 16-bit external Motorola 68000, then clocked up to 12.5 MHz. IBM had briefly considered the 68000 before launching the first PC, opting for the 8088 instead. Getting more performance from Intel was becoming urgent for IBM.

On the horizon, clouds were gathering. A fledgling company, Sun Microsystems, had launched their first "workstation" running a UNIX variant on the 68000. Apple was using the 68000 in the expensive but innovative Lisa with its GUI and there were rumors of another machine soon to debut in 1984.

Having reached a defining moment, Intel faced the possibility of losing their leadership position almost as quickly as they had established it. The 80286 microprocessor launched in 1982. It offered a full 16-bit architecture internally and externally, sans the address-data multiplexing of the 8088. By Intel's admission, most of the technology world did not see the new part as a massive leap, but as just an incremental improvement over the 8086.

Reversal of Fortunes

The marketing machine at Intel went to work, conceiving the "Checkmate" initiative – and hit the road to tell their story in over 200 cities reaching over 20,000 engineers. They went to IBM, to Microsoft, and to new companies just joining the scene with names like AST Research and Compaq who were producing clones that could run the exact same software.[5]

Intel seized on the "exact same software" idea to build their core storyline, but added an innovative twist. Their pitch would turn a situation that, according to Intel marketing execs, was "three or four to one in favor of Motorola" to a complete reversal in favor of Intel. Winning back designers secured their advantage in personal computing, and they would never give it up again.

The lede of their story was a huge computational performance increase without any software changes. The 80286 also had a 12.5 MHz clock, along with improved pipelining, and highly flexible and fast addressing modes. They also had a roadmap to the 32-bit 80386, retaining code compatibility with further gains in speed for users.

For the first time, people were talking in terms of millions of instructions per second (MIPS) and instructions per clock cycle as metrics. The Whetstone benchmark for floating-point computation was popular, and the industry standard benchmark Dhrystone for

2

measuring integer performance was about to debut. The dark art of benchmarking was about to take center stage, playing a huge role in selection and evolution of microprocessors.

An example of competitive benchmarking took shape around the first of two big advantages in Intel's favor. When it came to string manipulation, Intel had instructions and hardware support better than alternatives. Business users wowed at the ability to type in textual data and automatically filter, search, and sort it quickly. The power was evident in popular applications like spreadsheets, word processors, and database management tools.

The second advantage was a stroke of competitive genius. Intel had integrated a potent new feature on the 80286: a memory management unit, addressing not only more RAM but enabling protected mode operation. Therein was the twist IBM, Microsoft, and others were looking for – and a wrinkle that gave Motorola a severe case of heartburn.

Motorola had an external MMU for the 68000, but it was slow. Sun took one look at it, and designed their own MMU hardware for the Sun 1. By integrating an MMU on chip starting with the 80286, Intel reduced system cost, improved external bus bandwidth, and made it easier for designers to use the feature. It was a complex feat of engineering, and it would pay off handsomely.

Protected mode would enable multi-user, multi-tasking operating systems like UNIX to run on 80286 hardware. Microsoft had a license for Xenix from AT&T, and they were just waiting for a platform it could run on effectively. With an MMU on chip, a single hardware platform could now serve the needs of both personal users running MS-DOS and departments running Xenix.

The battle for the processor socket in IBM compatible personal computers was effectively over, but the war for future microprocessor architecture was just starting.

In the microprocessor business, architecture is only part of the equation. The 80286 and the 68000 were the best available choices in 1983, but not solely based on technology. Success also depends on

3

being able to produce large, sophisticated parts cheaply and in volume. It also depends on portraying and executing a roadmap, something both camps did well for the years that followed.

There were other parts out there. Firms like National Semiconductor, Texas Instruments, and Zilog were able to scale their popular 8-bit microprocessors up to 16- and eventually 32-bit. Even so, they found themselves unable to compete on a broader scale beyond embedded applications. While they usually lack gigantic volumes of their personal computing counterparts, embedded design wins can be lucrative with longer life cycles and less pricing pressure.

Image 1-1: Sophie Wilson, Chris Turner, Steve Furber, Chris Serle, Hermann Hauser, Christopher Curry at the BBC Micro 30th anniversary in 2012

Photo credit: Trevor Johnson, under Creative Commons Attribution-Share Alike 2.0 Generic license, https://creativecommons.org/licenses/by-sa/2.0/legalcode

On that backdrop, we now inquire about what we see as the most important technological development of 1983, one that would in time free mobile from the "brick". Why, in the midst of all this, would anyone consider jumping in and designing yet another 32-bit microprocessor architecture? On the market since the end of 1981, the BBC Micro was the pride and joy of Acorn Computers, about to become the birthplace of just such an effort.

Fast, for an 8-bit Machine

Designed to spread computer literacy in the UK and backed by the British Broadcasting Corporation (thus the name BBC Micro), Acorn had based it and several other successful designs on the venerable MOS Technology 6502. This was the same microprocessor found in the Apple II, Atari, and Commodore 64.[6]

An 8-bit engine with a 16-bit address bus, the 6502 was fabbed in 8 micron, packaged in a 40-pin DIP, and clocked at 1 or 2 MHz. Its design team, led by Chuck Peddle, defected from Motorola to form MOS Technology with the idea of making an improved 6800, compatible with existing peripheral chips.[7]

One might ask what an improved 6800, with many concepts that carried over into the 68000, meant. The overriding goal of the MOS Technology design circa 1975 was reduced die size, wiping out unnecessary portions of circuitry and redesigning others for efficiency. Fewer transistors, precious in 8-bit designs, meant more parts on a wafer, better yields, and lower costs.

By streamlining the state machine with more clock-free stages and avoiding microcode by using hardwired logic, the 6502 designers created a core that could execute instructions in half the clock cycles of other designs. A slower external clock speed also meant less expensive memory and peripherals, further reducing system cost.

Also important was the idea of interrupt handling and context switching where a minimal register set is vital. The 6502 used six to be exact: accumulator, two index, status, stack pointer, and program counter. It also implemented a "zero page," a concept borrowed from Digital Equipment Corporation and the PDP-8 architecture. This provided direct access to 256 bytes with an 8-bit address skipping a high-order address byte.

The 6502 was fast for an 8-bit machine, inexpensive, and critical to Commodore – so much so, they bought MOS Technology when Texas Instruments all but cornered the calculator IC business, nearly driving MOS insolvent. While that and second sources for the 6502 stabilized supply, the acquisition doomed timely progress on the architectural roadmap.

Chip designer Bill Mensch lost interest post-acquisition and defected again, forming the one-man Western Design Center and creating an errata-reduced version of the 6502. In 1983 when Acorn visited his office, he was working a 16-bit upgrade called the 65816 – but there was no 32-bit enhancement on the drawing board. 6502 enthusiasts would only take on a 32-bit redesign many years later.

Without 32-bit or an MMU on the near-term roadmap, personal computer vendors were fleeing the 6502. Acorn had been pondering another direction, in fact several, for some time.

To speed up the BBC Micro, Acorn had a created expansion strategy to add a second processor: Tube, a loosely coupled asynchronous message-passing interface and host protocol. Tube used an ASIC to create several FIFO buffers that isolated the co-processor from the host, meaning each could run much more independently while exchanging data via DMA.[8]

Just about any CPU that could fit on a card could be wedged in a Tube slot. The most obvious starting point for a second processor was a 6502, followed quickly by a Zilog Z80 to run CP/M. Then, just for grins, Acorn created a Tube experiment with an 80286 – and the results were underwhelming.

It was a poorly kept secret that if one wanted to tie an 80286 in knots, the best way was to hit it with a lot of interrupts, especially external hardware interrupts. The 68000 was better which is why real-time operating system developers generally favored it and avoided the 80286. Nevertheless, even the 68000 was still prone to run away with lengthy, uninterruptible instructions in some worst-case situations.

The Tube protocol hammered those interrupts, and exposed poor data movement capability. Benchmarking found neither of the major processors nearly as efficient as the 6502 and its small register set, plus Acorn's highly tuned machine code and BASIC interpreter. With their ancient 8-bit machine outrunning 16-bit and partial-32-bit parts, Acorn engineering teams led by Sophie Wilson and Steve Furber became convinced that their next solution had to be full 32-bit.[9]

Scanning the field with that in mind turned up the National 32016, with a smallish set of 15 registers and a full 32-bit instruction set with a 16-bit external bus. It was faster, but still too slow as a Tube second processor, with similar issues of long interrupt-proof instructions and limited memory bandwidth.

If You Can't Join Them ...

With the oncoming requirements of high-level programming languages, graphical games and user interfaces, and multi-user operating systems, nothing on the market was providing the type of performance breakthrough Acorn was looking for. Word was starting to spread on something big brewing in the Bay Area. Reduced Instruction Set Computing, or RISC, was about to disrupt the entire microprocessor landscape.

Berkeley RISC – the direct forerunner of what would become Sun SPARC, and inspiration for the Intel i960 and AMD 29000 – and the MIPS effort at Stanford had both begun under the DARPA VLSI Program. The RISC concept profiled what instructions were actually used by complex software like UNIX, ripping out complexity and transistors needed for any instruction rarely required.[10]

A redesigned RISC instruction set focused on load/store operations and simpler addressing made for a much more efficient 32-bit pipeline. Registers were a subject of controversy, and the two approaches diverged somewhat. MIPS took the path of many fast registers, while Berkeley RISC went with a register window approach, dedicating multiple blocks of smaller register sets with only one set visible in each procedure.

Redesigned compilers for each architecture, which understood how to translate code for the pipeline and registers efficiently, took over from there. The resulting software simulations were stunning and, after some gnashing to map these new architectures onto transistors, so were the potential die savings.

The Berkeley RISC-I circa 1982 was 44,500 transistors, compared to the 80286 weighing in at a hefty 134,000, and the 68000 somewhere near 68,000. That would presumably translate to power consumption savings as well but Sequin and Patterson never mention "watts" in their RISC-I disclosure. An 80286 was around 3W, and a 68000 around 1.4W – both were headed the wrong direction in transistor count and power as their roadmaps unfolded.

RISC was looking like a fantastic idea, but not a solution that Acorn or anyone else could lay their hands on easily. Neither Berkeley RISC, nor MIPS, nor a litany of other RISC architectures soon to debut had chips available for sale in 1983. None of them were a sure bet given the dynamics of adoption cycles and the details of manufacturing and software support.

The experience of the visit to the Western Design Center had left two impressions with Wilson and Furber. The first was the 6502 line had served its purpose and its successor, the 65816, was not a big enough reach given what was happening with RISC. The second was a far more important observation. Instead of using a huge team with expensive CAD equipment, Mensch was doing his design on an Apple II mostly by himself with only a couple of interns.

As Furber put it coolly: "Well, if they can design a microprocessor, so can we."[11]

ARM1: A Chip is Born

Acorn knew what did not work; next was to build a road for something that did. The map was marked with intimate knowledge of the 6502, the benchmarking experience, and the Berkeley RISC concept.

Wilson used all that, working on a simulator of a new, unnamed 32-bit RISC instruction set in BASIC. Its focus was load/store operations where data processing instructions acted only on registers with most instructions executing in a single cycle. Running the simulator on a

6502 in a Tube slot of a BBC Micro was more than enough to illustrate the potential.

With all that in the mélange, the decision Acorn was about to undertake doesn't sound so crazy after all. Furber and Wilson, along with Andy Hopper of the Cambridge Computer Lab who had dropped the RISC bug in their ear, were scheming their next move. They had been in constant dialog sharing all these ideas with Hermann Hauser, co-founder of Acorn. All agreed the time was right; the formal Acorn RISC Machine project launched in October 1983.[12]

With a new RISC instruction set mostly in hand, the team set off on designing a processor to run it, and getting that processor built by some entity. The EDA industry was in its infancy and there were no foundry-agnostic toolsets or IP libraries; the process of chip design and fabrication were inextricable. Selecting a design partner for the processor would make or break the project.

Acorn had enough experience with chipsets, like the Tube ULA built by Ferranti, to know they needed some help. VLSI Technology was making a name as an ASIC company, with several parts in the IBM PC, and already supplying some parts to Acorn. They had a design flow with cell-based routing, and a fab.

Hopper persuaded Hauser to jump in, on the basis the computer company of the future would have to know how to design chips. Acorn recruited a compact team of chip designers, led by Robert Heaton, featuring names like Jamie Urquhart, Dave Howard, and Harry Oldham. They dug into the VLSI Technology software tools – installed on-site by none other than Paul McLellan of SemiWiki blogging fame – running on Apollo workstations, and were ready to go.

From formal inception, it took about one year to design the microprocessor from scratch. There were prevailing concerns that huge companies with vast resources would spin complex chips repeatedly, typically five to ten times, before getting them right. Acorn could ill afford that path. RISC changed the equation, simplifying the task of processor design.

Simplicity had another dramatic impact. The design that Furber, Wilson, and the team created had 25,000 transistors as handed off to VLSI Technology in September 1984. As Wilson later described, "MIPS for the masses" had been the rallying cry, and power efficiency was a somewhat accidental side effect in the first instantiation. It would prove to be a much bigger revelation soon enough.

The wait after handoff must have been agonizing knowing that if everything went right something magical could happen that would transform Acorn. VLSI Technology delivered samples from their 3 micron fab in April 1985 to what, by all accounts, was a very excited Acorn team.

On April 26, 1985, a 6 MHz ARM1 chip powered up for the very first time – and ran the entire instruction set flawlessly, something unimaginable for that era. By comparison, Berkeley RISC-I suffered four restarts indicating the degree of difficulty with tools, verification, and handoff.

Image 1-2: ARM1 processor on evaluation board, circa 1985

Photo credit: cropped still image from "The first ARM processor in the world with Sophie Wilson (Part 2)", ARMdevices.net, YouTube, https://www.youtube.com/watch?v=re5xAqgKqc0

Furber related that even he was surprised at the results. Wilson tells a story that the ARM1 sample did not power down properly once during some testing. They soon discovered they had forgotten to connect the power supply – the chip ran on leakage from I/O pins.[13]

After a couple months of testing the ARM1, they decided to tell the world. Furber called a tech reporter on one day in July 1985, saying Acorn had been working on a new microprocessor design and had it working. The reporter's response, "I don't believe you. If you'd been doing this, I'd have known," hanging up with irritation.

For the time being, the secret of the ARM1 processor was safe and the journey just underway.

Chapter 2: Working it Out

If the annals of technology innovation have taught us anything, it is that the best technology does not always win – right away, or sometimes at all. With marketing superiority on its side, a good product can suppress a great one without enough reach.

Even with a remarkable accomplishment like the ARM1 design to its credit, Acorn was still very short on reach. Competing not as a PC company but as a semiconductor design firm selling microprocessors would require very different skills. As Intel "Checkmate" had demonstrated, larger, better known brands with marketing clout could easily overwhelm others vying to compete on their turf.

Olivetti Rides Into Town

For ARM technology to survive past infancy, Acorn would first need to save itself by drastic measures then redefine how they would compete.

Despite the popularity of the BBC Micro, in 1985 Acorn found itself awash in inventory and red ink as creditors lurked. Olivetti came to the rescue, and with its successive rounds of cash infusion averted an immediate financial crisis. After some organizational and financial cleanup, it became clear an all-new product was required beyond the stopgap BBC Master in development.[14]

Both Carlo de Benedetti, Chairman of Olivetti, and Hermann Hauser of Acorn had their eyes on the same target: business computers. Businesses were where the big money was. IBM was enjoying huge success building personal computers dressed in gray flannel suits, not toys designed for games.

Up until the arrival of the IBM PC, most personal computers targeted home and enthusiast use. Many were "wedge" designs, with a keyboard built into the CPU base. Peripherals were external. Tape or floppy drives were in their own shoebox-like cases, and often a portable TV served as the display. Software predominantly locked into brands, with little to no portability between machines.

IBM stood in stark contrast, with machines serious about business. Its most advanced machine entering 1985 was the System Unit 5170, better known as the PC AT, with the Intel 80286 inside. Microsoft MS-DOS 3.0 and a spate of business titles took advantage of the increased processing power, and offered the allure of software investment protection across compatible machines.

Following their established formula, the IBM base unit contained the motherboard, power supply, and floppy drives in one case. A large CRT sat on top, displaying primitive character graphics in shades of green. A roomy keyboard, which was descended from a generation of legendary IBM data entry terminals, completed the hardware.

Renegades had other ideas, more like business casual. A big trend was the luggable, a design pioneered by Kaypro and Osborne and taken to the next level by Compaq. These were suitcase-sized, with motherboard, power supply, floppy drives, and a small CRT all in one box, and a keyboard usually in a detachable cover. They could be set up in conference rooms, placed near scientific instrumentation, or even taken into the field where AC power was available.

Acorn had conceived its first business foray in late 1983, dressing up the BBC Micro into the ill-fated Acorn Business Computer (ABC). It featured a unified enclosure with a full-size green phosphor monitor, motherboard, power supply, and floppy drives, augmented by a separate keyboard.

While the look was a departure, the architecture of the ABC borrowed directly from the BBC Micro. It packed a 6502 mainboard and one of several Tube second processors productized from the experiments leading up to ARM1. The most successful of the ABC variants was the Cambridge Workstation with a 32016 hanging around in second chair.

Market timing is everything. Shortly after Acorn's ABC announcement the Apple Macintosh debuted with a similar unified design metaphor but with a more dramatic execution. It was mouse operated, featuring a GUI on a high-resolution grayscale CRT with pixel graphics that shamed monitors found on most other computers. (High-resolution displays are in Apple's DNA.)

The Macintosh was small, portable, and powerful. Its molded plastic case, adorned with signatures of the design team on the interior, contributed to its uniqueness. So did its software, incompatible with anything, which slowed its acceptance in businesses. In the workplace, the original Mac was mostly a novelty, used to draw diagrams or create presentation visuals.

Where the Mac gained more initial success was for educational use, with young minds finding self-expression through intuitive click and drag. Heavily discounted Macs found popularity among university students and staff, and leveraged a growing PC counter-culture among creatives. The groundbreaking design had definitely turned heads across the industry. It also hit Acorn right where they had made the most headway to date.

Pinched between the Mac on one side and the PC-compatible juggernaut gearing up for the newly announced Intel 80386 on the other, the ABC was doomed as soon as it debuted. Acorn all but withdrew it from the market.

Meanwhile, Acorn was adjusting to life as part of Olivetti. The major premise of the deal that made it attractive to Acorn, besides the badly needed cash, was access to Olivetti's global channels to extend Acorn's reach. Having a channel and being able to use it effectively are two very different things.

Fixated on competing with IBM, de Benedetti had issued instructions to his sales force not to sell anything except IBM compatibles. The Acorn product line was decidedly not IBM compatible, nor would it be. That proclamation left the BBC Master drifting as a result with only moderate sales.

How to Dabble in Business Computers

It was becoming clear Olivetti was little to no help beyond stalling creditors. With not much to sell, Acorn inventory and liabilities continued to pile up. Chris Curry, co-founder of Acorn, later lamented in an interview:

"After that reality became known, we should have sued [Olivetti] because they breached the contract. But, of course, we didn't behave like that, and afterwards Olivetti exercised its right to take 75% of the company and put in their own controlling management and gradually shut the place down, completely destroying everything that was there."[15]

Not quite everything, fortunately.

Acorn had ARM technology that could compete in business computers, at least in theory. Olivetti was completely oblivious to the potential. It is easy to assume they wore blinders, focused on an all-out pursuit of IBM. Let us give them credit for some insight and factor in what else was happening in the industry.

ARM1 was certainly fast, but not ready for prime time. Acorn finally briefed Olivetti on the technology. What they saw probably seemed like little more than an engineering prototype – certainly not a PC or Mac killer in waiting. The ARM1 as a second processor on a Tube card shackled to its BBC-era 6502 host was far from a sleekly packaged business computer system.

Perhaps more of a concern was Acorn MOS: the homegrown, character mode, single-tasking operating system. Acorn developers and customers were used to it, but the rest of the world was expecting more. Olivetti was in PC mode, focused on Microsoft operating systems. In turn, Olivetti was beholden to its major investor AT&T who had their own operating system.[16]

Any advanced operating system for 32-bit machines would naturally draw comparisons to AT&T's brainchild, UNIX, or to the Mac Finder and similar GUI platforms derived from Xerox PARC research. To succeed in business computers, the ARM architecture would definitely need a powerful, native, multi-tasking OS.

However, Acorn was facing a lot more than just designing a new machine and operating system around the ARM processor. Several other threads of activity were retracing the boundaries of computers in the mid-1980s.

IBM was mulling a course change. The prevailing versions of Microsoft MS-DOS and the IBM PC AT supported 16-bit data and 20-bit addressing for so-called "real mode" operation. PC compatibility had strong benefits, but the blade was cutting both ways. IBM began to rethink their systems approach, in the name of fostering innovation and bolstering profits, starting with their operating system.

OS/2 was initially a joint venture between IBM and Microsoft. In short, it established a multi-tasking model, took advantage of the new 80286 protected mode, and changed much of how the underlying BIOS worked. It was still able to run MS-DOS programs for compatibility. Soon to come was a GUI called Presentation Manager. OS/2 targeted a new machine: the Personal System/2, cast even more deeply in the IBM business attire.[17]

Microsoft was off working in parallel on Windows, which would put a GUI on MS-DOS. After its maiden voyage in 1985, its first real success would be the next release accompanied by point-and-click versions of Excel and Word. Even so, it would be years and more releases before Windows would have a major impact on the industry. OS/2, while arguably better at the onset, would ultimately fall victim to the Microsoft marketing machine.

It's Not Easy Being Different

Others were discovering just how tough competing with IBM was. Only a few weeks before the ARM1 first silicon arrived at Acorn the recently high-flying Apple found itself in a nosedive. Sales of the Mac through its first year were disappointing, at less than a tenth of expectations. Blame was making the rounds as the stock price plummeted to a historical low.

Once fast friends, Steve Jobs and his handpicked marketing guru John Sculley had turned to mortal combat. Frustrations and disagreements were increasing. Fed up with each other, they both approached the Apple board of directors. Each made a case that the other be relieved of his duties.

Like many technologists, Jobs was too close to the prodigy he birthed and raised. He thought the problems with sales of the Macintosh 512K were simple: pricing and advertising. The Macintosh Office concept placed Apple in the printer business with a networked LaserWriter supporting Adobe PostScript. Desktop publishing had debuted with a release of Aldus PageMaker.

Sculley understood the problems were deeper, having to do with a "toy" still too personal, not business enough, and lacking compatibility to compete head on with IBM and their ecosystem. Apple II was long in the tooth, new Mac product schedules were slipping, and inventory was growing. There were already enough questions about Jobs and his temperament, his willingness and ability to manage cash flow and budgets and schedules, and perceptions of Apple on Wall Street.

Mike Markkula and the rest of the Apple directors did not need much persuading. Commenting on the dust-up more openly only after Jobs' passing, Sculley said, "Steve didn't at that age know much about running companies." During that soliloquy, he keenly observed there is a big difference between leading innovation and managing a company in the midst of heavy competition.[18]

The Apple board demoted Jobs from his faux "Chairman" playing CTO role on May 24, 1985, tossing him unceremoniously in a penalty box.

Five months later Jobs resigned, was asked to leave, or was fired from Apple – the story varies depending on who is doing the telling. He would form NeXT, creating an even edgier machine with an object-oriented operating system and development environment. A NeXT cube would ultimately wind up in the hands of Tim Berners-Lee as he wrote the code for the World Wide Web.[19]

NeXT was part of a new class of machines taking shape: the engineering workstation. These high performance computers did the heavy lifting in computer-aided design (CAD) and in writing advanced software. The 80386 and 68020 each had MMU technology and were capable of running UNIX or BSD and a GUI. As workloads increased, workstation users clamored for more performance than either popular CISC processor family provided.

Workstation vendors began moving to RISC in 1986. Hedging their bets, IBM was among the first to dive in. Their near-RISC processor,

ROMP, hovered nearly five years while an operating system strategy gelled. It first appeared in the IBM 6150 RT in January 1986. AIX debuted simultaneously, running on top of a virtualization microkernel along with other operating systems.[20]

HP was pursuing the RISC trail, too, but more cautiously. Their first PA-RISC "processor" was TS-1 launched in March 1986 inside the HP 9000 Series 840. It was a six-board implementation using TTL chips. A chip-level PA-RISC processor, the NS-1, would come a year later.[21]

1986 also marked the debut of the first RISC microprocessor for merchant sales. John Hennessy and friends from Stanford formed MIPS Computer Systems (now part of Imagination Technologies) two years earlier. Building on their DARPA research exploring RISC architecture, MIPS secured venture capital and set off on readying a chip and an optimizing compiler. Shortly after IBM and HP tipped their RISC plans, MIPS announced their first product: the R2000 processor with their first customer workstation vendor Prime Computer.[22]

Time was running out for Acorn to make an impact.

ARM2 Catches the Tube
The processor core would be ARM, but what the Acorn machine would look like and what operating system it would run were undecided. Creating a competitive business computer was vexing much larger companies. Workstations were new and exciting and more of interest to Olivetti as a complement to their PC strategy. However, Acorn's strength traced back to educational markets.

As part of their research efforts, Acorn had quietly opened a research center in Palo Alto to look more closely at Xerox PARC and their WIMP technology. WIMP stood for windows, icons, mouse, and pointing, the same ideas that had gone into the Apple Macintosh and were now heading into RISC workstations.[23]

Based on that research and scanning the competition, the path Furber and Wilson came up with for the next ARM implementation was as a multimedia engine, capable of supporting not only general purpose computational needs, but graphics and sound. As is often the case in

EDA, the current chip helps design its successor. ARM1 went to work in simulations of architectural improvements and development of code for a production version of a chip.

ARM2 was still compact, around 25,000 transistors, fabbed in 2.5 micron at VLSI Technology. System interfaces expanded to support a 32-bit data bus and a 26-bit address bus. The register count totaled 27, with 16 accessible at once, and there was no on-chip cache.[24]

Three steps enhanced performance in ARM2. First was refinements in the three-stage instruction pipeline, including one stage dedicated to barrel shifting. Second, clock speed increased to 8 MHz.

The third and most significant breakthrough set the tone for future versions of the ARM architecture. Most processor architectures at the time performed multiplies with lengthy sequences of additions and shifts in software – painstakingly slow, impervious to optimization, and consuming cycles while other operations waited.

To increase efficiency, ARM2 added 32-bit multiply and multiply/accumulate instructions. What the ARM architecture now had was rudimentary DSP capability, an advantage in dealing with audio synthesis. There was also a co-processor interface added with a floating-point unit in mind, although Acorn never actually created one for ARM2.

Four new Acorn chips were ready in 1986: the ARM2 processor, a memory controller, a video controller, and an I/O controller. However, a computer without an operating system does not ship, and the operating system intended for ARM2 was in huge trouble.

The team in Palo Alto had the basics of the ARX operating system running, but release of the microkernel design with a windowing interface was dragging out interminably. "ARX was late, very late. It became a black hole into which we poured effort," said Wilson. Productizing a full multitasking, multithreaded, multi-user operating system may have been the bridge too far for Acorn.[25]

Spurring interest in ARM, getting more software written, and helping sales of the BBC Master were urgent. It was time to release something with ARM in it. The solution: drop an ARM2 processor on a Tube card, package it with enhanced BBC BASIC, and release it as the ARM Development System. This got the academic community talking, and they began porting many high-level languages to ARM.

Getting a system released was the next priority. Deciding ARX would never finish, Acorn decided on a pivot: they went back to the BBC with a plan for a revamped BBC-like operating system on ARM2. It was a bit of a shock when the BBC bought the idea. A 12-month crash program ensued, bootstrapped with application programmers who were suddenly developing an OS. Tribal lore says the OS project name, "Arthur", came from a directive: "ARM by Thursday."[26]

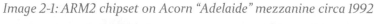

Image 2-1: ARM2 chipset on Acorn "Adelaide" mezzanine circa 1992

Photo credit: Paul Vernon, Retro-Kit,
http://www.retro-kit.co.uk/page.cfm/content/Upgrading-an-Acorn-A3010-with-
an-ARM3-processor/

By August of 1987, the first models of the Acorn Archimedes family were ready. They featured ARM2, its companion chips, and the Arthur project rebranded as RISC OS. During testing, another incredible power-related anomaly showed up: in an early Archimedes unit, the ARM2 needed to be off for over a half a minute to reset reliably. Back EMF from the system fan was enough to keep the chip partially alive.

(Now you know where that note in any computer manual from that era came from.)

Cloners Take Control

Archimedes was fast, but Acorn customers and sales channels were now totally confused. The machine was relatively expensive for educational use and incompatible for business use; however, it was of some value as a programming workstation and hobbyist platform. Sales would be reasonable, but not the home run Acorn was so desperately seeking.

The delays in getting ARM2 out the door for the first time proved costly in the bigger picture with the competition running away rapidly. Strangely enough, Olivetti was helping make a lot of that happen on the PC side.

IBM decided they were tired of cloners siphoning off profits and were about to flip the table. As part of their new system strategy with OS/2 and the new Personal System/2 machine debuting in April 1987, they decided to break their own PC compatibility under the guise of more performance.

A key feature of PCs was the ability to plug in third-party expansion cards via a bus slot. Micro Channel Architecture (MCA) superseded the 16-bit Industry Standard Architecture (ISA) bus with a 32-bit bus for more bandwidth. In addition to faster clocking and improved power and ground routing, MCA included support for burst mode transfers and bus mastering. It also pioneered a jumperless configuration approach, a predecessor to "plug and play".[27]

IBM heavily patented MCA technology, closing the door they had sloppily left open for cloners in the formative PC years. Licensees were slow to embrace the idea, fearing IBM control and reluctant to pay fees to use their technology. Olivetti was one of only a handful of adopters of MCA, although IBM did make substantial use of MCA in their RISC workstation families.

However, IBM was still a competitive threat when it came to business machines; after all, that was their middle and last name. The cloners did not take kindly to what amounted to fighting words, perhaps nowhere more than at Compaq. They were riding success of their sturdy packaging, quality, and 100% PC compatibility, running the exact same shrink-wrapped software that an IBM machine would.

Compaq CEO Rod Canion was not about to pony up just to have the non-exclusive privilege of following IBM down the MCA road. He sensed there had to be an option. He opened a product strategy session in October of 1987 with this, "I'm having a real problem accepting the idea that we can't come up with a way to avoid having to switch to Micro Channel-based products."[28]

After some hesitation, his brain trust spoke up and collectively formed a plan: Compaq would design a completely backward compatible 32-bit bus interface and slot definition, shop it to every PC competitor not named IBM, get Microsoft on board, and make the chipsets supporting it available without royalties to anyone who wanted them. It was open source hardware before there was such a thing.

The "Gang of Nine" – Compaq, AST Research, Epson America, HP, NEC, Olivetti, Tandy, Wyse Technology, and Zenith Data Systems – stepped on stage together in September 1988. They proclaimed the Extended Industry Standard Architecture (EISA) as their bus architecture moving forward.

Normally, such a move against a bigger competitor would be suicidal. In this case, the combined market share of the Gang of Nine outweighed IBM, even before the emergence of brands like Dell and Gateway. The cloners wrested control of the next phase of the PC market away from IBM.[29]

Withering Fire from Workstations

In workstations, things were heating up – figuratively and literally. With the perception of performance at nearly any cost, workstation processor developers were not as constrained by nuisances such as cost, size, and power consumption. Applications were heavily optimized for a particular workstation family, and compatibility and interoperability were low to nonexistent on the list of concerns.

The theme of the workstation game was to get faster. After a few years of 680X0 dominance in machines from firms like Apollo Computer, new RISC workstations and processors for them were coming from every direction.

Sun Microsystems was leading the new pack. They took Berkeley RISC architecture into their own design, SPARC I. Multiple vendors, notably Cypress, Fujitsu, LSI Logic (a direct competitor of VLSI Technology), TI, and Weitek built first generation chipsets with a processor and floating-point unit. With the SPARCstation 1 a huge hit, Sun was pursuing an entire SPARC roadmap to keep pushing the performance envelope and maintain their lead.

MIPS had found an ally in another Stanford-rooted firm, Silicon Graphics (SGI). SGI was enjoying the ride as the entertainment visual effects rendering workstation of choice, thanks largely to their "geometry engine" chip. With the IRIS 4D, SGI went all-in on MIPS, eventually buying the chipmaker (and later spinning it back off). The R3000 second-generation processor would raise the stakes even more, pushing a 1.2 micron part as high as 33 MHz.

IBM, HP, and Digital Equipment Corporation (DEC) were also betting heavily on RISC workstations. IBM was developing POWER1, a ten-chip monstrosity made in their own fabs, for the RS/6000. HP was also fabbing their own PA-RISC parts and had the NS-1 chip in several systems. DEC had been tinkering with their PRISM architecture, but opted for the MIPS R2000 for their DECstation 3100 launch, and was beginning to think about the even bigger Alpha project.

Intel, AMD, and Motorola developed merchant RISC parts, with success in high-end embedded applications. Intel actually had two competing projects, the i960 and the i860; both were lost in the shadow of the 80386 franchise. AMD had the Am29000, finding homes in laser printers – including the Apple LaserWriter family. Motorola showed up fashionably late with the 88000.

By 1988, all these contestants were making things increasingly uphill for Acorn, even with an expanding Archimedes family carrying ARM2 processors succeeding in British educational markets. Archimedes would sell for several more years, but nowhere near RISC workstation volumes of the leaders.

Image 2-2: Acorn Archimedes A3000, circa 1989

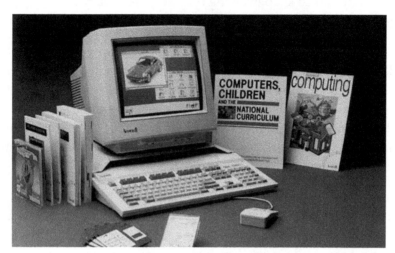

Photo credit: Chris Whytehead, Chris' Acorns, under Creative Commons Attribution-ShareAlike 3.0 Unported license, http://creativecommons.org/licenses/by-sa/3.0/legalcode

Olivetti was not in great financial shape either, under the same withering fire from everywhere. Perhaps the greatest contribution they had made to Acorn at this point was not interfering with the ARM architecture development. That was about to change, at least behind the scenes.

Groping for a way to salvage some value, Olivetti quietly started shopping ARM technology looking for a buyer.[30]

Internal units of Olivetti balked, all too closely tied to Intel and the PC compatibility dogma. The newly formed STMicroelectronics (then operating as SGS-Thomson) passed, having invested in British transputer maker Inmos and their occam language a few years earlier. Siemens was approached, but incorrectly assumed that if Olivetti wasn't going to use ARM, it wasn't worth buying. They even pitched Larry Ellison, long before Oracle had any conscious thought of becoming a hardware company.

25

ARM3 Plows Ahead

No takers would later prove to be a blessing in disguise. Unloved but undaunted and still funded, the Acorn research team continued. They realized they had to keep evolving the ARM architecture to be successful. The ARX operating system experiment had not been a total wipeout; it provided insight into the next processor enhancements.

ARM3 was a dramatic step forward in performance, introduced in 1989 with several new features. The biggest was the addition of 4KB of on-chip L1 cache; the implementation was small and simple to avoid problems other vendors were having with more sophisticated cache schemes. Clock speeds revved up to as high as 33 MHz fabbed on the improved 1.5 micron VLSI Technology process.[31]

One of the pitfalls the ARX team had found was critical. Frequent switching in and out of kernel mode to change contexts, a common operation in a multi-tasking environment, clobbered performance. The solution was typically mutual exclusion, or mutex – a way to prevent two competing processes from modifying a shared resource simultaneously.

Designers added the SWP instruction to ARM3, a single instruction that performed an atomic read and write to memory. This not only helped with reducing the context switching times, but also in creating message passing semaphores between tasks. It would also come in very handy for multiprocessing in later enhancements.

When the parts were tested, it was clear the ARM3 processor had competitive performance. However, sans L1 and companion chips it had a dramatically lower transistor count, smaller die size, and lower power consumption than any RISC alternative. This was becoming more than serendipity; it was a core competence.

What was missing was marketing reach. A brilliant research team and some awesome parts simply were not enough to win. The ARM architecture gasped for air without design-in momentum, a roadmap with frequent planned improvements, a widely accepted operating system and expansion interface, and a sales team.

Buried inside of Acorn, in turn trapped inside of Olivetti, even the advanced ARM3 didn't stand a fighting chance of competing in either PCs or workstations.

Selling ARM parts to other computer manufacturers was difficult. Ironically, the effect traced to the miserable experience of the 6502 being captive to Commodore, the very problem the ARM architecture was fashioned to solve. Acorn was incompatible with PCs, and effectively locked out of workstation vendors heavily invested in developing their own RISC processor architectures.

Other RISC merchant solutions – notably MIPS R3000 and AMD 29K – were not just workstation parts. They were gaining popularity in embedded applications. In embedded, the lower power consumption of the ARM architecture could be brought to bear as a competitive advantage.

Under the Acorn fabrication deal, VLSI Technology had acquired rights to sell ARM processors but had not aggressively exercised them. With other chips in many places, including Apple, IBM, and Olivetti, they had a fantastic set of industry contacts. They started spreading the word, adding to voices from computer science academia who understood the potential.

Shortly, the first serious inquiry on the ARM architecture for an external design win would come not from some random industry sales lead, but from an old friend in a new place.

Chapter 3: Writing on the Wall

By chasing the business computer and workstation trend, the Acorn research team had been trying to overcome weaknesses instead of optimizing the strength of the ARM architecture: targeting embedded applications.

Originally, the objective was to produce a 32-bit processor simpler than the existing CISC alternatives and thereby potentially faster. The ARM3 processor core was proving itself more efficient than other RISC parts. A combined advantage in speed, power consumption, and die size put the ARM architecture in a position to go where few other processor architectures could.

Opening the Apple Door

People on the outside had noticed. The ARM Development System was proving itself in various compiler and software projects across the academic community. Whispers also reached Cupertino.

With Steve Jobs out of the way, John Sculley was steering Apple very differently. Organizational changes included the formation of the Advanced Technology Group (ATG) in 1986. ATG would house many cutting-edge hardware and software research projects over its decade of existence. Some delivered high visibility results, such as QuickTime. Some were stealthier.

Mac was the sacred cow, but Apple II was the cash cow. The Apple III, still based on the 6502 processor and not enough of a stretch, was finally detached from life support and pronounced dead. Sculley plowed investments back into the Apple II product line. The Apple IIGS was nearing release, with the incrementally more powerful 65C816 processor, carefully avoiding encroachment on Mac space.

Researchers are usually undeterred by annoyances such as cash flow and product positioning. ATG had executive backing, money, talent, and ideas, and hunted for projects. Tom Pittard and Paul Gavarini of ATG spotted the ARM architecture, rightly inferring Acorn had shared 6502 experience and motives.[32]

Investigation began. Pittard and Gavarini went to work on the Mobius project. Their two-year effort created a board using a VLSI Technology ARM2 chip plus software emulating the entire Apple desktop computer lineup: a 6502 or 65C816 running Apple II code, and a 68000 running Mac code. All emulated code ran faster on the ARM2 processor than the corresponding native versions.[33]

Mobius boldly explored some of Apple's technology problems, but created a potentially dangerous set of marketing nightmares. Blurring the lines between the two major Apple hardware product lines made few friends internally. Mobius terminated quietly – but Pittard kept the prototype in his office.

Friends in the Neighborhood

The writing was on the wall. Outside of the Acorn Archimedes and its decade-long run, and goodwill from Apple and other researchers, there were no business computer wins in the foreseeable future for the ARM architecture. Adding to the pressure of trying to compete in business computers was a surging Acorn executive brain drain. Gone but still conveniently nearby, the former leaders were in and around the greater Cambridge area pursuing various avenues of serial entrepreneurism.

Chris Curry co-founded Acorn in 1978, and was its first major executive to step aside. He had helped form a company publishing the preeminent journal *Acorn User* in 1983. When Olivetti moved in during 1985, Curry departed and founded General Information Systems, venturing into smart cards and readers.[34]

Hermann Hauser was the other Acorn co-founder and the mentor for Furber and Wilson. He stepped aside upon the Olivetti takeover, but remained in the Olivetti fold becoming vice president of research, and soon co-founded the Olivetti Research Laboratory (ORL).[35]

Andy Hopper was the co-inventor of the Cambridge Ring. He co-founded Orbis to commercialize the technology, and that firm became the networking division of Acorn. His planting of the Berkeley RISC paper around Acorn led to initiation of the ARM architecture. Soon after Olivetti arrived, Hopper departed and founded Qudos, a CAD and chip prototyping firm. He then co-founded ORL with Hauser.[36]

It must have been those and other voices Steve Furber and Sophie Wilson were hearing at night. The notion was circulating around Cambridge that perhaps the ARM architecture could only thrive if it were free from control of Olivetti and Acorn. How to accomplish that would be easier said than done.

In 1988 Furber, Wilson, and their team were in the throes of development on ARM3. They certainly felt the Olivetti straight jacket becoming tighter every passing day. Hauser's departure from ORL was perhaps the clearest signal, as were the futile attempts by Olivetti to find an outright buyer for their creation.

Urgency to do something radical securing the future of the ARM architecture was building. In their spare time, the duo had begun work on a business plan for a stand-alone entity. They had the ARM processor designs, a fabrication partner in VLSI Technology, and substantial high-level programming language support.

Best Strategy Available

A lot was still missing, starting with positioning. Low power 32-bit RISC was still a nascent idea, seemingly wedged between 8-bit microcontrollers, merchant RISC offerings from MIPS, and a gaggle of Sun SPARC licensees. Yet, embedded RISC was clearly the best strategy available for the ARM architecture as the business computer doors were swinging shut with a resounding thud.

Lessons learned over the last several years provided some insight. Intel had proven the value of marketing and roadmap execution. The one-man-plus-interns operation of the Western Design Center was slow, hard to scale, and largely uncompetitive for new design wins. MIPS and Sun Microsystems had swept up many potential merchant licensees for RISC microprocessors. Microcontroller space was messy – a raft of inexpensive, low margin, low pin count, low performance parts with applications coded in assembly language.

What was the ARM product to be, exactly? How would it compete for design wins against larger, established firms? Would it be finished silicon, a processor design service, both, or something else? How would product or service pricing work? What would pre-sales and post-sales support look like? Who would run a stand-alone company? How would it scale? Where would the capital come from?

Among these and a thousand other burning questions, one loomed largest: How many units would sell? "I could never get the numbers to work. You have to sell millions before royalties start paying the bills. We couldn't imagine selling millions of these things, let alone billions," said Furber.[37]

Perspective from the personal computer and workstation experience colored that opinion. It was clear new applications would be required in places other than the desktop. Consumer electronics were not yet absorbing volumes of processors. Automobiles also were not yet ready for big volumes. Were there other segments that would soon need millions of low power ARM processors?

Analog mobile phones were a hot ticket as 1G cellular networks proliferated worldwide. Motorola expertise in miniaturized RF technology set the benchmark for handheld phones with the DynaTAC 8000X in 1983, and others soon followed. Nokia, operating under the Mobira brand, introduced the compact Cityman 900 in 1987. Samsung produced its first handheld mobile phone, the SH-100, in 1988.

Microprocessors and analog phones were not an obvious match, but a transition was imminent. The Confederation of European Posts and Telecommunications (CEPT) had formed the Groupe Speciale Mobile, or GSM, in 1982. The GSM charter was to design a pan-European mobile technology, and by 1988 they completed a first set of specifications for a new, digital mobile network with deployment commitments from 13 countries.[38]

GSM was also tinkering with a new idea: short message service. Phone networks have signaling paths used to set up calls before voice communication begins. SMS borrowed those paths when idle to send short text messages, settling on 160 characters. GSM fully embraced SMS as part of their specifications. Mobile phones were about to become not only bearers of voice, but of data.

Both these factors pointed toward a coming digital revolution for the handheld mobile phone. A low power, embedded processor like the

ARM architecture could enable phones to operate more efficiently and securely, opening a new set of services driving huge demand. It was just a matter of time.

Another idea was about to set mobile ablaze immediately.

Applying for College

The battle between Steve Jobs and John Sculley did not end with the departure of Jobs from Apple – in fact, it intensified. Jobs formed NeXT with every intention of ripping the educational market from the jaws of Apple with better technology and marketing initially focused on colleges and universities. There was also a hint of vendetta. "Part of Steve wanted to prove to others and himself that Apple wasn't just luck," said NeXT publicist Andrea Cunningham.[39]

Jobs brought six key Apple employees with him including Dan'l Lewin, who had created the Apple University Consortium. Lewin led NeXT marketing and fostered the concept of a "scholarly workstation" developed from extensive interviews with and advice from collegiate faculty and students. With the backing of billionaire Ross Perot and others, NeXT embarked on a three-year mission culminating in October 1988 with the launch of their new workstation.

NeXT was an insurgent in an uphill battle against Apple and a bevy of workstation manufacturers. Observers quipped NeXT ought to be renamed "Eventually" in response to ongoing product delays. Sculley was not prepared to discount a possibility of their success given the charisma of Jobs and the high profile support he garnered. Apple was preparing a bold response.[40]

Critics had been faulting Sculley for a lack of product vision since the Jobs departure. They mistook an absence of public statements from Apple for lack of progress. In the background, with the Apple II under control, Sculley had his technologists in ATG off researching the next big thing.

One of the bigger ATG projects was Aquarius. Initially started by Sam Holland in 1986, ATG funneled millions of dollars into a Cray X-MP/48 supercomputer and engineers simulating a quad-core RISC design intended to update the Mac. To throw competitors, reporters, and Wall Street off the track, a cover story emerged that the Cray was an industrial design engine, working on Mac enclosures. After three years of few results despite leadership changes, Aquarius was canned. Fortunately, the Cray did save Apple millions of dollars designing Mac plastic and more.[41]

Why Aquarius didn't start with the ARM architecture, especially considering its existence was known within ATG from the Mobius project (and perhaps several others, with rumored experimental graphics accelerator and printer boards), is a mystery. Part of it was no doubt political; there were career paths and stock options at stake. Aquarius was under the watch of Jean Luis Gassée who was willing to toss copious amounts of money at the Mac to make it more successful.

More likely, there was a sense that at the time Apple could not compete with the likes of Intel and Motorola in designing and producing a high-end processor for the Apple flagship. The ARM business model was still a dream, entirely unproven. There were also strong Apple technical voices, most notably Steve Sakoman, who loudly gave the Aquarius efforts no chance of succeeding. Many engineers ran away screaming from the project, wanting nothing to do with a potential flameout.

On the other hand, the failure of Aquarius and their overlooking of the ARM architecture may have been a stroke of luck. Had Acorn engaged Aquarius, they would have been squarely under the gun to make quad-core work flawlessly during development of ARM3 when they were just learning about cache and the SWP instruction. The science of multiprocessor bus sharing and cache coherency was in its infancy. A failure there may have been equally disastrous for both Apple and hopes for a startup around the ARM architecture.

Navigating Toward a Vision

There was no shortage of big ideas. Jobs had done Apple a massive favor – by choosing to attack their existing education market with high performance, expensive technology, and taking a long time to bring out a complete solution. Sculley's book "Odyssey: Pepsi to Apple" debuted in August 1987, before Jobs officially launched the NeXT workstation.

Shaped by discussion with Apple fellow Alan Kay, Sculley outlined what he called the Knowledge Navigator as an epilogue to his book. Before the World Wide Web debuted, imagination had Knowledge Navigator traversing information highways using voice and touch commands, even incorporating the idea of intelligent assistants. Sculley described his idea in sweeping, high-concept terminology, somewhat removed from current reality.

Bud Colligan, director of higher education marketing at Apple, was growing tired of the "no vision" knock. He saw Knowledge Navigator as an opportunity to take back the high ground in education. The forum presented itself: Sculley was slated as keynote speaker at Educom, a leading education trade show, in October 1987. In parallel with writing text for the speech, Colligan decided to go the next step, engaging ATG's Mike Liebhold as part of a team to create a story portraying what Knowledge Navigator could be.[42]

In six weeks, starting from Sculley's overarching narrative, Colligan and his team created a short video. It depicted a professor who comes to work, checks email, engages in online research, collaborates with a colleague via video, and other tasks – all on a tablet-like device. Educators were appeased at the preview, but probably grasped the difference between vision and actual product.

The big splash would come at the following Macworld. Jean Luis Gassée literally had nothing he could share publicly with a mainstream audience, including technology journalists and analysts, about upcoming Apple product strategy. Colligan was asked to reproduce the Educom keynote, with updated text, revised demos, and an enhanced version of the Knowledge Navigator video. This time, it went viral.

In just over five pre-recorded minutes of video broadcast during January 1988, Apple had gone from having a product with no vision to having a vision with no product.

Debuting the Knowledge Navigator video wasn't totally a gamble for Gassée. He had been writing on the topic of complex shape recognition since 1985, predicting handwriting recognition would become a key technology within five years. In March 1987, he persuaded Steve

Sakoman to stay at Apple to pursue a stealth project on the idea: Newton. Sakoman had recruited Steve Capps back to Apple, and was building a small Newton project team off-site.

Unfortunately, they were conceiving "a monster in a box." As a research project, Newton was free of budgets and oversight, given carte blanche by Gassée. What began with a $2495 target for a small tablet quickly turned into a specification for a letter-sized slate with a touch screen, hard disk, and infrared port – and a price tag estimated between $6000 and $8000.[43]

Image 3-1: Apple "Cadillac" slate prototype

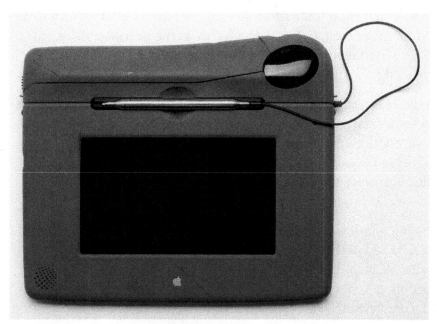

Photo credit: Grant Hutchinson, under Creative Commons Attribution-NonCommercial-NoDerivs 2.0 Generic license, https://creativecommons.org/licenses/by-nc-nd/2.0/legalcode

Adding to the missteps, Newton started with the wrong processor. In another attempt to develop an architecture they could control, Apple went to one of the co-creators of the original Berkeley RISC concept. David Ditzel, a well-known Silicon Valley evangelist on the topic of RISC, was exploring the C-language Reduced Instruction Set Processor

(CRISP) at AT&T. Apple funded the project, naming it Hobbit and casting in millions of dollars to productize the chip.[44]

Keeping Up Appointments

Apple was pouring kerosene on the "personal digital assistant" (PDA) fire, but they were not the only ones chasing the idea. Most notable was Jerry Kaplan of Lotus Development fame with GO Corporation and their PenPoint OS – developed on Intel processors. The search was on for truly handheld hardware.

Discussion on PDAs had also made the rounds in Cambridge a decade earlier. Hermann Hauser first met Sophie Wilson in 1977 when Hauser was a physics student and Wilson was studying microprocessors. The conversation started with Hauser, notorious for a short memory and missing appointments, asking, "I want to have this electronic pocket book. Can you advise me about it?" That thought morphed and grew into a design for the first Acorn personal computer.[45]

Hauser had not forgotten his PDA wish. In an attempt to turn Olivetti around, Hauser had his ORL team hard at work near the close of 1988. They set a goal: integrate a telephone, scanner, printer, and electronic paper into a book-sized computer. Olivetti had much of the technology for a handwriting recognition platform, but completely overlooked the ARM processor under their noses.[46]

Shortly thereafter, Hauser departed to form Active Book using his own money, additional funding from Olivetti, and other venture capital. He planned an integrated chipset, codenamed Hercules, to power the A4-sized tablet device. He knew exactly where to get a processor core for such a chip.

Turning to Acorn, Hauser licensed an ARM core in early 1989. He felt from experience and trust in his friends that ARM2 had enough processing power for handwriting recognition. The next request: reduce its power consumption.[47]

Most microprocessor designs of the day were dynamic designs with a constantly running clock required even if work was not underway. To reduce power to levels appropriate for a battery-operated handheld device, microprocessor designers were turning to static designs, able to slow down or even completely pause the clock without losing information in registers or calculations in the pipeline. This would widen the inherent power consumption advantage of the ARM architecture.

The result of a quick design turnaround effort was the ARM2aS, a fully static 1 micron CMOS processor core. It included the SWP instruction from ARM3, but omitted any cache. Active Book would only produce a short run of prototypes to support various demonstrations, but they drew the attention of AT&T and others with a platform that changed perceptions of mobile hardware.[48]

After six years of stepwise refinement, the completion of static core intellectual property (IP) was the tipping point for the ARM architecture. The ARM2aS arrived not a moment too soon, ready for embedded duty.

Overpromise and Underperform

Back at Apple, the Newton project was not going well at all. Larry Tesler, Vice President of Apple ATG, had many issues to deal with. Egos were extremely hard to contain. Promises made to engineering staffers said there would be no marketing people and no compromises. Newton was bloated, with three processors included in its initial concept to run everything.

The AT&T Hobbit processor was still exclusive to Apple. Many designers saw it as elegant in theory, an efficient stack-based architecture. In the real world, Hobbit limped along, nowhere near the finish line. Tesler later described Hobbit as "rife with bugs, ill-suited for [Newton], and overpriced." He may or may not have been looking for a different processor; nonetheless, one found him.[49]

In the afterglow of Mobius, Tom Pittard did a presentation for Apple engineering teams on his benchmarks a few months after work halted. Heads turned. Of particular note were results from Pittard's Lisp benchmarks on ARM2.[50]

Lisp was more than a passing fancy at Apple. Most embedded projects were coded in C. Drawing on the Xerox PARC experience, Apple was finding object-oriented languages better suited for GUIs. At the dawn of the mobile age, the thinking was to carry a Mac-like user interface onto the smaller Newton screen. Apple had just purchased Coral Software and their Allegro Common Lisp, a $400 tool providing a complete Macintosh toolbox using object-oriented extensions for windows and menus.[51]

Tesler, a veteran of Xerox PARC and an expert on GUIs, saw Pittard's results. He grasped where the ARM architecture could take Newton. Word on the adventures of Active Book had spread to Cupertino, now on full alert for PDA competition. John Stockton of VLSI Technology was quick to chime in as to the technical virtues of the ARM architecture. Sculley reached out to Hauser who brokered a meeting between Apple and the ARM architecture team. Tesler liked what he heard in the preliminary discussions, including ideas for what could come after the ARM2aS.

1990 brought rapid and decisive political change at Apple. Not long after the promotion of Michael Spindler to Apple COO in January, Steve Sakoman resigned abruptly. Jean Luis Gassée also resigned with a transition period, surreptitiously planning to take Sakoman with him to form Be Incorporated.

Sculley laid the fate of Newton on a somewhat reluctant Tesler's desk. After a short evaluation period reviewing the status, he chose to accept the mission.

For Newton to succeed, Tesler first had to clean up ATG dealings. He wasted no time. First was a brief, unsuccessful attempt to combine Newton with another ATG PDA project led by Bill Atkinson, Andy Hertzfeld, and Marc Porat – later spun off as General Magic. With that off the table, he reaffirmed funding for Newton with the Apple board, and went to work.

"All these decisions had been made [on Newton] and I really disagreed with almost every one," Tesler said. The list started with the flailing Hobbit processors and their deepening money pit for ongoing development. His concerns extended to the overall high-priced design philosophy, the physical size, the operating system, and the wireless connectivity.[52]

Called on the carpet for an update on Hobbit, AT&T made an epic blunder. Mistaking exclusivity for account control, they demanded "several million" more in non-recurring engineering funds just to make Hobbit work. At least that was the plan; success was far from assured given the AT&T futility to date. Enough was enough for Tesler.

Style, Substance, and Saxby

Change had also come to Acorn. After three passes at developing a business plan, both Furber and Wilson realized their passion was creating technology, not the ongoing operation of the business. Furber departed for a faculty position at the University of Manchester (at the urging of Andy Hopper); he continued to consult on ARM technology issues while working on new research. Wilson made "a very difficult decision" to stay behind with Acorn, with the freedom to pursue new projects while still being available to consult for ARM.

A team of 12 Acorn engineers now drove the ARM architecture forward, along three disciplines. There were four chip designers with VLSI expertise: Jamie Urquhart, Harry Oldham, Dave Howard, and John Biggs. Systems engineering also had four designers: Tudor Brown for video and memory interfaces, Mike Muller and Al Thomas as systems architects, and Pete Harrod as floating-point expert. Software came from another four engineers: Lee Smith and Andy Merritt for software tools, David Seal for algorithms, and Harry Meekings for C compilers.[53]

Negotiations reached a critical point. Apple needed a processor. Acorn wanted to monetize an exit strategy for the ARM architecture. VLSI Technology had a deep interest in the outcome. The ARM engineering team was ready to form a company with Apple as the lead customer supporting the next phase of development beyond ARM2aS. Planning began with the objective of creating a new joint venture between the three parties.

Who would run the new firm? ARM engineers had a depth of engineering experience, and a newfound relationship with Apple technologists, but little knowledge of what it would take to run a semiconductor startup long term. They needed a leader with the right combination of experience.

At Apple's behest, executive search firm Heidrick & Struggles – the same firm that had recruited John Sculley – began exploration. The name that appeared most prominently on their radar: Robin Saxby.

Saxby was a veteran of Motorola, ascending through the ranks from field application engineering to overseeing sales of microprocessors – predominantly in embedded segments. He was involved in the formation of Motorola Microsystems, initially building VERSAbus boards and systems based on 68000 processors running the UNIX System V operating system.

Image 3-2: Robin Saxby

Photo credit: ARM

In one of his leadership development exercises during his Motorola tenure, Saxby had written a business plan for spinning out the Motorola microprocessor operation based on design services. Motorola passed on the idea. Dusted off, the concept would prove useful for an ARM business model.[54]

Startup experience was also vital in the choice. Since 1986, Saxby had been part of European Silicon Structures, a pioneer in silicon compilation and e-beam fabrication for semicustom designs. "The ES2 ideas were good, it was just 22 years ahead of its time," Saxby mused. In spite of e-beam difficulties, ES2 had gained vital experience in rapid prototyping and distributed design and manufacturing with facilities scattered throughout Europe. Saxby was running the US division of ES2, trying to clean up its strategy, when the call came about ARM.[55]

Europe is a cozy technology community. Saxby had been friends and ski buddies with Hermann Hauser since the 1970s. He had seen papers on the ARM architecture as it unfolded. He was not a huge fan of Acorn or Olivetti, but the allure of a spin-off backed by Apple had tremendous appeal. Saxby was introduced to Tesler, and Malcolm Bird, technical director at Acorn.

Obviously, Acorn didn't quite know what they were in for by licensing a processor. Saxby did. His mantra in creating a business around the ARM architecture: "We have to be the global [embedded] standard. That's the only chance we've got." Acorn was still harboring hopes of the ARM architecture landing in business computers. Saxby nodded politely, but never subscribed to that idea, prepared to bet entirely on embedded applications from day one.

To win, the startup would have to pivot from captive Apple supplier to embedded RISC processor vendor selling IP globally. Acorn, Apple, and VLSI Technology were mostly on the same page, and wanted Saxby as their leader. The joint venture structure: Apple brought £1.5M ($2.5M) cash in exchange for a primary stake and a board seat for Tesler. VLSI Technology kicked in unlimited, free design tools and support valued around £250,000 for a minority stake. Acorn contributed IP valued around £1.5M, plus their ARM development team.[56]

Saxby knew what he had to work with in ARM technology. He wanted a better grasp of his people, hoping to see how to organize them for the challenge ahead. Before accepting the offer to become CEO, he asked Jamie Urquhart and Tudor Brown for a team meeting with all 12 ARM contributors present. A friendly gathering took place in a local pub – with the ARM team arriving fashionably late, five minutes before Saxby

42

was about to leave thinking he had been stood up. (Had he left, that would have changed history entirely.) Saxby settled on Urquhart as sales director, Mike Muller as marketing director, and Brown as engineering director.[57]

Styletheme Limited formed on October 16, 1990, as the joint venture holding company. ARM-related IP transferred into a subsidiary, Widelogic Limited, on November 12, 1990. These off-the-shelf trade names obfuscated corporate matters until all legal requirements on two continents were satisfied.[58]

November 27, 1990, marked the official public announcement of the new ARM entity. The joint venture became Advanced RISC Machines Holdings Limited, with Saxby as Chairman and CEO, and the IP subsidiary was renamed Advanced RISC Machines Limited within a few days of the announcement.[59]

Image 3-3: ARM Partner Meeting with VLSI Technology, circa 1991

Photo credit: Lou Kourra, VLSI Technology

ARM would shortly find its first home in a barn in Swaffam Bulbeck just outside of Cambridge. One of Saxby's first jobs was to find furniture for next to nothing. He won a large conference table (pictured above) in a coin flip with an office furniture purveyor, and lost a game of billiards attempting to win desks and drawers.[60]

Fortunately, the game of semiconductor technology is nothing like billiards. The real work of making the ARM architecture the worldwide standard for embedded applications was about to begin in earnest.

Chapter 4: In the Right Hands

Viewed in their purest form, embedded computers are dedicated to an application. Programmed once, they run a fixed set of tasks, usually with minimal user input. They often reside inside a larger system. Typically, they survive with constraints in size and power and heavily optimized designs are the norm. Hardware debug hooks provide visibility into details of real-time behavior.

In contrast, personal computers and workstations serve users as needed and depend on frequent interaction. Size and power are usually less constrained, in favor of providing more resources to deliver higher performance and better flexibility. They run various programs on request and can change their behavior anytime just by adding the right peripherals and loading new software.

Floating-Point for Acorn, ARM6 for Apple

If the goal for Advanced RISC Machines Limited was devising the global standard for embedded processors, how would they satisfy Acorn? What were they thinking in taking on Apple as a customer? What else would be required for achieving success with the new embedded strategy?

Keeping Acorn happy would turn out to be straightforward. From their perspective on the desktop, no radical departure in architecture was necessary, only incremental improvements need apply. What Acorn wished for most was a floating-point accelerator chip communicating over the co-processor interface added during ARM2 development.

As part of the formation agreement, Robin Saxby agreed to commit half of ARM's resources for one year to support development of the FPA10 floating-point chip for Acorn. He was skeptical of the sales forecasts however – and he was right. First-year FPA10 sales to Acorn totaled a whopping 500 units which would have been a disaster in the absence of other opportunities. The project was not entirely a bust. Floating-point capability would later prove useful, development costs were contained, results were published, and Acorn was sated.[61]

Saxby understood the risks: "If we'd done [only] the pure Acorn roadmap, we'd have been dead in five seconds." Out of the starting gate, the other half of Saxby's resources would go toward his new best friends at Apple.

Creating an application processor for an Apple PDA would be a giant leap forward; other potential ARM customers were bound to notice. The objective was development of the ARM6 processor core and a complete chip, the ARM610. New monikers were used reflecting a fresh start for ARM's numbering scheme and business model. Assuming Newton made it to market, given Apple's reach, even a "failure" in this context would likely turn out to be significant in terms of unit shipments for ARM6. The development effort would also be significant.

Image 4-1: Die photo of ARM610 processor fabbed at GEC Plessey

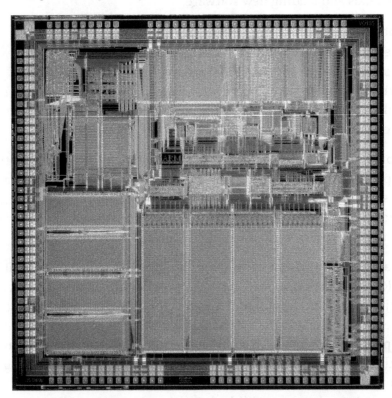

Photo credit: Pauli Rautakorpi, under Creative Commons Attribution 3.0 Unported license, https://creativecommons.org/licenses/by/3.0/legalcode

The static core design technology from the ARM2aS was a must-have for ARM6, but Apple had more on their wish list that reached deep into the hardware and software architecture. The biggest change was a move to 32-bit addressing, from the 26-bit address bus in all prior ARM implementations; to avoid breaking everything, both modes would require support.

Modifications rippled through the ARM6 register set with 31 general 32-bit registers and 6 status registers. These registers were windowed in a suite of six processor modes. Program counter operation also had to change for full 32-bit support. One new register, the Saved Processor Status Register (SPSR), aided in using virtual memory and reducing the difficulty in tracking page faults. For the first time, both big endian and little endian byte ordering were supported with hardware switching between modes.[62,63]

Augmenting the ARM6 core, the ARM610 included a new memory management unit (MMU) and 4kB of cache as well as an eight-deep write back buffer. Another first was addition of IEEE 1149.1 boundary scan support. The ARM610 sported 360,000 transistors fabricated initially in 1.0 micron, clocked at 20 MHz, and packaged in a 144 pin TQFP measuring 22x22mm. A late life shrink to 0.8 micron would produce a final version clocked at 33 MHz.[64]

After only 11 months of development by ARM, Apple had the first samples of ARM610 silicon in their hands for testing by October 1991.

Pocketing the Newton, Seeking $3T

When John Sculley and the Apple board gave Larry Tesler the green light to proceed with the Newton project in April of 1990, they also set a target for release: April 1992, with a price of $1500. Executives had bought into a mock-up consisting of only notional software running HyperCard stacks on Mac hardware. Two years was not much time to translate it into an actual handheld prototype.

The first Newton concept was a 9" x 12" slate known internally as Figaro. Pieces had been prototyped over four years of research. Penciled in for the integrated product were three processors. Before the badly played AT&T gambit, Tesler had an endgame in mind: two AT&T

Hobbits and one ARM610 – sight unseen. He based that on the status of Hobbit, Tom Pittard's ARM2 benchmark results, and roadmap discussions with the ARM development team.

As design efforts progressed, Figaro took on all the functionality engineers wanted. However, it was not anywhere near the mandated $1500 price point with estimates ranging from $4000 to $6000.

Word went out to lighten the Newton ship, fast.

Three young guns responded. Steve Capps, Michael Tchao, and Mike Culbert favored a more aggressive approach: Pocket Newt, measuring 4.5" x 7" with just one ARM610 inside. The backup plan was a mid-sized 6" x 9" unit, which Tesler thought might be more achievable. His main concern was miniaturization. Apple manufacturing had zero experience building anything that small. Tesler knew the smaller the device, the harder it would be to fit everything and obtain acceptable manufacturing yields. He kept all three alternatives open.[65]

With Capps pushing an optimistic schedule and Tchao unabashedly lobbying Sculley for Pocket Newt, the manufacturing decision was critical. Who knew how to pack a lot of electronics in a small footprint, with quality, and in volume? The Japanese. A waiver cleared the way to go outside the friendly confines of Apple. After teams vetted Matsushita and Sony, Apple decided to cut a deal with Sharp – at that time the world's largest LCD panel manufacturer and already building the successful Sharp Wizard personal organizer.

Newton options narrowed to one; mid-size vanished and gigantic went on indefinite hiatus. The freshly minted ARM610 silicon dropped into the waiting socket of "Junior," the Pocket Newt prototype. An epic software siege began, with Newton teams feverishly working an extremely buggy pile of complex code. Even Tesler would find himself coding before it was all over.

Sculley had enough confidence in progress on Newton to go on stage at CES Las Vegas on January 7, 1992. Without mentioning Newton, he made a compelling pitch for PDAs and digital convergence. His punchline: the possibility of a $3 trillion market for devices and content within a decade.[66]

48

Two Failures in Recognition

On May 29, 1992, Apple brought several Newton prototypes to CES Chicago for a demo during Sculley's keynote. That turned out to be excellent planning; the first one died on cue, affirming the hazards of live trade show demonstrations and the frailty of the still-early prototypes. Unfazed, Capps picked up a second unit and proceeded to fax a pizza order built with topping icons dragged and dropped on a virtual crust using the pen interface. It was quintessential "vaporware", yet it was the stuff of imagination and feature stories in tech journals.[67]

After months of bone-crushing debugging of thousands more software flaws and a tortuous release-to-manufacturing, the original Apple MessagePad was proclaimed ready. It debuted for orders on August 2, 1993, at a price of $699. Within seven months, the original MessagePad became the MessagePad 100 with a new release of the Newton operating system and a price drop to $499.

Image 4-2: Apple Newton MessagePad

Photo credit: Apple, Inc.

However, it still had issues. Handwriting recognition software was spotty, its inaccuracy lampooned by everyone from *Doonesbury* to *The Simpsons*. Infrared transfers were iffy. Battery life, even with a miserly

ARM610 processor at 20 MHz, was short on four AAA alkaline cells. On the plus side, its original 336x240 pixel display was crisp and responsive, and Wi-Fi could be added via PCMCIA. Ongoing operating system improvements in new models and a mid-life kicker to a next-generation ARM chip, a bigger 480x320 display, and IrDA helped.[68]

According to Dataquest, Apple sold 60,000 MessagePad units in its first full year of 1994, rising from nothing to third in PDA sales. Every one of those packed a $20 ARM chip inside, a home run for Saxby's team albeit later than hoped. Apple's primary PDA competition, shipping 100,000 units in 1994: the HP 95LX, a clamshell palmtop running Lotus 1-2-3 on an NEC V20 clone of the Intel 8088.[69]

History has overlooked what Newton might have become. Tesler had hired a computing anthropologist, Eleanor Wynn, to bring the "voice of the customer" to the project. From her interviews, she correctly predicted most of the success for Newton, beyond gadget geeks and programmers, would be in vertical markets, such as first responders, healthcare, and insurance. Tchao wanted more than just vertical applications. He ran his own focus group, and concluded that more people would want Newton if it were small, and handled natural handwriting.

Both pre-market consumer studies concurred that a cell phone feature should be included in Newton – advice immediately dismissed as uneconomical to build. That sounds odd, since those kind of concerns hadn't stopped the Newton project team from piling other exotic features onto Figaro. Once Pocket Newt won the shootout, adding an analog cell phone was out of the question considering cost, schedule, already strained power and thermal budgets, and regulatory factors.[70]

Little did Apple realize that part of the answer was right in their hands. In progress was a shift from analog to digital technology that would reshape mobile.

Cell Phone Zero

Scientists at AT&T first conceived the notion of "cellular" in 1947, but had neither the technology nor regulatory clearance to proceed. The high-concept pitch was for exactly the mobile voice network we see today: low power transmitters organized in a grid, with automatic switching and call handoffs from tower to tower, and reuse of frequency spectrum with many channels.

What took shape starting in the late 1940s was a much simpler metropolitan wireless telephone service, created in cities across the US by AT&T and Motorola. These "0G" mobile radio telephone systems targeted utilities, truckers, and reporters – the mobile workers of the day. They deployed one big transmitter tower in each city, supplemented by several smaller receiver towers.

Mobile radio telephone offered extremely limited capacity, ultimately reaching only 40,000 subscribers in the US. Similar services would appear in countries worldwide over the next four decades. The biggest limitation of these 0G systems was that they supported only a handful of simultaneous callers within a city, and all calls required an operator. At one point, only 12 channels existed in all of New York City, and waits to place a call were typically 30 minutes.[71]

Recognizing the usefulness of mobile calling and the severe drawbacks of the primitive 0G system, AT&T scientists went back to work during the 1960s. Advancements in computers and RF technology made the cellular concept feasible. The result was Advanced Mobile Phone Service (AMPS), brought to the Federal Communications Commission (FCC) for approval in 1971.[72]

The biggest breakthrough making cellular service a possibility was spectrum availability. The limitations of channel counts on mobile radio telephone service were a direct result of an FCC decision in 1949 to allocate only a small set of frequencies to mobile service, holding more spectrum for two-way radio.

Subjected to AT&T's prodding, the FCC saw the problem and finally allocated 75 MHz to "common carrier mobile service" in 1970 and authorized a proof-of-concept. In 1974, the FCC undertook a series of decisions including allocating 40 MHz specifically to cellular services and establishing boundaries between telephone companies and competing "radio common carriers".[73]

Those decisions put a three-pronged supplier model in place: phones, network infrastructure, and carriers. Getting initial alignment in a heavily regulated environment with new technology and competitors was not easy. AMPS began limited network trials in 1978.

1G Rolls Across the Globe

While conditions stabilized in the US, many diverse automatic 1G cellular networks started springing up across the globe. In Japan, NTT launched the first commercial cellular system in Tokyo in late 1979, quickly covering the country. Nordic Mobile Telephony (NMT) debuted in 1981, appearing first in Saudi Arabia and eventually covering Scandinavia, the Netherlands, Belgium, Switzerland, Russia, and several Baltic nations. The UK adopted Total Access Communication System (TACS), a close cousin of AMPS, in early 1983. Appearing in 1986 were systems including C-Netz in West Germany, Radiocom 2000 in France, and RTMS in Italy.[74,75]

Rollout of US commercial cellular service based on AMPS began on October 13, 1983 in Chicago. The first phones on that system were "trunk phones." There were mountable in vehicles, but weighing hundreds of pounds not small enough for routine personal use – soon to change with the Motorola DynaTAC 8000X. In and around Chicago, AT&T provided the AMPS network infrastructure, and the carrier was Ameritech Mobile Communications.[76]

Although other 1G systems had a sizable head start, AMPS won in terms of rapid acceptance – eventually growing to 10 times the subscriber base of the next largest system, NMT.[77]

These systems all represented a huge improvement over mobile radio telephone networks. Calls were placed automatically without need for an operator, dialed just as on a conventional landline phone. Subscriber capacity and signal strength improved as towers sprang up across the landscape. More businesses saw the value of mobile phones as productivity tools. Consumers who could afford the price snapped up the latest handheld phones, as status symbols.

As amazing as it was, 1G analog technology still left a lot to be desired.

Analog voice transmission was unencrypted, meaning eavesdropping was as simple as setting up a receiver at the right frequency and modulation. Phones were unlocked: good for consumer portability, not so fantastic for carriers trying to monetize networks. International travelers quickly discovered roaming was largely a myth outside of Scandinavia, with phones rendered useless on regional networks that were using a different technology.

Spectrum has always been precious. 1G systems generally utilized frequency-division multiple access (FDMA), with the full spectrum subdivided into frequency channels, and each channel holding one user at a time. This allowed spectrum reuse between adjacent towers. Nonetheless, as subscriber counts grew rapidly, designers were turning to narrowband versions of the standards to try to pack more channels in the same space – which increased interference.

Transmit power at the analog mobile unit was high, usually one to three watts, to overcome noise and maintain a somewhat reliable connection. Talk time for a first generation battery-powered handheld mobile phone was typically less than 60 minutes. Handheld phones became hot during use, and concerns were growing over high frequency radiation precariously close to human brain cells.

GSM, chartered in 1982, was a slow, political waltz for its first two years. In their regulatory role, CEPT had set aside a small chunk of spectrum for "pan-European cellular radio service", but not much else. Technical details remained for the GSM committee to work out during their biannual meetings. Wrangling was intense, no surprise given the diversity of 1G implementations. History was not on the side of unified European efforts, but the winds were shifting in favor of political and economic cooperation. Motivated by beating the US to the next mobile standard, everybody stayed in the game.[78]

Three factions existed: the French and Germans who often cooperated on matters where industrial might was at stake, the Scandinavians who had a block of common technology in NMT, and a swing vote of the Italians and British courted by both sides hoping to secure enough support for any standard.

Fight for a 2G Future

Attention crystallized around several competing proposals for digital radio as the basis of 2G technology. Companies serving defense markets had a huge body of research and experience with digital radio, spread spectrum, and encoding technology. The German firm Standard Elektrik Lorenz AG, or SEL, was at the time a subsidiary of US telecommunications and defense contractor ITT. Using concepts proven on the Boeing E-3 Sentry, better known as AWACS, SEL came to the front teamed with Alcatel of France in October 1984.[79]

What would become known as the CD-900 proposal employed wideband time-division multiple access (TDMA). In TDMA, a single frequency channel is divided into multiple time slots. Interference between users diminishes with channels encoded and decoded digitally instead of relying on increasingly sharper, bigger, power hungry, and more expensive analog filtering.

TDMA introduced a new element: synchronization. A mobile phone grabs an available time slot from a base station and holds it for the duration of a call. Once synchronized, a TDMA radio only needs to transmit power during its assigned time slot resulting in considerable power savings for a phone – another big plus.

Competition to the SEL/Alcatel wideband TDMA concept surfaced: a wideband TDMA system from Philips, a narrowband TDMA system from Bosch, and a small French firm LCT with narrowband TDMA plus frequency hopping. The Scandinavians responded with all narrowband TDMA proposals from Ericsson, Nokia, Televerket, and Elab – a university group from Trondheim, Norway, and the smallest of the entrants – rounding out the field.

GSM established six selection criteria for 2G cellular: efficient use of spectrum; best sound quality; greatest potential for development of handheld phones; greatest potential for data transfer; lowest cost of mobile phones; and lowest infrastructure cost. Five of these could be evaluated on paper, but one – sound quality – could only be substantiated in real-world testing. By November 1986, these eight groups moved into the watershed Paris field trials.[80]

The two Franco-German wideband TDMA proposals with 2 MHz channel width had a checkmark against them in spectrum efficiency. If the narrowband systems with 300 kHz channel width underperformed, the competition was open. Elab brought two secret weapons to their effort. One was a Viterbi algorithm for equalizing demodulated signals. The other was a simulation of their solution, and those of the competitors, run on a Cray supercomputer at the Norwegian University of Science and Technology.

Amid the clutter of buildings and other obstacles on the streets of Paris, the Elab system shined as predicted by its researchers. They altered frequency bands during trials with equally good results, something none of the other contestants did. After extensive debate along political lines regarding rural versus urban infrastructure, voice coding, modulation, frequency hopping, mobile handset production, and spectrum issues, narrowband TDMA became the preferred approach in GSM.

With Stephen Temple at the helm, GSM secured agreement with the September 1987 Copenhagen Memorandum of Understanding, initially signed by representatives of 15 network operators in 13 countries. The agreed-upon goal: place GSM systems into service by 1991. The European Telecommunication Standards Institute (ETSI) was created in 1988 to oversee development and rollout of GSM. Specifications for infrastructure tender followed shortly.[81]

The Scandinavians took the July 1, 1991, goal very seriously. Most credit Nokia with the win. On that exact date, the former prime minister of Finland called the mayor of Tampere, Finland, on a Nokia-supplied GSM infrastructure operated by Radiolinja, using a Nokia GSM car phone in Helsinki. A few weeks earlier on June 11, Ericsson had demonstrated a GSM call for Mannesmann on their infrastructure – using a Motorola International 1000 GSM car phone, while driving around Dusseldorf – but had no subscribers, and no handsets. Ericsson-powered GSM systems were also ready to go on July 1 in Copenhagen and Stockholm.

A new, unofficial definition for GSM emerged: "God Send Mobiles!"[82]

Licensed to Process

ARM was also seeking immediate help by the close of 1991, divine or otherwise. For "voice of the customer" to work, ARM needed actual customers. Salaries were frozen and cash was tight. Apple silicon for Newton was under control but still two years from volume shipments. VLSI Technology was building parts for Acorn and Apple while exploring for other big ARM wins.

Robin Saxby was busy running his story past every contact in his extensive network looking for licensees for ARM. His original business plan called for establishing partners in the US, Europe, and Japan. His Christmas 1991 gift to ARM employees: a backdated check for a tentative licensing deal with Plessey, which would become formal after parent GEC approval in mid-1992. GEC Plessey immediately stepped into production with the ARM250, a design based on the ARM2aS static core, and the FPA10 floating-point chip for ARM3 customers.[83]

With momentum building and licensing agreements on two continents, in 1992 ARM announced QuickDesign – a design service for embedded controllers. Leveraging VLSI Technology and GEC Plessey expertise in design and fabrication, ARM could now offer customization of parts for embedded OEM customers.[84]

Chatter was making the rounds about the ARM610 and the capability for custom ARM designs. Saxby was shuttling back and forth to Japan, supporting a seminar binge reaching out to technology firms. He worked out a £650,000 venture funding deal with Nippon Investment and Finance as a contingency plan in case other deals did not materialize. Sharp, intrigued by what they saw in their Newton licensing deal with Apple and the ARM tour of Japan, inquired.

One large customer prompted Sharp's intense interest in the ARM architecture: Nintendo. Negotiations were not easy. Saxby relates, "On my tenth trip to Japan [since joining ARM], Mike Muller came with me, and we went to Nara [home to Sharp's Advanced Development and Planning Center]. We saw a Sharp sign and I got Mike to take a picture of me standing under it – for luck." Sharp signed on as the third ARM licensee in March 1993; their first part was the 20 MHz LH74610.[85]

Dealing for DSPs

The desperate shortage of GSM phones was starting to ease. A joint venture of Racal and GEC Plessey built the Orbitel 901 bag-phone. It was the first to receive official GSM type approval, and the first to send an SMS message.

For handheld GSM phones, it looked like a three-way race was developing. Motorola launched the International 3200, a revamped handheld brick design, but without SMS capability. The capable Nokia 1011 appeared next, becoming the first mass-produced GSM handheld phone. Ericsson responded with a hasty respin of their "Olivia" platform into a digital version, the GH172.[86]

The European marketing team of Texas Instruments (TI), led by Gilles Delfassy, observed the state of GSM affairs from their base in Nice. They saw the sweat pouring off brows of engineers at phone manufacturers under pressure to shrink designs and ship digital handsets. There was an immense opportunity developing for smaller, lower power DSP chips to handle the new processing requirements.

TI had ventured into the high-end DSP market in 1982, with parts used in niche applications such as defense communications, radar, and medical imaging. Wally Rhines (currently CEO of Mentor Graphics) led the TI microprocessor group during the early DSP push, "We were struggling to find higher volume applications for DSPs. For us, nirvana was to be adopted in a cell phone."

The first level was reached in a 1987 deal with Ericsson where TI set up a 0.5 micron wafer fab for Ericsson in exchange for deeper collaboration on Ericsson parts. Initially, the focus was on cellular base station products. Ericsson had a funny view of the world, thinking that handsets were just an extension of the cellular network. Quarterly meetings between TI and Lars Ramquist, CEO of Ericsson, eventually convinced him they needed DSPs in GSM cell phones.[87,88]

The second level should have been a TI deal with Motorola. The two companies liked each other, having worked together on Six Sigma quality programs. In the early 1990s, the Motorola cellular operation favored buying non-Motorola chips whenever possible. The premise was saving Motorola semiconductor capacity for external customers and avoiding a double financial whammy if there were ever a downturn in mobile business. TI finally won a DSP socket for GSM phones, but Motorola was still preoccupied with AMPS.

The slow uptake at Ericsson and Motorola left TI seeking another GSM handset partner looking to move more quickly and in big volumes. Sporting two dozen large chips inside, the Nokia 1011 screamed for better digital integration that DSP could provide. Improved processing could cut manufacturing costs, lower power, increase performance, and allow addition of advanced user interface, data, and security features.[89]

Delfassy and his TI team organized a legendary 3-day workshop for Nokia in Finland, featuring technical discussion interspersed with various recreational excursions. The exercise cemented a roadmap using TI DSP technology for voice coding, modulation, and baseband processing in future Nokia GSM phones.[90]

Image 4-3: Wally Rhines at Texas Instruments, circa 1984

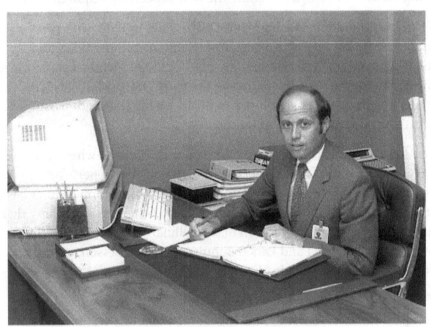

Photo credit: Walden Rhines

Coincidentally, as 1992 ended, other TI teams in the US were engaged in preliminary discussions with ARM about automotive applications. Both discussions bubbled up chain. Rich Templeton, today CEO at TI who was then running the microprocessor group, put an ARM license agreement on the desk of his boss – Wally Rhines, Executive VP of TI's semiconductor group – for signature.

Rhines was not easily convinced, "We can't compete with the Japanese in manufacturing [a reference to DRAMs], and now you're telling me we can't even compete with other companies in design of a microprocessor core to embed in a baseband chip?" Templeton persisted, citing advantages of working with ARM and synergy between TI's two biggest opportunities. Rhines held off.[91]

To see just how good the digital handset opportunity was, TI rolled the dice and introduced ARM to Nokia.

ARM teams had seen this movie once before and knew what to expect. They went into the Nokia meetings prepared with a roadmap for their next core: ARM7. It was planned as a performance bump to ARM6, debuting in 0.8 micron for faster speeds and lower power. Cache doubled to 8KB, and both the translation look-aside buffer in the MMU and the write-back buffer doubled in size as well. An enhanced hardware multiplier also helped with performance. For the first time, ARM planned features supporting embedded designers with hardware debug and in-circuit emulation capability.[92]

Nokia had big plans for their software and was ready to sign up for a new application processor for their GSM phones – except for one detail.

Thumbing the Way Ahead
RISC architectures were more efficient than CISC architectures on many single instructions and in most short- to mid-length sequences of operations. However, in longer sequences of typical programs, early RISC compilers tended to generate significantly more instructions compared to CISC for the same compiled source code. This difference in code density meant more memory was usually required to support a RISC processor, both for storing code and executing it. ARM was the

most efficient RISC option, but not nearly as good in code density as Nokia's favorite 16-bit Hitachi H8 CISC core.

Approaching the intersection of innovation and rejection, with a TI licensing deal about to skid out of control, Mike Muller and his team decided to attempt running the red light. If it was 16-bit memory Nokia wanted, it was 16-bit memory they would get. Starting on the flight home, the ARM brain trust drafted their plans to neutralize the code density objection.

Their creative architectural solution added a preprocessor unit near the front of the pipeline capable of decoding either a new set of simplified 16-bit instructions or the existing set of full 32-bit ARM instructions. These 16-bit instructions known as Thumb would map into 32-bit counterparts on execution, leaving the balance of the processing pipeline intact.[93]

The Thumb instruction set produces code only 65% the size of ARM code, and runs at 160% the speed of comparable ARM code using 16-bit memory. Both instruction sets are available on a per-routine basis, leaving designers the flexibility to opt for performance or code density as needed.[94]

Adding Thumb instructions to the ARM7 roadmap quickly converted Nokia from skeptics to unmitigated supporters. Wally Rhines finally signed the ARM licensing agreement for TI, then the sixth largest chipmaker on the planet, in May 1993. (Rhines would later tell Saxby, "I think [ARM] is going to make it.") The Nokia win and ARM7 plan were still top secret. TI cloaked the deal as intended for their Prism library of mixed-signal blocks targeting automotive applications, vaguely describing customized DSP cores combined with ARM6 cores.[95]

ARM had just been trying to land a major deal but was about to accomplish far more with ARM7 and Thumb. "Voice of the customer" led to a breakthrough in embedded scalability. Lines blurred between 16-bit and 32-bit processor architecture, and TI traced a new path toward multicore system-on-chip (SoC).

The digital mobile device onslaught was about to be unleashed.

Chapter 5: Coming on Strong

Ten years into their technology journey, ARM was finally ready to have fun in the financial sense. By the fourth quarter of 1993, volume shipments of Apple Newton running on the VLSI Technology-built ARM610, plus several other parts shipping from VLSI and GEC Plessey, had a stream of revenue flowing.

Change was sweeping across the semiconductor industry. Intel introduced Pentium earlier in the year. Apple, IBM, and Motorola launched the PowerPC initiative two years earlier, and design-ins were underway. The advent of GSM networks ignited a fuse for a coming explosion in digital mobile handsets. DSP technology pushed into new areas. Fabless technology was also making a dent; new names were popping up.

Custom Chips, ARM7, and a Star

A sign of change appeared in October 1993. Attempting to break the dominance of Nintendo and Sega in game consoles, the 3DO Interactive Multiplayer was an open gaming console design with its hardware licensable to manufacturers. Panasonic was first to release a 3DO unit. On its motherboard sat two large 3DO ASICs for video acceleration, a video DAC, a CD interface chip, and a custom audio DSP, surrounding a VLSI Technology ARM60 processor.[96]

"To be successful [in game consoles], you need custom chips, high manufacturing volume, and tons of marketing," 3DO founder Trip Hawkins observed. When Sony entered the segment at the end of 1994 with a $499 PlayStation, 3DO's fate was sealed. Competing for game titles against a massive Sony marketing spend of over $2B proved futile. The trend toward custom chips, however, was spot on – and not just for game consoles.[97]

Strategically, ARM was all about custom chips and "turning enemies into friends." Their business model centered on the strength of their IP, an ecosystem of design licensees, and an extremely compelling roadmap. A cheaper, faster path to market was for design teams to collaborate with ARM technologists, license a core, and create exactly the silicon needed for a unique device.[98]

Image 5-1: VLSI Technology ARM60 processor in Panasonic FZ-1

Photo credit: cropped still image from "What's inside a 3DO (FZ-1)",
Legion2000, YouTube, https://www.youtube.com/watch?v=9okLali9Xcs

The finished ARM7 core was unveiled at the Microprocessor Forum event on October 20, 1993. Without its cache the new core checked in at 35,610 transistors. Silicon footprint was 3.1mm x 1.9mm in a 0.8 micron process. Power consumption at 20 MHz running on a 3V supply was 33mW. VLSI Technology had the new ARM700 processor ready for immediate sampling.[99]

Along with extensions for JTAG debugging and connecting in-circuit emulators, ARM outlined details of the ARM7DM extension, adding a single-cycle hardware 32x8 multiplier array for DSP-like operations. Array iterations could quickly complete a 32x32 multiply within four passes.[100]

With fabrication partners established and a growing portfolio of IP, the ARM business model moved into its next phase. Instead of a generic "ARM license", ARM could grant rights for a specific core, or for a version of the instruction set.

The first licensee of the ARM7 core was Cirrus Logic, signing on in December 1993. Earlier in the year, Apple announced new licensing agreements – including deals with Motorola, Kyushu Matsushita Electric, and Siemens – for Newton technology. Cirrus Logic, an up-and-coming fabless firm, became an authorized supplier of "Newton-compatible chipsets" and had bigger aspirations.[101, 102]

Keeping ARM ahead in the race had become never-ending work, and 1994 brought a flurry of design activity. One of Steve Furber's brightest graduate students at Manchester – Simon Segars – had been at ARM a couple of years, employee #16. He led a development team readying the promised implementation of the Thumb instruction set in an ARM7 core variant. Another ARM team was working on defining the ARM8 core for the all-important roadmap.[103]

Image 5-2: Simon Segars, circa 1997

Photo credit: ARM, via IEEE Micro July/Aug 1997

Fall of Hobbit, Rise of Consulting

One company's fun is often another company's disaster.

AT&T, after the Apple spurning, continued with the Hobbit processor looking for a win. Jean-Louis Gassée's new firm, Be Inc., fired up prototypes of the BeBox sporting two Hobbit 92010 chips and three AT&T DSPs. That configuration never sold. Be converted to dual PowerPC 603 processors for its production designs.[104]

Persevering, the Olivetti-to-AT&T connection resulted in AT&T backing PDA startup EO Inc. with roots in Hermann Hauser's Active Book, and the hardware side of Jerry Kaplan's GO Corporation. The AT&T EO Personal Communicator hit the market in April 1993 with a Hobbit chip inside. Monstrously overpriced, it started at $1999, with a cellular modem inside its six-pound frame.

Analyst estimates indicate a paltry 10,000 EO units sold. AT&T abruptly cancelled Hobbit in January 1994. The ironic twist: EO had prototyped on ARM and went to production with Hobbit, while Apple prototyped Newton on Hobbit and went to production with ARM. (Apple spinoff General Magic flirted briefly with Hobbit; its Magic Cap licensees, Motorola and Sony, launched on the Motorola 683xx later in 1994.) Facing an insurmountable crisis of a complete redesign without capital, EO ceased all operations a few months later.[105,106,107]

That Larry Tesler wager on ARM was now looking very, very good. Others were lining up to place their bets on the ARM architecture.

Pursuing "emerging markets" and convergence, the sixth ARM licensee in May 1994, was Samsung, aiming toward PDAs, disk drives, cell phones, and set-top boxes. Licensee number seven was Asahi Kasei Microsystems (AKM) in August 1994, bringing expertise in mixed signal chipset design for communications applications – essential for integrating GSM and other digital handsets.[108, 109]

Existing licensees were continuing innovation. Sharp shipped its first ARM part in March 1994: the LH74610 based on the ARM610 running at 20 MHz. ARM and VLSI Technology released the ARM710 processor in July 1994, the successor to the ARM610. They then introduced the ARM7500 in October 1994, a powerful system-on-chip in a new 0.6 micron process. It combined a 33 MHz ARM7 core with memory controller, video, audio, and I/O in a 240 pin quad flat pack. Its first customer was Online Media, a new division of Acorn building set-top boxes using asynchronous transfer mode (ATM) switched networking.[110,111,112]

ARM was also adding talent, enabled by Samsung kicking in a substantial sum of money for their license. Headcount numbered around 70 in mid-1994. In September, ARM pried Warren East away from TI after they closed an operation in Bedford. His charter: to handle the burgeoning trend of customers wishing to co-design chips with ARM. He formed a consulting operation to handle initial design discussions with licensees which would help keep design engineers more focused on core development projects.[113,114]

StrongARM and ARM7TDMI Arrive

One of those new discussions was already in progress. Digital Equipment Corporation had their eyes on supplying the PDA market too. Teams led by Dan Dobberpuhl toyed with the idea of reducing their Alpha architecture to come up with a lower power, yet still fast, RISC chip.[115]

Alpha parts were fabbed at DEC in 0.75 micron, ran at 200 MHz, and chewed up 26W at a core voltage of 3.45V. Reducing the core voltage to 1.5V cut power consumption to 4.9W, but also cut clock speed, affecting performance. It was still a very long pull to a sub-1W design suitable for handhelds.[116]

Rich Witek and Jim Montanaro had recently rejoined DEC, forming an Austin design center. During their first tenure they were integral parts of the Alpha design team. They knew what they were facing. Their audacious response after preliminary investigation: approach ARM and merge what DEC knew about high performance with what ARM knew about low power to create a new core.

DEC grabbed the latest ARMv4 instruction set and ideas from the outline for the ARM8 core, then went to work with ARM engineers in cahoots. On February 6, 1995, ARM and DEC jointly announced a license and a project name: StrongARM. (Curiously, the press release mentions the not-yet-announced ARM8 core.)[117]

Exactly one month later, ARM publicly introduced the Simon Segars project. Launched on March 6, 1995, the ARM7TDMI core changed everything. While earlier ARM7 variants would be available for some time, a new line was drawn. Most future licensees would head straight toward ARM7TDMI and its successors for its advantages in embedded implementations.[118]

The ARMv4 instruction set ditched the legacy 26-bit addressing mode, which few outside of Acorn were using. In its place, the long-awaited 16-bit system plan hatched on a plane ride back from a visit to Nokia was finally ready. Simplification of register definition and instructions allowed design of an efficient three-stage fetch/decode/execute pipeline. Eventually, all ARM instruction sets prior to ARMv4 became obsolete.[119]

The decode stage of ARM7TDMI operated as usual on 32-bit instructions for full performance and software compatibility, or transparently decompressed a subset of the most used instructions encoded in 16-bit for better code density and lower cost memory subsystems. Software designers could use either or both instruction sets in the same program. In the designation, 'T' represents the 16-bit Thumb instruction set (officially, the ARMv4T extension). 'D' is the JTAG feature, 'M' the fast multiplier, and 'I' the ICEbreaker in-circuit emulation capability first introduced in the basic ARM7 core.

Segars later characterized ARM7TDMI as "72,000 beautiful transistors." The blend of small silicon footprint, performance, low power consumption, and the addition of 16-bit code density brought ARM even more notoriety and interest. With licensees proliferating on various processes, just how small, how fast, and how much power was becoming a matter of the licensee's fab technology.[120]

Adoption and Advancing Processes
Atmel, an expert in EEPROM that was just moving into 8051 microcontrollers with its 8-bit AVR architecture not yet conceived, saw an opening. They acquired Saxby's former employer, ES2, in a complex transaction starting in April 1995. Atmel ES2 took out an ARM7TDMI license in July, hoping to use their advanced 0.5 micron process to create new microcontroller designs.[121,122]

NEC licensed ARM7TDMI in September 1995, becoming tenth on the list of ARM licensees. This was a strange twist, because NEC was also a licensee of MIPS architecture. They had announced the MIPS R4300i in 0.35 micron just a few months earlier with a claim of offering "64-bit performance at a price less than most 32-bit processors." Steadily, MIPS was making a strategy shift from solely high-end workstation processors toward lower power embedded parts. The R4300i consumed 1.8W at 100 MHz. Set-top boxes were a major point of application overlap, and Acorn and others expressed some displeasure at the unusual move by ARM – but not enough to thwart it.[123,124]

Nearly three years after their first GSM foray in the forest with Nokia, and after patiently waiting for ARM to bring the Thumb instruction set to reality, TI was ready to show their hand. In early October 1995, they had evaluation samples of their TMS470 microcontroller powered by ARM7TDMI. These used TI's TGC3000 technology, in 0.6 micron. The 74,203-transistor core took up only 4.8x4.8mm, clocked at 40 MHz. It sat next to a 100,000-gate array that enabled addition of customized digital logic.[125]

A few days later at the Microprocessor Forum on October 11, 1995, Rich Witek of Digital Semiconductor previewed the StrongARM SA-1 core. It was still a few months from production, but the initial results were mind-blowing.

DEC had cranked up a 0.35 micron, low voltage CMOS technology using 2V logic transistors and 3.3V I/O. In a break with previous ARM cores, DEC moved from the simpler von Neumann approach with unified cache to a Harvard architecture with separate data and instruction caches. Pipeline stages increased from three to five. Improvements were made in branching, single cycle shift-adds, the fast multiplier, and a five-port register file. They crammed 115,000 transistors in less than 4.3x4.3mm. At 160 MHz, the SA-1 core burnt only 120 mW of power – achieving close to 400 MIPS per watt, ten times better than contemporary desktop processors. All this was completely ARMv4 instruction set compatible.[126]

Symbios Logic brought ARM deeper into a new segment. When they licensed ARM7TDMI at the end of October 1995, Symbios held 28 percent of the SCSI (Small Computer System Interface) host adapter chipset market. SCSI is a high-end disk storage interface for servers and single board computers. Accelerating storage channels would later prove to be a competitive battleground.[127]

LG Semicon was looking to diversify beyond DRAM and add processor technology. They licensed the ARM7 core and ARM710 macrocell in November 1995. They were after what was becoming the list of usual suspects: PDAs, set-top-boxes, communications platforms, and high-end consumer electronics.[128]

ARM8, SA-110, and a new EPOC

Landing between ARM7TDMI and StrongARM, ARM introduced their not-so-secret ARM8 core in November 1995. Retaining the von Neumann unified cache to keep die size small, ARM8 instead turned to a double data rate memory interface, or DDR. They appropriated the five-stage pipeline idea, with prefetch, decode, ALU operation and shift, memory access, and register write-back stages. This bumped up the clock cycles per instruction from 1.9 to 1.43. They targeted 0.5 micron processes, avoiding overlap with DEC. While improving on ARM7 performance and completing the transition to ARMv4, the 72 MHz ARM8 core found itself immediately in a dangerous middle ground, without Thumb and far short of StrongARM.[129,130]

Closing out 1995, ARM went back to the low end of the roadmap. The ARM7100 integrated the ARM710 macrocell with a DRAM interface, LCD driver, PLL clock multiplier, serial ports, IrDA port, timers and real-time clock, and other microcontroller-style features. Cirrus Logic was gearing up to build parts.[131]

Four companies joined the licensee roster in 1996. Oki was first in January, choosing ARM7TDMI for semi-custom parts in segments including automotive, computer peripherals, PDAs and phones. Alcatel was next in February, with their Mietec ASIC subsidiary picking ARM7TDMI saying it was "20 to 30 percent better in benchmark tests" compared to other processor cores. Yamaha went for ARM7DI and ARM7D in March, targeting advanced sound generators and other uses. Rohm rounded out the list in November, selecting ARM7TDMI for hard disk drives, computer peripherals, and cell phone ASICs.[132,133,134,135]

Four chip announcements also highlighted 1996. On February 5, DEC introduced the SA-110 StrongARM microprocessor, in 100, 160, and 200 MHz versions. With caches, it came in at 2.5M transistors, with a die measuring 7.8x6.4mm. In an inexpensive 144 pin plastic package, the 160 MHz version consumed 450 mW and was just $49 in 10K quantities, with the 100 MHz version even cheaper at $29.[136,137]

Cirrus Logic presented the CL-PS7110 processor, their implementation of the ARM7100, in July 1996. Simultaneously, Psion Software plc threw in its support for this "PDA on a chip" running the EPOC32 operating system. EPOC32 was the upgrade of the 16-bit operating system used in the popular Psion Series 3 PDA since 1991, also sold as the Acorn Pocket Book. It was obvious the NEC V30H processor was about to lose a socket to the ARM ecosystem.[138,139,140]

VLSI Technology announced the ARM810 processor in August 1996, carrying its progression into a third generation. It was available as either an ASIC core or packaged in a 144-pin QFP and drew 500 mW at 3.3V. 10K prices were $25.[141]

TI revealed the multicore combination many were waiting for in November 1996. Their news indicated they had been shipping a c470 microcontroller version combining a TMS320C54X DSP core with an ARM7TDMI core on the same part to Nokia for several months, and were ready to release it generally. They were targeting not only GSM handset designs, but also any digital baseband need, including DECT for home wireless phones, and ERNES for paging.[142]

Image 5-3: Nokia 8110i, the first GSM phone with an ARM (baseband) core

Photo credit: Krystof Korb, under Creative Commons Attribution-ShareAlike 2.0 license, https://creativecommons.org/licenses/by-sa/2.0/legalcode

ARM sources confirm that indeed, Nokia had been shipping the TI-designed baseband ASIC in a GSM phone since March 1996. Best known as the phone Neo used in the first "Matrix" film several years later, the Nokia 8110 featured a sliding cover and a unique "banana" curvature. Its user interface processor was still the Hitachi H8/3001, soon to be outgrown by software demands. The title of "first GSM phone with an ARM core" rightly belongs to the Nokia 8110.[143,144]

When it came to ARM developments, Apple had a definite advantage with inside information. From all the available choices, they jumped on a StrongARM SA-110 for a major upgrade to the Newton, squeezing out 162 MHz. The MessagePad 2000, previewed in October 1996, also contained the Cirrus Logic Voyager chipset. It had four chips: one for a group of CPU-related functions including LCD control, analog functions including the pen digitizer and touch-pad interface, a PCMCIA controller, and an infrared transceiver.[145,146]

RISC Leaders, Windows CE, and Loyalty

Technology never stands still, and success is rarely unnoticed for very long. ARM was winning in embedded RISC, but by no means had a monopoly as competitors advanced.

NEC, perhaps torn internally by the ARM7TDMI licensing, and probably stung by the prospect of losing more V30H design-ins, surged back with a new MIPS part. The VR4101 processor debuted in August 1996. It was an integrated 64-bit processor with lower power consumption in a 160-pin package. At 33 MHz and 3.3V, it consumed 250 mW. It came in at less than $25 in 100K volumes.[147]

Hitachi was steadily improving its relatively new SuperH processor family. From its inception, it was a 32-bit RISC processor with a 16-bit instruction set. Riding on the Sega Saturn game console with two SH-2 chips inside, Hitachi laid claim as the top RISC supplier worldwide in 1995. The SH-3 core added an MMU and improved cache to the architecture. In September 1996, the SH7708 arrived – 60 MHz, 3.3V, 600 mW, in a 144-pin QFP, and priced at $25 in 10K quantities. They had also added a noteworthy SH-3 licensee: VLSI Technology.[148,149]

Then, Hitachi and NEC dropped a bombshell. They had been working with Microsoft on a new operating system: Windows CE, specifically designed for "the new category of handheld PCs." Only SH-3 and MIPS processors were included in the reference port for manufacturers.[150,151]

Bill Gates strode on stage to unveil Windows CE in Las Vegas at Comdex 1996 on November 18. He touted a lineup of seven announced "pocket PC" devices based on one of the supported Hitachi or NEC processors. It was an impressive roster: Casio, Compaq, HP, Hitachi, LG, NEC, and Philips had pledged support.[152]

Microsoft was in charge – and ARM and Motorola were behind, perhaps a little, perhaps a lot. This was a wake-up call, with a message that semiconductor providers no longer dictated events. Without the right software support, even the most power efficient processor did not stand a chance of securing design wins.

Two weeks after the Comdex demo, Microsoft gloated that they were busy at work on Windows CE with Motorola for PowerPC 82x parts and with ARM and their licensees Cirrus Logic and Digital Semiconductor.[153]

ARM countered with its version of the story on the same day, effusing how important the new Microsoft partnership was. The list of operating system support for ARM had grown from humble beginnings with Acorn RISC OS. One of the more important mobile operating systems cited was Accelerated Technology Nucleus (later acquired by Mentor Embedded). In a possible oversight, they neglected to mention Psion EPOC32 – which would soon become prominent.[154]

1997 ushered in six new ARM licensees. Rockwell licensed ARM7TDMI and ARM810 in January for modems using their K56Plus technology. Lucent Technologies, then the leading supplier of standard cell ASICs, signed in April, targeting ARM7TDMI for mixed-signal ASICs for digital cell phones and modems. Philips Semiconductor also joined in April, picking up ARM7TDMI for microcontrollers – setting off a bogus rumor of a suspected 8-bit ARM core. Sony and Hyundai both announced on ARM7TDMI in July. Sony was after a wide range of consumer and professional media products. Hyundai was seeking a new market for code division multiple access (CDMA) PCS phones.[155,156,157,158,159]

The last announced licensee of 1997 resolved a bit of drama. LSI Logic was a direct competitor of VLSI Technology. LSI CEO Wilf Corrigan had been pursuing Robin Saxby for an ARM license for years, dangling large sums of money. Out of loyalty to his joint venture partner (VLSI Technology), Saxby refused, "All you're going to do is compete with VLSI. When you can get me some new business Wilf, I'll consider giving you a license." As a result, LSI licensed the ARM7TDMI for the print server business of Emulex and others, creating a version synthesizable in their CoreWare design methodology on their 0.25 micron G10 process.[160,161]

Seeking to get on top of operating system ports and avoid a replay of the Microsoft episode, ARM and Sun Microsystems formalized an agreement for JavaOS in February 1997. Driven by Sun's "the network is the computer" strategy, JavaOS was gaining popularity. ARM was inside network computers from Acorn, Oracle, and Wyse.[162]

Then, two mobile devices made the biggest splash in the industry since the Apple Newton.

Symbian, Nokia 6110, and ARM9TDMI

In June 1997, Psion released the Psion Series 5 PDA, priced at $699. Its EPOC32 operating system ran on an 18 MHz Cirrus Logic CL-PS7110 with 4 or 8MB of memory. The palmtop design featured a sliding clamshell, measuring 170x90x23 mm and weighing only 354g. It had a backlit, grayscale 640x240 pixel touchscreen, and a miniature QWERTY keyboard. There was a CompactFlash slot for expansion, and power came from two AA batteries.[163,164]

The Series 5 sold well – a "constant 20K units per month" in 1998 according to Psion. The PDA software race was on, with Palm enjoying a substantial lead, and Windows CE gaining strength along with EPOC32. In June of 1998, Psion Software teamed with Ericsson, Motorola, and Nokia, turning their EPOC32 code over into a new joint venture: Symbian.[165,166]

Image 5-4: Psion Series 5mx

Photo credit: Georg Dembowski

Setting the record straight, the *second* GSM handset with an ARM core made its entrance in Beijing in November 1997: the Nokia 6110, with a TI c470 codenamed MAD2 running everything. The 6110 reverted to the familiar Nokia "candy bar" shape, measuring 47x130x28mm and weighing 143g. Life on its lithium ion battery was outstanding, with talk time of 5 hours and 270 hours of standby time. Its software handled SMS messaging, stored 50 phone numbers, offered 35 ring tones, and introduced the legendary Nokia "Snake" game.[167,168]

The Nokia 6110 roared across the globe rapidly. Dan Hesse, then CEO of AT&T Wireless, labeled the 6110 "the best wireless phone on the market, bar none" – high praise considering the Motorola StarTAC was the primary competition. It shipped over 3 million units in its first year, propelling Nokia to the top position in cellular handset share for the first time in 1998.[169,170]

Overwhelming adoption of the ARM7TDMI, and the tepid reception to ARM8, clearly indicated the Thumb instruction set had to be integral in future releases. Simon Segars and his team had their response. The ARM9TDMI core appeared at the Microprocessor Forum in October 1997. Giving in to the trend, it went with a Harvard memory architecture and a five-stage pipeline but kept branching in the pipeline simple. It was designed to a 0.35 micron rule set, occupying 4mm x 4mm, and clocked up to 150 MHz. Power was 1.5 mW per MHz at 2.5V.[171]

Simultaneously, ARM showed the ARM940T, a macrocell implementation with 4K data and 4K instruction cache and a write buffer. It incorporated the new Advanced Microcontroller Bus Architecture, or AMBA, as an aid in standardizing system design around their IP. The ARM940 used a simpler memory protection unit instead of a full MMU, defining eight regions of data and eight regions of instruction memory.

Hijacking and Brinksmanship

ARM was whittling away at licensing the list of top ten semiconductor firms. Two names near the top were still not ARM licensees: Intel, the world's largest semiconductor company in 1997, and Motorola, the third largest. They were about to take two radically different paths.[172]

DEC sued Intel in May 1997, alleging Pentium infringed on ten Alpha-related patents. Intel countersued. After the US Federal Trade Commission strongly suggested that Alpha needed to survive for competitive reasons, the parties reached a settlement in October. Intel would buy DEC's Hudson, Massachusetts, semiconductor fab for $700M, hire all Digital Semiconductor employees except those working on design of Alpha, and agree to provide 7 years of foundry services for Alpha processors. The FTC was still unhappy, but ultimately capitulated in April 1998.[173,174]

Under cover of an Alpha smokescreen while few noticed, Intel hijacked StrongARM in the deal.

Meanwhile, Motorola was being Motorola. A four-alarm dumpster fire raged in 1997. First, TI helped Nokia get to GSM phones, and Nokia did the rest, taking a big lead in digital and stealing market share. Next, a delayed response to GSM from US customers lulled cell phone head Bob Weisshappel into staying the analog course. He rationalized the situation logically, "Forty three million analog customers can't be wrong." (Recall that Motorola had a GSM handheld phone first, and built a reasonable GSM phone share in Europe. Blindly listening to customers can be bad.)[175]

When the US carriers finally got on board with digital, they decided what they needed was CDMA – and with Motorola not in the CDMA handset game, they turned to upstart Qualcomm for phones. Open conflict flared between new CEO Chris Galvin and Weisshappel, who hated the idea of paying chip royalties to catch up in digital and stopped buying Qualcomm chips in 1995. Tensions came to a head with the Weisshappel sarcasm, "I guess I'll just buy Qualcomm," a fitting epitaph when he left Motorola soon thereafter.

Chip royalties were a four-letter word throughout Motorola. Saxby had approached his former employer several times. ARM eventually got an audience with Hector Ruiz, a rising star in Motorola's semiconductor operation who would later become sector president. Their meeting went well until Ruiz blurted, "And of course, we won't be able to pay you any license fees, or any royalties." ARM was not sure they'd heard that correctly.[176]

Motorola badges in the 1990s came with a can of kerosene for fire starting. Ruiz had poured the contents on the table, and proceeded to strike a match. He revealed to ARM that Motorola SPS had something like 200 engineers working on a new low power processor – not 683xx, or ColdFire, or PowerPC, but another entirely new embedded RISC core. They were cooperating on the design with Motorola's cellular handset operation.

So much for warring tribes and that don't-buy-phone-chips-internally theory. Moreover, so much for an ARM license at Motorola, at least for the time being.

In October of 1997, at the same Microprocessor Forum event where ARM9TDMI took the stage, Motorola disclosed their self-proclaimed "ARM killer". The M-Core microRISC engine borrowed heavily from ideas in ARM, SuperH, and the just-introduced MIPS16 architecture; a 32-bit core with a 16-bit instruction set, a four-stage pipeline, and 16-entry register file. This gave it similar code density advantages. The

M200 family was fabbed on 0.36 micron, initially clocked at 50 MHz. It achieved 0.41 mW per MHz at 1.8V.[177,178,179]

Solid Profits and Momentum

Despite the hyperbolic death threat, ARM had little reason for concern.

Concluding its seventh full year of standalone operation, ARM published impressive financial results for 1997. Revenues were £26.6M, up 59% over the previous year. Profits were £5M, up 35%. Employee headcount totaled 274.[180]

Analysts brought more good news. Fueled by domination in the printer segment, the Sony PlayStation, and deeply embedded applications such as network routers and set-top boxes, MIPS had overtaken Hitachi SH. They stood solidly first in market share somewhere between 44M and 48M units. The latter estimate indicated they had even overtaken Motorola 68K. Hitachi SH checked in second, at 20.6M units.[181]

ARM was in third place in embedded RISC processor unit shipments. They shipped 9.8M units for the year, and ARM was the fastest growing entry with a 133% upturn over the previous year. Intel's i960 was close behind at 9.4M units, followed by PowerPC at 3.8M, both overtaken by ARM during the year.[182,183]

Momentum belonged to ARM, thanks mostly to ARM7TDMI and a wide variety of consumer device applications. The Apple Newton, Psion Series 5, and Nokia 6110 were just the tip of the digital mobile device iceberg. A wave of smarter devices was coming, powered by increasingly sophisticated yet still very efficient ARM cores.

Chapter 6: Making the Cortex-A List

Reaching the near-10 million ARM processor annual run rate went far beyond any dreams in the Imaginarium of Professor Steve Furber and Sophie Wilson.

ARM was poised for far more. Closing 1997, eight licensees were producing ARM-based parts, and more were coming online. Variety was also on the rise for ARM and its customers with an increasing mix of processor cores, system-on-chip designs, and fabrication processes. The next phase of ARM's growth meant expanding efforts to adapt and verify more of its IP in less time.

ARM's IPO, and ARM10

Apple, ARM's primary investor (still holding 42.3%), was heading in the opposite direction in a tumultuous 1997. A billion dollar loss piled up on a second straight year of revenue decline while operating cash dwindled. Layoffs did not help. Midway through the year, Steve Jobs (back in charge after Apple acquired NeXT) began an epic housecleaning of management and products to reverse Apple's misfortunes.[184,185]

In July 1997, Jobs persuaded the Apple board to part with CEO Gil Amelio. Shortly thereafter, Jobs became "interim CEO". In another July move, Larry Tesler stepped down from the ARM board of directors and would soon leave Apple, one of many casualties in the restructuring. Gary Wipfler, the finance mastermind who ran Apple Sales International, replaced Tesler on the ARM board.

Needing more capital to fuel expansion, and with Wipfler eyeing a quick source of cash, ARM management decided to take the company public. On April 17, 1998, the new ARM Holdings, plc issued 11,730,000 shares of stock, divided across the London Stock Exchange and NASDAQ, netting ARM £36.4M. Apple instantly unloaded 18.9% of its stake, a gain of about $24M before foreign taxes. In October, Apple sold again gaining nearly $32M before tax, lowering their percentage of ARM to 19.7%.[186,187]

ARM7TDMI drew more followers in 1998, including HP, IBM, Matsushita, Seiko Epson, STMicro, and Toshiba. Its popularity suggested adding AMBA for integration ease; ARM reengineered processor versions of the ARM710T with an MMU for PDAs, the ARM720T adding features for Windows CE, and the ARM740T with the memory protection unit for embedded. ARM also retooled the core into a synthesizable ARM7TDMI-S version, configurable with industry-standard EDA tools. National Semiconductor became its first licensee.[188,189,190,191]

Interest was also building around ARM9TDMI. Companies started taking ARM licenses more quietly, keeping them private. Four undisclosed firms signed. Industry sources pinned a going rate of $5M on a license fee for the latest core, a figure CEO Robin Saxby did not dispute when queried.[192,193]

VLSI Technology teamed with Ericsson for two generations of integrated parts for digital handsets – and had their third generation running. The VLSI VWS22100 OneC GSM platform, a derivative of a part developed for Ericsson, became available for OEMs in November 1997. It was a single-chip customizable GSM baseband part based on ARM7TDMI and an OakDSPCore from DSP Group.[194]

As big as GSM was, CDMA was becoming even bigger. In April 1998, LSI Logic announced its single-chip CDMA baseband processor architecture using ARM7TDMI and dual OakDSPCores. VLSI countered with its single-chip CDMA+ solution in June, illustrating how quickly derivative designs took shape. Qualcomm, the progenitors of CDMA, took an ARM7TDMI license in July. They were developing their MSM3000 single-chip CDMA baseband solution claiming to enable data speeds at 64 Kbps and above.[195,196,197]

At the Microprocessor Forum in October 1998, ARM gave a forward-looking preview of the ARM10T core under development in its new Austin design center. Climbing back up the performance ladder but still low power, the AMBA-enabled ARM10T targeted up to 300 MHz in 0.25 or 0.18 micron processes and beyond, later becoming the first GHz-clocked ARM core. It relied on a new six-stage pipeline with an issue stage and additional address calculation hardware in the execute stage. It also added a 64-bit external memory bus and a new fast 16x32 hardware multiplier. Also new was an optional vector floating-point execution unit. Supporting the core was a new instruction set, ARMv5TE. [198,199]

HP previewed plans for their next-generation handheld PCs in October 1998. Previous Jornada models ran on Hitachi SuperH processors. HP made the switch to an Intel StrongARM SA-1100 processor that supported the latest Microsoft Windows CE version 2.1. With that, Intel had their first big StrongARM win. [200]

Shipments of ARM processors in 1998 totaled 51 million units sending ARM shares skyrocketing to a four-for-one split in April 1999. (Analyst Andrew Allison understated the ARM shipments figure, estimating just 38 million. He placed MIPS at 50 million units shipped and Hitachi at 26 million.) [201,202,203]

Image 6-1: ARM celebrates its IPO at the NASDAQ

Photo credit: ARM

Original Partners Part Ways

The original triumvirate of ARM backers capitalized in different ways during 1999. Over the course of the year, a refocused, slowly recovering

Apple continued to cash out. They sold 32.6 million ARM shares and gave up their board seats as their stake shrank to about 6%. [204]

Acorn, operating as Element 14, vacated its investment entirely. Its market capitalization sank to less than the value of their ARM holdings. In a complex £270M transaction, Acorn sold to Morgan Stanley and delisted; shareholders received two ARM shares for every five Acorn shares. [205]

VLSI Technology had sold about one fifth of its stake in the ARM IPO. In April 1999, it pared about half its remaining holdings, selling 1.1 million ARM shares. Philips then acquired VLSI Technology in May for $1B, sweetening an earlier hostile offer VLSI rejected. [206,207]

The Ericsson-VLSI partnership deepened. Ericsson invented Bluetooth, a new short-range wireless interface in 1994, hoping to replace serial cables. With IBM, Intel, Nokia, and Toshiba, Ericsson formed the Bluetooth Special Interest Group in 1998. Introduced in March 1999, the VWS26001 combined an ARM7TDMI core with an Ericsson Bluetooth core on a single 8x8mm, 96-pin chip. Again, VLSI showed how flexible their ARM-based designs were for wireless chips. [208,209,210]

TI was also moving forward. They announced the Open Media Application Platform, better known as OMAP, in May 1999. The goal was mating a 130 MHz ARM9 core with a 320 MIPS TMS320C55x DSP core and dedicated logic on a single 0.15 micron chip optimized for Symbian EPOC. Nokia immediately endorsed it. [211]

Headlining the Embedded Processor Forum in May 1999, ARM unveiled ARM9E. It backfilled the ARMv5TE instruction set and the fast 16x32 multiplier from ARM10T into ARM9TDMI. This gave ARM9E basic DSP capability, in a compact design – 2.7mm^2 on 0.25 micron, only 30% more than the original ARM9TDMI. Lucent Technologies grabbed one of the first licenses citing opportunities with hard drive manufacturers. [212,213]

For easier integration and reuse of IP, ARM introduced two innovations later that May. AMBA 2.0 increased performance with the Advanced High Performance Bus (AHB), adding split transactions, hidden arbitration, zero-turnaround, plus support for 128-bit bus widths.

PrimeCell peripheral libraries were written in VHDL and Verilog with test benches for SoC verification. Original PrimeCell functions included an SDRAM controller, UART, synchronous serial, real-time clock, audio codec, smart card interface, and color LCD controller.[214]

In August 1999 at HOT CHIPS, synthesizable ARM946E-S and ARM966E-S macrocells appeared based on ARM9E. ARM946E-S was similar to the ARM940T with cache, write buffer, and memory protection unit. ARM966E-S shed memory protection and replaced cache with a new feature: tightly coupled memory, or TCM, made for real-time applications. LSI Logic licensed both macrocells for their synthesizable CoreWare library.[215]

So much progress in hardware left ARM needing more software resources. Spend £1.1M, get 25 experienced software developers – such was the case when ARM purchased their Cambridge neighbors, Micrologic Solutions Ltd, in October 1999. ARM had been using Micrologic on a contract basis, so bringing the team inside made sense. Demand was on the rise for optimized algorithms such as connectivity protocols and audio codecs.[216,217]

Combined, these efforts were unstoppable. ARM shipped 182M processors in 1999, moving to the lead in embedded RISC. There was plenty of upside; only 19 of 37 licensees were shipping parts, with the rest in development. Saxby estimated about half of the licensees were involved in mobile devices.[218]

Foundries, Investments, Extensions

With the number of fabless semiconductor firms increasing, ARM began establishing formal partnership agreements with foundries. UMC joined the ARM Foundry Program in February 2000 and TSMC quickly followed in March. These were under a new "per use" license, lowering the cost of entry for foundries and smaller firms with a model based on the number of design projects.[219,220]

ARM made three equity investments during 2000. The first was a £1.3M equity stake in m-commerce IP provider Parthus Technologies plc, also an ARM7TDMI licensee (who would soon join with the DSP Group to form CEVA). CoWare, creator of IP models for system-on-chip design and verification, got £2.1M. Cambridge Silicon Radio (CSR), who had announced their BlueCore solution for Bluetooth powered by ARM cores, received £0.7M.[221,222]

Mobile technology was advancing. Support was building for the Sun Microsystems vision that handsets should run compact, low power implementations of Java. An early example was upcoming i-mode phones from NTT DoCoMo in Japan running DoJa.[223]

Improved Java performance was one of three announcements ARM made during October 2000. Jazelle, officially the ARMv5TEJ extension, added 12,000 gates and 8K of microcode for interpreting Java bytecodes in front of the ARM pipeline. This compared to a Java hardware coprocessor approach other RISC architectures were taking. Simulations indicated Jazelle was eight times faster than a software Java virtual machine running on an unaided ARM9.[224,225]

A set of single instruction multiple data (SIMD) extensions highlighted a preview for the upcoming ARMv6 instruction set. These helped media streaming, providing flexible word-width math acceleration for a 75% performance boost – again, without adding a hardware coprocessor and its power use.[226]

SecurCore debuted with the SC100 core, a hardened version of ARM7T designed for smartcards and SIMs. It contained anti-counterfeiting measures, and protection against side channel attacks that sought to deduce activity from analyzing power consumption of a core.[227]

Intel was ready with their new ARMv5TE core in August 2000. The XScale core, as the name suggested, could range from 200 MHz at 40 mW up to 1 GHz at 1.5W. It incorporated dynamic voltage management to aid in matching performance to workload.[228]

Frio was the code name for a new 16-bit DSP architecture Intel had been plotting with Analog Devices. Hailed as the Micro Signal Architecture, the endgame for Intel was to combine an XScale core with an MSA core, similar in concept to TI OMAP. Intel had visions of mobile devices implementing their Personal Internet Client Architecture, or PCA, revealed in Tokyo in September 2000. (At Analog Devices, Frio morphed into Blackfin.)[229,230]

Competing with TI's head start was an optimistic goal. In addition to Nokia, both Ericsson and Sony were committed to OMAP for phones. Ericsson and TI were developing Gigacell, adding enhanced 3G capability around the cores. Sony added a Symbian license for its mobile efforts.[231,232]

Analog Devices also announced their AD20msp430 SoftFone chipset for GSM in January 2000, blending their ADSP-218x DSP core with an ARM7TDMI core in one chip and the companion Othello 2.5G GPRS radio in a second chip. SoftFone introduced entirely RAM-based software, allowing operators to customize phones easily with downloadable updates.[233]

Lucent raised the stakes in April 2000, reporting they were first to silicon with ARM10T. Their strategy targeted both CDMA handsets and infrastructure. For handsets they had ARM9E and the EVRC PRO speech coding chip. For infrastructure they had the more powerful ARM10T and variants of the new StarCore DSP family, jointly developed with Motorola.[234,235]

China was an untapped market. ZTE, then a sizable GSM and CDMA infrastructure provider, was looking to expand its nascent mobile phone operation. Through a joint venture, they licensed ARM7TDMI and PrimeCell in October 2000 for the ZCP320A communication processor.[236]

Smartphones Come, Holdouts Go

Feature phones with basic talk and text capability were well under control. Nobody had yet heard the term "smartphone". Primordial attempts had closed in on the right combination of elements.

IBM was first to go fishing with "Angler" prototypes at Comdex in 1992. After a year of development with BellSouth, Simon launched in November 1993. It was a head-shrunken PC with a 4.5"x1.4" touch screen and an analog cellphone. Inside was an X86-compatible Vadem VG320 processor running an embedded version of MS-DOS. Simon was oversized (200x64x38mm), heavy (510g), hungry with a one hour talk time, and expensive with an $899 price tag.[237,238]

The Nokia 9000 Communicator came in August 1996, packing an Intel 386EX and running GEOS. It was a candy bar phone when closed, but when unfolded longitudinally a large LCD and physical keyboard appeared. At 173x64x38mm and 397g, it was 27mm shorter and 113g lighter than Simon, and thanks to a GSM cellphone it had a 3-hour battery life. Its 1998 successor, the 9110 Communicator with an AMD 486 still running GEOS, shrank further to 158x56x27mm, got 144g lighter at 253g, and doubled battery life to near 6 hours.[239,240]

The Palm-powered Qualcomm pdQ followed in September 1998 combining functionality of a Palm III with a CDMA phone. It was familiar to Palm users with built-in and downloadable apps. The pdQ measured 157x67x35mm and weighed 229g with a numeric keypad that flipped out to show the full 3.5" screen. Its battery life was too short at 2.5 hours, and it was rather slow.[241]

Ericsson brought the R380 in November 2000, the first phone running Symbian ER5u on an ARM processor. This 130x50x26 mm, 164g GSM phone had a battery life of 4 hours. With its numeric keypad closed, a small LCD display was exposed. Flipping the keypad open uncovered a 360x120 pixel touchscreen, running a complete GUI – faster and smoother than any smartphone to date. Apps included a WAP browser, SMS messaging, email, and organizer features, but no others could be downloaded.[242,243,244]

Advanced operating systems on ARM processors had the formula for smartphone size, performance, power consumption, and application ecosystems. Nearly everybody in the mobile industry could see where things were headed.

Everybody, except Hector Ruiz. His short but turbulent three-year reign at the top of Motorola Semiconductor ended well for him. In January 2000, Jerry Sanders tapped him as president of AMD and heir apparent to the CEO.[245]

During and shortly after his tenure, things hadn't gone so well for Motorola. In response to overcapacity concerns Ruiz started the "asset light" initiative, consolidating fabs and sending about half of chip production to foundries. Multiple reorganizations created an exodus of talent. Missed commitments at the mid-range and high-end of the PowerPC roadmap left Steve Jobs and other customers fuming.

M-Core did not go as planned, either. It certainly hadn't killed ARM, or even slightly flesh wounded them. In fact, it did not get far beyond Motorola internal use. Staffers, including design center leader Jim Thomas, were fleeing to work elsewhere – many heading to Intel to work on their next ARM project. [246,247]

Even good things went south. The king of PDAs in 2000 was Palm with some 70 percent market share. Since 1996, all the millions of Palm and Palm OS-licensed units ran on variants of the Motorola MC68328 DragonBall processor. Palm, just off its IPO in March 2000, turned toward ARM for its smartphone future. They pre-announced their intent at their first major analyst briefing in April, two years before the ARM-enabled Palm OS 5 would be ready. [248,249]

That was probably the straw that broke the camel's back. In December 2000, Billy Edwards, VP of strategic planning for Motorola SPS, gave a carefully worded statement in London. He grudgingly acknowledged, "The embedded market is exploding – it's bigger than we expected", and that ARM was an "almost de facto standard". Saxby had won his personal quest; Motorola became an ARM licensee, at last. [250]

Thriving in a Meltdown

ARM processor shipments for the year 2000 exceeded 400M units. 2001 found ARM, its partners, and its people, fulfilling their commitments – in spite of the dot-com meltdown in progress and difficult conditions for telecom firms. [251]

TI began shipments of the OMAP1510 in February using a special TI-enhanced ARM925 core paired with a TMS320C55x DSP core. The list of OMAP supporters was impressive. There were the usual mobile device names: Nokia, Ericsson, Sony, Symbian, Microsoft, and Sun Microsystems. Joining them was a new name quickly building market presence: Handspring, founded by the inventors of Palm. [252]

ARM released the Jazelle extensions in both ARM926EJ-S and ARM7EJ macrocells during April, along with a software toolkit. The ARM926EJ-

S was an immediate hit, generating 16 licenses in its first year of availability, and would grow to be the most widely licensed ARM core to date.[253,254,255]

The ARMv6 instruction set details revealed at the Microprocessor Forum in October 2001 showed much more than SIMD extensions were coming. There were memory subsystem improvements with a tightly coupled, faster DMA controller and redesigned cache. From the TI relationship came an understanding of multicore support with ways to operate on shared memory and synchronize data between cores. There were also very un-RISC like enhancements essential for embedded use. The first was support for bi-endianness, referring to how 8-bit bytes are ordered within a 32-bit word, either high-to-low or low-to-high. Another was hardware support for unaligned data, handled by generating multiple memory accesses and avoiding data abort exceptions. The next processor core would be both faster and more flexible.[256]

Nintendo shifted its fortunes from consoles to gaming handhelds. The Game Boy Advance made its Japanese debut in March 2001, running on a Sharp ARM7TDMI processor with a Z80-compatible coprocessor. Measuring 145x25x82mm and weighing 140g, it provided 15 hours of game play on two AA batteries. It would be the first in a line of Nintendo handhelds based on ARM.[257]

Nokia made its next smartphone move in June 2001. The Nokia 9210 Communicator upgraded to a 52 MHz ARM9 processor running Symbian 6.0. It was the same size and just a few grams lighter than its predecessor but with two important differences. When its clamshell opened, it revealed a 640x200 pixel color display. It was also "open", supporting a developer ecosystem for downloadable Symbian applications and ringtones.[258,259]

One of the wounded telecom firms was Ericsson. Rumors swirled as losses piled up and market share eroded. Ericsson's ability to match the pace of consumer-friendly handset designs from Nokia and Motorola – about to launch the incredibly small, light, elegant V60 phone on GSM – was in question. What they needed was design and branding help, and a partner committed to the same processor and operating system technology. The logical choice: Sony. Negotiations leaked in April 2001 became official by August with the formation of Sony Ericsson Mobile Communications.[260,261]

After nearly 11 years in the chair, Robin Saxby was also ready for change. He believed strongly in succession planning. Several years earlier, he had suggested to the ARM board that he would like to step aside as CEO before age 55.[262]

Choosing the new face of ARM was easy. The new leader would be the man who had been in front of customer after customer in successful consulting engagements since 1994: Warren East. Minimizing market ripples (and perhaps exercising caution after 9-11), a single paragraph in an October 15, 2001 quarterly earnings report ushered in the transition. East was promoted to CEO of ARM Holdings plc, and Saxby would remain as Executive Chairman of the board.[263]

Against an otherwise horrific year for most of the semiconductor industry – which shriveled 31.7% by iSuppli estimates – ARM thrived. Semiconductor partners increased to 77 with 33 of them shipping product. Reporting of unit shipment counts changed, with annual figures amassed on a September baseline for more accurate reporting at financial year-end in December. Compared to 367M units from October 1999 through September 2000, the corresponding 2001 shipment figure was 420M units for a 14% gain.[264]

XScale, ARM11, and OS Contenders

For the smartphone, the path was becoming clear. Running sophisticated operating systems with color GUIs and robust applications would take faster processors and more memory.

Two advanced cores came to the front. In February 2002, Intel debuted their first XScale entrants. The 400 MHz PXA250 and the 200 MHz PXA210 were fast but a tad slower than the 600 MHz offering touted nearly two years earlier.[265]

There was nothing slow about the ARM11 core – the last of the ARM "classic" cores – announced in April 2002. It combined the ARMv6 instructions and Jazelle acceleration with every architectural wrinkle

ARM had developed to date. Its longer eight-stage pipeline featured out-of-order completion of some instructions along with improved branch prediction and vectored interrupts. Models suggested speeds of 350 to 500 MHz on 0.13 micron with 0.4mW/MHz operation, and speeds over 1 GHz on 0.1 micron processes.[266]

Image 6-2

Classic ARM processor cores

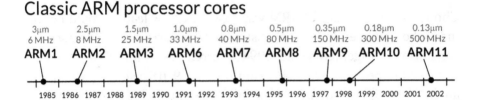

ARM11 processors followed quickly in October 2002 in the ARM1136J-S and ARM1136FJ-S with the 'F' signifying an added floating-point co-processor. The day after the processor announcement, new ARM11 licensing agreements from Qualcomm and TI were a clear sign of rapid mobile adoption.[267,268,269]

Five smartphone operating system contenders were in the mix. Plans for Symbian OS v7.0 leaked in February 2002 with a new set of 3G features including GPRS for data. Shipments of Palm OS 5 commenced in June. Microsoft branded its "Stinger" platform as Microsoft Windows Smartphone 2002 in October. Some companies, including Motorola, were even tinkering with an open source Linux approach for handsets.[270,271,272,273]

The fifth contender was pushing business email. Research In Motion (RIM) took their popular "pager" based on an Intel 386EX, rewrote their operating system around Sun's Java 2 Platform Micro Edition (J2ME), rehosted it on an ARM7EJ-S core, and added GSM voice capability. The BlackBerry 5810 launched in April 2002. It wasn't a perfect smartphone, requiring earbuds and a cord-dangled microphone to place calls, but it hit the target with a devoted base of business users and their circles of influence. It was small (117x79x18mm), light (133g), and leveraged the popular RIM thumb-board users loved.[274]

During a second straight tough year for the semiconductor industry ARM's 2002 financial results wavered with uncertain forecasts even prompting a 12% headcount reduction to 721 employees. Shipments moved slightly higher at 456M units, surpassing a milestone of over 1B ARM cores since the journey began.[275]

Chip partners numbered 108 with two prominent SoC vendor additions. The first was Broadcom, unannounced at the time, perhaps due to sensitivity over their being a MIPS partner through the 2000 acquisition of SiByte. The second was MediaTek, a fabless powerhouse in Taiwan who was then a leader in CD and DVD drive controllers. A new architecture licensee also came from Taiwan. Faraday Technology, a spin-off of foundry UMC, licensed the ARMv4 instruction set to design a series of processor cores.[276,277,278]

Seagate also joined on with their first effort incorporating multiple ARM966E-S cores in the Cheetah disc drive family. Flextronics signed on in a new category of "licensing partner", expanding its design services portfolio by enabling sub-licensing of ARM cores to contract manufacturing customers.[279,280]

AMBA 3, TrustZone, MIPI, and a Gift

Seeking stability in 2003, ARM redoubled its efforts in integration and improving system-level functions around the core. Both Cadence and Synopsys announced EDA optimization approaches to cut design times. A SystemC interface specification for AMBA 2 launched early in the year enabling high-level modeling of bus interconnects and furthering IP reuse. Then, the introduction of the high-performance AXI protocol brought together a collective of knowledge from over 25 silicon and EDA partners. As part of the AMBA 3.0 specification, AXI added support for multiple outstanding bus transactions that helped bursts, and a uni-directional channel that easily bridged clock domains.[281,282,283,284]

With smartphone operating systems that could download applications proliferating, security in mobile gained attention. TrustZone established a hardware security framework at the core level, protecting both on-chip and off-chip memory and avoiding insecure software-only solutions. TrustZone first appeared in new ARM1176JZ-S and ARM1176JZF-S cores.[285,286]

Blending code density and performance, ARM introduced its Thumb-2 technology. Since the Thumb instruction set appeared, ongoing improvements in memory chip density and cost relieved constraints on code density. Where Thumb used two distinct instruction streams, one for 16-bit and one for 32-bit, Thumb-2 combined both. This delivered a 26 percent memory reduction over pure 32-bit instructions and 25 percent better performance than 16-bit code. Faster execution enabled clock speed reduction, saving power. The ARM1156T2-S and ARM1156T2F-S cores were the first to incorporate Thumb-2.[287,288]

(Funny story from ARM sources: "Thumb" was initially an internal code name for the project, a pun describing the small extension at the end of an ARM. It stuck as the official product name. The next project was "Wrist", but prior to release the official name became Thumb-2.)[289]

TI and STMicro also had their eyes on better system integration. The OMAP architecture was good for promoting CPU-DSP integration, but building phones meant adding other peripherals. More required customization was slowing phone designs. First, TI and STMicro defined OMAPI in 2002 creating some profiles for common hardware and software drivers. They quickly realized they needed to go farther and gain more industry support.

OMAPI grew from a two-company specification into a not-for-profit organization for broader industry participation. The MIPI Alliance – the Mobile Industry Processor Interface – formed in July 2003 with the addition of ARM and Nokia. Its vision was to stimulate design of both mobile SoCs and peripheral chips making sure the value chain aligned from silicon to software.[290]

Two other processors debuted. Trying to replicate the deeply embedded popularity of ARM7, ARM created the ARM968E-S, the smallest, lowest power variant of the ARM9E family. Retaining the benefits of TCM, it was 20 percent smaller and 10 percent more power efficient than the ARM966E-S.[291]

Intel previewed its next XScale part: "Bulverde", the PXA270. It included several mobile-friendly features: SpeedStep, a dynamic voltage and frequency scaling (DVFS) tactic, and Quick Capture Technology for dealing with video and still images from camera sensors.[292]

Handspring unveiled its ultimate creation in June 2003, the Treo 600. Featuring Palm OS 5 running on a TI OMAP 1510 at 144 MHz, it combined the familiar Palm touchscreen features with a physical thumb-board. It was a slimmer 112x60x22mm, 163g unit ditching the flip cover used on previous Treo devices. It introduced a 640x480 pixel rear camera and offered 6 hours talk time and 240 hours standby. The smartphone had arrived, and Palm wanted it back – they acquired Handspring and its defector-founders for $192M, strengthening the new Palm to compete with Nokia, Motorola, RIM, and Sony Ericsson.[293,294]

Cameras were suddenly in. On the heels of the Handspring announcement, the Nokia 6600 appeared also sporting a 640x480 pixel rear camera – and would become the first million-unit selling camera phone. Its ARM9 processor at 104 MHz ran Symbian OS v7.0 with Nokia's iconic Series 60 software. It checked in at 109x58x24mm and 122g with a stylish oblong shape.[295,296]

Motorola was betting on Microsoft. The two collaborated on the MPx200, putting Windows Smartphone 2002 on a TI OMAP 710 at 133 MHz. Still no Motorola chip, as neither the i.MX1 family nor the brand new Motorola i.MX21 processor with a 266 MHz ARM926EJ-S core were inside. Motorola still had the formula for a small flip-phone; the MPx200 measured 89x48x27mm and weighed 116g, but it was missing a camera.[297,298]

A stealthy Palo Alto startup was also interested in digital cameras. Fresh off designing the ARM7-based Danger Hiptop (also known as the T-Mobile Sidekick), Andy Rubin formed Android, Inc. His vision was developing location-aware consumer devices that could better adapt to user preferences. He had the right idea, just too small a market in digital cameras. Rubin pivoted to work on an OS for smartphones, but ran low on capital. Android avoided premature extinction thanks to an envelope from Steve Perlman containing a gift of $10,000.[299,300]

ARM was printing money. Their so-called stabilization year of 2003 ended with 71% unit growth on 782M units shipped, a function of many previous licensees moving to production. Several new licensees came from China, including Datang and Spreadtrum.[301]

MPCore, NEON, and "The Keynote"

All the hard work of accumulating a stellar list that now totaled 128 semiconductor licensees entering 2004 was about to pay off. Even amidst industry-wide challenges, ARM tripled its net cash position since 1999 while also nearly tripling its annual research and development investments. This pointed at something big coming – likely several things.

In May 2004 at the Embedded Processor Forum, ARM announced they had been working with NEC on a breakthrough that would repeal Moore's Law. It was multicore, almost a full year before Intel debuted their first dual-core part. The ARM MPCore synthesizable multiprocessor contained one to four ARMv6 cores with full cache coherency and configurable power management technology allowing DVFS and complete shutdown of unused cores.[302]

Next were two multimedia breakthroughs. First, ARM unveiled a collaboration with Imagination Technologies on the PowerVR MBX graphics accelerator core, adding full OpenGL ES compliance. OpenGL was already very popular in workstations, and this step unified the game and multimedia communities around an open standard suitable for graphics rendering in mobile devices. It was the beginning of the mobile GPU.[303]

SIMD extensions featured in ARMv6 helped, but the demands of multimedia and transcoding were steadily increasing. Intel had tweaked their desktop MMX technology for SIMD, starting with the PXA270, into a more compact mobile variant, iwMMXt. Calling the bluff, ARM previewed NEON, featuring a full 64/128 SIMD instruction set operating in its own pipeline and 32 dedicated registers. NEON doubled the ARMv6 SIMD performance.[304,305]

Of the many licensees signed during 2004, three new names stand out. MobilEye, an Israeli developer of vision-based advanced driver assist systems (ADAS) for automobiles, licensed the ARM946E-S core for its first generation EyeQ product. Marvell disclosed a full ARM architecture licensing agreement, with their first 500+ MHz processor cores mostly captive to Marvell SoCs but also incorporated in some high-volume ASICs. Huawei, then little known outside of mainland China, signed on for ARM7TDMI and ARM926EJ cores.[306,307,308]

On the phone front, BlackBerry kept doing what they were doing, but added color with the new BlackBerry 7200 series running BlackBerry OS 4. After several attempts, Sony Ericsson had its first big smartphone hit with the K300.

During 2004, ARM shipped 1.3 billion cores. ARM also completed a $913M acquisition of physical library provider Artisan Components, vastly expanding its SoC capability. This drove ARM employee headcount to 1171. Basking in success, they created a new forum for their ecosystem.[309,310]

At its inaugural Developers' Conference in October 2004, ARM went after a microcontroller (MCU) breakthrough. While ARM cores, particularly ARM7TDMI, deployed in various MCUs to date, there was still an air of disdain. Many engineers and analysts saw 32-bit cores as overkill, adding unnecessary device cost and complexity where simpler 8-bit and 16-bit designs would do just fine.

The trump card was development and lifecycle costs. ARM was building a new story where software and tools were portable from a low-end MCU core to a mobile SoC core to a high-end multicore processor. As devices became more sophisticated, scalability and feature integration were becoming more important. That left the 8051 and PIC architectures in a lurch, without an upward scalability story. It also put MIPS in a position of having to catch up in downward scalability.

Warren East used "The Keynote" to launch the brand. He outlined three tiers in the new ARM strategy: the Cortex-A family for application processors, Cortex-R cores for real-time embedded needs, and Cortex-M cores for MCUs. And yes, the Cortex naming convention is A-R-M.

Image 6-3: Warren East

Photo credit: ARM

ARM then put the Cortex-M3 processor on the table without showing the rest of its hand just yet. The Cortex-M3 core was extremely compact and low power at just 33,000 gates (exact transistor counts depend on synthesis results). It was fast for its size, with all the embedded benefits of tightly coupled memory and peripherals, and the performance plus code density of Thumb-2. It featured a new interrupt mechanism, Tail-Chaining, which cut interrupt handling overhead as much as 70 percent. Also introduced was a new single-wire debug interface, reducing pin count, a sensitive area for MCU stalwarts.[311]

ARMv7, Cortex-A8, and Android

Everyone knew this thing called the ARM Cortex-A core was coming – but what was it? By this point, ARM and its licensees had displaced virtually all other processor architectures in mobile phones. The challenge for 2005 was to keep the smartphone advance going.

Some of the dots connected when ARM explained its new instruction set, ARMv7, at the 2005 Embedded Systems Conference in San Francisco. Reiterating that the A profile was for "sophisticated, virtual memory-based operating systems and user applications", ARMv7 incorporated recent technology announcements – namely Thumb-2 and NEON. A new addition was called Jazelle RCT (runtime compilation target), enhancing just-in-time and dynamic adaptive compilation. This would improve performance and code density for Java and similar environments – potentially reducing code footprint by a factor of three. ARMv7 retained 32-bit instruction set compatibility all the way back to ARM7TDMI, paving the way for easy forward migration.[312,313]

The Cortex-A8 processor came dressed to kill at the second ARM Developers' Conference in October 2005. It was a complete ARMv7 implementation plus AMBA 3 AXI and TrustZone support, and fully packaged with an Artisan Advantage-CE library. Its 13-stage superscalar pipeline backed a configurable level 2 cache, delivering 2.0 DMIPS/MHz – a level only reached previously by desktop processors. Without NEON, L2 cache, and trace technology, a Cortex-A8 fit in $4mm^2$ at 65nm.[314]

Support for Cortex-A8 was instantaneous. Samsung, TI, and Freescale (the spun-out entity from the processor operations of Motorola) were first, along with EDA tool vendors Cadence and Synopsys, and operating system providers Microsoft and Symbian.

It was the first note of the death knell for Intel XScale, at least as an applications processor. The gap in processor design elegance that DEC had initially established had closed quickly. As ARM progressed to Cortex-A8, gaps in low-power DSP integration for 3G, multimedia such as mobile GPUs, and advanced OS features such as Java performance blew wide open.

One of the problems at Intel was (and still is) sales force synergy; selling parts for PCs and parts for mobile devices requires two vastly different skill sets and compensation strategies. Without a robust design win pipeline, momentum wanes. The last major design wins for XScale in mobile devices were unwinding.

The very thin Motorola Q was announced in July 2005, measuring 116x64x11.5mm and weighing 115g. Its design was similar to BlackBerry devices, with a 320x240 pixel color display, a physical thumb-board, a multi-directional center button, a 1.3 MP camera, and a thumb wheel on the side for rapid scrolling. Microsoft Windows Mobile 5.0 ran on a 312 MHz PXA270 processor. Unfortunately, Q shipments didn't begin until the end of May 2006 after resolving major FCC certification delays.[315,316]

In a puzzling move, Palm introduced the Treo 700w – a Windows Mobile 5.0 phone. Other than the stubby antenna, lower resolution display with touch capability, and twice the thickness of the Motorola Q, the Treo 700w was nearly identical. However, Palm was not the same company it had been.[317]

PalmSource, the software unit separated from hardware teams post-Handspring to avoid competing with customers, struggled. An ambitious rewrite of Palm OS to Cobalt (version 6.0) flamed; not even the hardware side of Palm would use it. The death spiral started. ACCESS bought PalmSource in September 2005, plans shifted to Linux, and all its relevance in mobile was lost.[318,319]

RIM capitalized on those stumbles, launching the BlackBerry 8700 on an XScale PXA901 at 312 MHz. It checked in at 110x69.5x19.5mm and 134g with an improved 320x240 pixel display and the full QWERTY thumb-board. It had broad cellular network support with the addition of faster EDGE data transfers.[320]

Nokia dwarfed all three of those smartphone contenders combined. The N70 was running Symbian OS 8 with the Series 60 user interface on a TI OMAP 1710 at 220 MHz. The N70 lacked a QWERTY keyboard, still using the numeric keypad to tap out SMS messages. Its 2 MP camera with 1600x1200 resolution was taking much better photos, rivaled only by the Sony Ericsson D750.[321]

Microsoft, RIM, and Symbian were about to have company.

Andy Rubin was looking for a buyer for Android. Google was paranoid that Microsoft would win with Windows Mobile and lock Google out of mobile search engines. Smartphone operating systems and applications were massively fragmented, giving Google fits in compatibility testing. Google needed a smartphone strategy, fast.

Rubin had Android code working, and had a relationship with Larry Page from the Sidekick days. Just two weeks earlier, Rubin had been laughed out of a meeting with Samsung executives, an utter cultural mismatch. An email to Page secured a meeting. The Rubin attitude, prototype, and story clicked instantly. Google invested $50M in July 2005 to buy the eight-person Android team and their prototype operating system.[322]

ARM kept plowing ahead. In 2005, a year expected to be flat, shipments were 1.7 billion units – more than 1 billion into mobile – and revenue grew 14 percent. New headliners were making news. Actel was the first FPGA vendor to join the ecosystem, developing an ARM7 soft core. NVIDIA licensed the ARM11 MPCore, looking to couple it with GPU technology. Renesas grabbed the ARM1136JF-S for phones, and the ARM946E-S for consumer devices. Marvell had moved from captive to merchant provider, sampling its Feroceon core developed from a 2003 architectural license.[323,324,325,326,327]

Calm before Disruption

In some ways, 2006 represented a relative calm for ARM after intense effort and before the coming storm of developments that would disrupt mobile. The Cortex-A8 won acclaim from industry publications, and more deals with licensees. ARM counted 2.45 billion processors shipped, but stopped counting licensees, moving to a count of semiconductor partners shipping and total number of licenses outstanding. This reflected how many firms were now holding multiple licensees, and different types of licenses, with varying royalty implications.[328]

Nokia and RIM continued to ascend, securing the top two smartphone spots. Motorola was on yet another comeback trail, riding the Q and Microsoft Windows Mobile in North America and the A1200 "Ming" running Linux in China. Few outside the walls of Google had heard of Android yet.

ARM took the time to pitch their non-mobile story, seeking to diversify. They emphasized hard disks, printers, automotive, and other applications in the launch of the Cortex-R4 in May 2006. It included a lockstep feature, allowing two cores to run the same code in safety-critical applications. Trends pointed to multiple cores in smartphones, and Cortex-R was also positioned for 3G baseband processing.[329]

Intel, falling behind more every day in mobile, capitulated. They sold the XScale application processor lines to Marvell in June for $600M. Intel put a happy face on the news, saying they wanted to concentrate on WiMAX. Marvell was thrilled, with much bigger plans for ARM and phones – as Marvell CEO Sehat Sutardja would quip years later, "Who wants a dumbphone?"[330]

Indeed. However, who would make better smartphones? Rumors were flying about a new name about to enter the phone business. Two other firms were also plotting their moves. With the origin story of ARM processors complete, an even wilder ride of evolution of mobile devices with ARM technology inside began.

Part II:
EVOLUTION

Chapter 7: From Cupertino ...

Observed in hindsight after the iPhone, the distant struggles of Apple in 1997 seem strange, almost hard to fathom. Had it not been for the shrewd investment in ARM, Apple may have lacked the cash needed to survive its crisis. However, cash was far from the only ingredient required to conjure up an Apple comeback.

Apple found its voice and immense profits from a combination of excellent consumer-friendly designs and relentless lifestyle marketing. No technology company in history has undergone a greater transformation, reaching a near-religious status with its followers. At its head during the makeover was its old leader, chastened but not quite humbled.

Better Call Steve

Steve Jobs rev 2.0 publicly insisted he did not want to be Apple CEO again, preferring a role as advisor returning after a self-described NeXT "hiatus". In fact, by May 16, 1997, he had taken *his* company and the CTO role back, and taken a lot of good people and products to the woodshed. He then took to the pulpit at the close of the Apple Worldwide Developer Conference (WWDC).[331]

Jobs walked on stage, sat on a wooden stool, sipped a beverage from a paper cup, expressed gratitude for the warm welcome, and proclaimed he would chat and take questions. The first inquiry: What about OpenDoc? It was one of dozens of cancelled initiatives. Jobs sarcastically but emphatically said, "What about it? It's *dead*, right?" Amid audience laughter, the befuddled developer who asked the question said he didn't know; it must be alive because he was still working on it.

Standing up and setting down the cup, Jobs began pacing. He first apologized to developers, saying he felt their pain. Folding his hands for effect, he then said exactly what a room full of tormented engineers wanted to hear. "Apple suffered for several years from lousy engineering management. I have to say it. There were people going off in 18 different directions doing arguably interesting things in each one of them. Good engineers, lousy management."

With disdain for what anyone outside his circle of trust might think, Jobs planted his key message: "Focusing is about saying no. Focusing is about saying no." We are not just killing stuff – we're *focusing*. Genius. For the next several years, probably three or four, he said the task was not to "reinvent the world" but to reinforce the Macintosh. He did not worry about being different for the sake of different; he wanted the Mac to be better, much better than the alternatives. The new operating system project Rhapsody, incorporating NeXT technology that would become Mac OS X, had to win with developers and third parties. That included Adobe and (gasp) Microsoft. He alluded to a less parochial strategy in the future, saying, "There are a lot of smart people that don't work at Apple."

After more Mac-related questions, there was a curveball: What do you think Apple should do with Newton? Jobs recoiled and laughed uncomfortably, muttering, "You had to ask that." He propped himself against a display table and paused an agonizing 15 seconds, staring at the floor. He sighed deeply, and finally slightly nodded his head in self-affirmation of what he was about to say.

In very measured tones, Jobs said rarely can companies manage two large operating systems, and he could not imagine succeeding with three. With Mac OS and Rhapsody, Newton made three – it had nothing to do with how good or bad Newton was, it was unsustainable. The follow-up: Have you used a Newton? The first one was "a piece of junk" he threw away. The Motorola Envoy lasted three months before it received a junk label. He heard the latest Newtons were a lot better, but hadn't tried one. Shouts from the crowd implored that he should.

Jobs was about to tread a fine line between calling the mobile baby ugly and tossing it in a dumpster, and positioning for a future he was already planning.

"My problem is ... to me, the high order bit is connectivity." In 1997, Wi-Fi was not nearly as pervasive or fast as it is today, and 3G mobile networks were still on the drawing board. He said it was about email, and to do email, you needed a keyboard and connectivity. He said he didn't care what OS was inside such a device, but he didn't want "a little scribble thing." That was the end of Newton.

Legions of the faithful waited nervously. The June 1997 cover of Wired depicted an Apple logo superimposed on a sunburst and wrapped in a crown of thorns, with the caption "Pray", a not-so-subtle reference. Gil Amelio resigned as Apple CEO in July, outmaneuvered and powerless to say or do anything else.

At Macworld Boston on August 6, 1997, Jobs announced a sweeping agreement with Microsoft. Tired of fighting unproductive IP battles, Apple and Microsoft settled and cross-licensed patents. Next came a five-year pledge for Microsoft Office on Macintosh, with parallel releases to Windows versions. Apple licensed Internet Explorer, and the parties agreed to collaborate on Java.[332]

To a chorus of boos and catcalls from the audience, Jobs revealed a Microsoft equity position in Apple to the tune of $150M in at-market purchases of stock. The shares were non-voting, allaying concerns. This was a clear signal to institutional investors that Apple stock was not only safe, but also a growth opportunity. Jobs declared, "The era of setting this up as a competition between Apple and Microsoft is over as far as I'm concerned."

Apple stock rose 33% *that day*, and Jobs secured the interim CEO role the next month, a title he kept for 14 years. Refocused, and financed in part with cash from sales of ARM stock, Apple began its recovery. Investors saw rewards as the stock climbed – rising 212% in 1998, and another 151% in 1999.[333,334]

Design and Digital Dreams

Restoring the shine to Apple would take more than a focus on new software. Jobs had always been passionate about design, evolving from early interest in Eichler-style homes in the Bay Area, to the gunmetal gray of Sony consumer electronics, to a simplistic Bauhaus style that permeated the Macintosh.[335]

Hartmut Esslinger of Frog Design was an early confidant of Jobs, creating the "Snow White" design language of the Lisa and Macintosh days. Esslinger also created the NeXTcube. Jobs turned to Esslinger in early 1997 as an advisor to help build his recovery strategy. Esslinger was the voice calling for making peace with Microsoft and Bill Gates, focusing a messy hardware product line, and elevating industrial design to the highest priority. [336]

Fixing hardware would take a strong manager. Jon Rubinstein managed hardware design at NeXT, then departed to help form what became FirePower Systems, a Mac cloner acquired by Motorola in 1996. Rubinstein joined Apple in February 1997 as senior VP of hardware engineering. His first months were spent scuttling projects, overseeing layoffs, and convincing key performers to stay for a strategy he knew was coming, but could not fully share. [337]

One of those key performers was Apple's young industrial design leader, Jonathan Ive. An employee since 1992, Ive and his team had redesigned the later versions of Newton and other products. Prior to Jobs' return, the industrial design team was sequestered off-campus with dwindling resources – even the almighty Cray supercomputer had disappeared in cost-cutting measures. [338]

Understandably discouraged, Ive harbored thoughts of quitting. Rubinstein intervened, telling Ive that after Apple was recovered, they "were going to make history". Ive still had a resignation letter in his back pocket when summoned to meet with Jobs for the first time in the summer of 1997. They clicked instantly. The first product of the Jobs-Ive partnership was the highly acclaimed translucent, egg-shaped iMac. It succeeded, buying Apple time for the next move. [339,340]

Esslinger had thought beyond a three-to-four year Mac reboot, suggesting the quest for Apple should be "digital consumer technology." This was more than creating smart, elegant devices; it would be a convergence play combining technology and content to deliver new experiences. It would pit Apple directly against Jobs' first infatuation – Sony, who Esslinger had also worked with and characterized as "asleep" – and firms like Dell, HP, and Samsung, as well as mobile device companies like Motorola and Nokia.

"Steve understood that both technology and aesthetics are a means to do something else on a higher level," said Esslinger. "Most people think features, performance, blah-blah-blah, whatever. Steve was the first to say, it's for everybody." The higher level: "Realize what people would love to dream."[341,342]

Music and dreams go hand in hand. In 1999, the MP3 file sharing service Napster debuted, forever disrupting music publishing. Users could easily browse and download songs to a PC, then transfer them to a personal MP3 player such as the SaeHan MPMan or the Diamond Multimedia Rio PMP300. Napster drew copyright infringement fire from artists including Metallica, Dr. Dre, and even the Recording Industry Association of America (RIAA) representing the entire industry. However, some lesser-known artists embraced downloading-sharing as a new channel, connecting with their listeners in new ways, and freeing them from album production costs.[343]

That sounded exactly like a job for a design-conscious Apple.

Sony dominated personal audio players in 1999, with its latest CD Walkman D-E01 (or Discman) featuring sophisticated "G-protection" for electronic skip mitigation. As a traditional music publisher, Sony was concerned with producing and selling CDs, delivering the highest possible audio quality, and maintaining copyright protection. Personal CD players had an inherent limit in physical size – the compact disc itself – and took considerable battery power to spin the disc.

Flash-based audio players offered smaller physical size and longer battery life, and were skip-free. Sony responded with the Walkman NW-MS7 in September 1999. It combined their MagicGate Memory Stick and proprietary ATRAC3 encoding format – offering higher sound quality than MP3 files. In May 2000, they launched the 'bitmusic' site in Japan offering digital downloads priced at ¥350 (about $3.30) per song. This strategy screamed end-to-end protection, built around emerging Secure Digital Music Initiative (SDMI) technology and a cumbersome check-in, check-out procedure implemented with the OpenMG specification.[344,345]

You're Doing It Wrong, Here's an iPod

The personal audio opportunity lay somewhere between two extremes. There were expensive, proprietary players delivering high quality, highly protected content. There were cheaper players spewing freely shared, lower quality files risking legal battles. A digital audio player as a peripheral to a Mac made sense for Apple, if they could safely piece together the rest of a differentiated solution.

In its first move into music, Apple secretly purchased rights to the popular Mac-based MP3 management application SoundJam MP in July 2000, and hired its creators Jeff Robbin and Bill Kincaid (who both worked for Apple previously). Robbin and his team went to work on their next "jukebox" software, launched on January 9, 2001 as the rebranded iTunes 1.0 for Mac OS 9. Incremental releases added support for Mac OS X in the following months.[346,347]

iTunes was a hit, compatible with the Rio PMP300 and newer players such as the Creative NOMAD Jukebox – but those devices weren't "cool" enough for Apple tastes.

An Apple-branded device could take control of the look-and-feel and enhance the user experience through better iTunes integration. It could also open a new segment offsetting the dot-com meltdown in progress. As part of a Mac media hub strategy leveraging FireWire as the interface for transferring large audio and video files, Rubinstein was tasked to make an Apple digital audio player happen.

Flash memory was still very expensive, and that limited how many songs an affordable portable audio player stored. On a factory visit to Toshiba, Rubinstein saw a new 5 GB 1.8" hard disk drive, and seized its potential. Creative was already using a 6 GB 2.5" Fujitsu hard drive in their larger CD-sized unit.[348,349]

Tony Fadell, a veteran of General Magic and Phillips, was starting Fuse Systems with the idea of a hard disk-based music player for homes. Just as things looked darkest and funding was running out, Fadell went on vacation. His holiday was interrupted by a Rubenstein phone call. Fadell was offered an eight-week contract, with few details.

Upon arrival, Fadell learned of the idea for "1,000 songs in your pocket". Foam mock-ups representing a device with a display and battery were created, and shown to Jobs, Rubinstein, marketing guru Phil Schiller, Ive, and industrial designer Mike Stazger among others. Schiller's input was to lose the buttons and add the iconic jog shuttle wheel. Ive and Stazger set off to create a case design. Fadell hired on to run P-68, the code name for the iPod project.[350]

FireWire offered a much faster interface than the prevalent USB 1.x of the day. The diminutive Toshiba hard drive was a huge advantage in capacity, size and weight, and still cost effective. A distinctive case design with a unique interaction method was on the way. What about the chipset and software? Audio decoding required DSP-like horsepower ... or an ARM processor.

There had been talk of a one-year development schedule, but as with any consumer electronics product, shipping for the holidays is crucial. The 2001 solution for iPod: bootstrap with external resources.

A then little-known fabless firm came into play. PortalPlayer formed in June 1999 from a group of National Semiconductor execs targeting digital media solutions for consumer devices. They evaluated MIPS and other RISC architectures for how well they could decode MP3s in software, and settled on ARM as their core. Their 'Tango' platform was SDMI-compliant with both MP3 playback and record capability, also supporting higher quality Advanced Audio Codec (AAC) formats.[351]

PortalPlayer did a first version of Tango, the PP5001, fabbed at Oki Semiconductor in 0.25 micron. It integrated the audio playback core, LCD driver, and USB interface. IBM and Sony were working with the PP5001 in 2000, but its 60 MHz single-core implementation using a proprietary co-processor proved too slow, and several flaws affected yields and performance.

Needing a reliable high-volume, high-performance chip to win customers, PortalPlayer engaged with eSilicon, a firm with more experience moving fabless chip designs into foundries for production. The new partnership redid the design, quickly creating the PP5002 with a dual-core 90 MHz ARM7TDMI, delivering 0.18 micron chips from TSMC in a 208-pin package. This time, it worked.[352,353,354]

Apple reportedly benchmarked nine MP3 chips, including parts from Cirrus Logic, Micronas, STMicro, and TI. When Apple called, PortalPlayer dropped everything. The PP5002 chip produced the best sound and was exactly what Apple was looking for, and they wanted to use it off-the-shelf. Fadell's team went to work on software for the PP5002, extending playlists, adding equalization, and improving power management among many enhancements.[355]

An application framework including user interface software came from another small firm, Pixo, run by ex-Apple engineer Paul Mercer. Efforts were made to obfuscate what Pixo was actually working on, with prototypes in shoeboxes, but one thing was clear: Steve Jobs was heavily involved. Notes would show up daily with requests ranging from changing fonts (Jobs insisted on Chicago) to increasing loudness to reducing menu clicks. The iTunes team joined the effort, adding Auto-Sync capability to their iTunes 2 release and harmonizing user interfaces for the device and the Mac.[356]

Image 7-1: Apple iPod

Photo credit: Apple, Inc.

Apple held a special event to announce the iPod on October 23, 2001. It was a stunning demonstration of how ARM-based chips could enable radically new software and design quickly, in this case just over eight months from concept to shipment. The $399 device with a 160x128 pixel display measured 102x62x20mm, weighed 184g, and offered up to 10 hours play time before needing a recharge. During the two-month 2001 holiday season, 125,000 units sold.[357,358]

On the way to nearly 400M iPod units shipped over its lifetime, three other developments stand out. Launched on April 28, 2003, the iTunes Music Store teamed Apple with publishers BMG, EMI, Sony, Universal, and Warner for over 200,000 downloadable songs. Each AAC-formatted song was just 99 cents. Over the next five years, Apple sold 4 billion songs.[359,360]

PortalPlayer said its actual orders from Apple were "100 times the original forecast." They grew up along with the iPod, issuing shares in a NASDAQ public offering in 2004. They moved into a third generation series of parts, starting with the PP5020 adding USB 2.0, FireWire, and digital video output, and shifted into TSMC and UMC for foundry services to support the huge demand.

iPods were about to change radically. The 84x25x8.4mm, 22g iPod shuffle broke the $100 barrier in January 2005 by discarding the display and hard drive, using 512 MB of flash and an ARM-based MCU to control it. Samsung then convinced Apple it could supply massive quantities of NAND flash memory at bargain pricing. (More ahead in Chapter 8.) In September, the iPod nano debuted, a fully featured small player – 89x41x6.8mm and 43g – with a 176x132 pixel display and up to 4 GB flash.[361,362]

Deal making became even nastier as the stakes rose. One day in late April 2006, PortalPlayer was selling chips to Apple. The next day, they were gone. Samsung unexpectedly announced they had replaced PortalPlayer as the processor supplier for future iPods, with an undisclosed ARM core on custom SoCs. Taken off guard, saying Apple "never talked to us" about changing chips, PortalPlayer considered legal action but thought better of it. PortalPlayer agreed to an acquisition by

NVIDIA in November 2006, its designs becoming the starting point for the Tegra mobile SoC family.[363,364]

Several more Apple surprise maneuvers were in progress.

ROKR Phones You'll Never Buy

Motorola's last flip phone hurrah was the RAZR V3, a sleek design carved from aircraft-grade aluminum. Just before its launch, new Motorola CEO Ed Zander and his team ventured into Apple headquarters in July 2004 to discuss a possible collaboration with his friend Steve Jobs: an iTunes-compatible phone.[365]

Zander handed Jobs a RAZR prototype, the first effort from the new and improved Motorola. Jobs fondled it with more than passing interest, asking a barrage of questions about its construction and manufacturing. A thought flashed through Zander's head: "That SOB is going to do a phone." If Zander had realized just how fast Apple was closing in, he might have backed off the deal.

Mobile phones grew in 2004 with a 30% increase to 674M units. Nokia grew units but shrank four points in share to 30.7%. Motorola grew a point in second at 15.4%, and Samsung grew two points in third at 12.6%, followed by Siemens, LG, and Sony Ericsson. Motorola thought an iTunes play could cut further into Nokia's share. Apple saw Motorola as a way into cellular carriers.[366]

The Motorola ROKR E1, a respun Motorola E398, measured 108x46x20.5mm and weighed 107g. Inside was the same engine powering the RAZR: the Freescale i.250-21 quad-band GSM/GPRS chipset. A DSP56631 baseband processor coupled a Freescale DSP core with an ARM7TDMI core. The phone attached via USB cable to iTunes running on a Mac or PC, and firmware allowed it to hold only 100 songs. A knob-joystick provided navigation.[367,368,369]

After numerous delays and consternation over its non-wireless download method, the ROKR E1 was ready to go. The exclusive carrier was Cingular, soon to become AT&T Mobility. Zander wanted to announce ROKR at a Motorola analyst event in July 2005. Jobs and

Cingular overruled him, opting for a higher-profile Apple event scheduled for September.[370]

Positioned behind carrier qualification and marketing concerns was a bit of subterfuge. Starting in February 2005, "Project Vogue" had Jobs in top-secret discussions with Cingular – with no Motorola in the room. Jobs was formulating ideas for his own phone, and had already decided he wanted Cingular as his exclusive carrier. Cingular initially balked, allowing the ROKR E1 to proceed.[371,372]

Some say Jobs didn't actually want ROKR to succeed. He definitely didn't like compromises in design and marketing, and he wasn't impressed with the ROKR E1 itself. Subterfuge was about to escalate, approaching full-scale sabotage.

On September 7, 2005, Jobs took the stage to discuss the digital music revolution. He invoked Harry Potter and Madonna before introducing iTunes 5. Using his signature "one more thing" hook, he then brought out the Motorola ROKR E1. 100 songs. USB cable. "It's basically an iPod shuffle for your phone." He then uncharacteristically botched the music interrupted by phone call demo, returning to dead air instead of the song. Wrong button, he claimed.

22 minutes later, Jobs blew the room up debuting the iPod nano.[373]

That explosion left Motorola covered in indelible bad ink. Zander blurted out "Screw the nano" in an interview a few weeks later. Those expecting an iPod-plus-RAZR, or even a sorta-iPod alternative, were disappointed. Reviews termed ROKR E1 performance as "slow" in both downloading and responsiveness. Competitive carriers scoffed at the wired downloads. At $249, ROKR E1 sales peaked at just a sixth of the weekly rate for the popular RAZR, with above-average customer returns, and then plummeted despite price cuts.[374,375,376]

Once you're gone, you can't come back. Motorola continued with ROKR phones – just without iTunes capability. Their next attempt, the ROKR E2 released first in China in June 2006, went with the Intel XScale PXA270 processor and bundled RealPlayer running on Linux.[377]

As it turned out, Jobs had played the ROKR card perfectly. Motorola took all the damage, and Cingular was unscathed. Next to a ROKR E1, a well-executed Apple phone could look fabulous. Customers would have seen the idea of an iTunes phone already, and be anticipating what Apple could do better. All that remained was to persuade Cingular, and actually deliver a better phone.

"Project Purple" and the iPhone

Apple had already started asking what-if touch interface questions as early as 2003, and in late 2004 discussion turned to phones. Software engineer Scott Forstall began recruiting within the company for the secretive "Project Purple."

Preparing to sneak out for his top-secret meeting with Cingular's Stan Sigman in Manhattan in February 2005, Jobs pressed the Purple user experience team led by Greg Christie for a hard-hitting presentation. He got it, and put Christie in front of Apple director Bill Campbell and Jonathan Ive to tell it twice again. Jobs wanted validation, but he also was assimilating details so he could deliver the pitch.[378]

Cingular likely understood what they were seeing was vaporware, but were nonetheless intrigued. An Apple smartphone with Wi-Fi and music capability could be a must-have for consumers – and Jobs offered an exclusive. In return, Jobs wanted control of design and marketing, and to be a mobile virtual network operator (MVNO), bundling service with phones sold in Apple Stores and online.

There were just a few problems. High profile MVNO deals such as Disney Mobile were making headlines, but no phone vendor had ever been granted control by a carrier like Jobs was requesting. An Apple phone could draw new subscribers, but how many, and how much data they would they pay for?[379]

To break the deadlock, Jobs turned to Adventis, a Boston telecom strategy firm who had consulted on the Disney MVNO. A team led by Raul Katz including Garrick Gauch and others descended on Apple headquarters, slides in hand. Jobs walked in, smashed his hands holding a pretend iPod and phone together, and stated his case for selling phones with voice and data for $49.95 per month.[380]

Adventis built a story. Jobs and Cingular's Ralph de la Vega ended up "talking past each other" at their meeting. Jobs framed his ask in terms of better phone design, too vague. Cingular execs thought in hard terms like phone subsidies, network infrastructure costs, and average revenue per user (ARPU). New-age technology vision ran into old school, we're-the-phone-company conservatism. However, Jobs and de la Vega forged a personal bond that grew to trust.

CSMG acquired Adventis and continued discussions with Eddy Cue, Jobs' designee. In early 2006, Gauch built a detailed model of long-term value (LTV) with variables including ARPU, customer churn, and cost per gross addition (CPGA). Calculations showed ARPU improved $5, churn reduced significantly, and an unsubsidized Apple phone for $500 reduced CPGA by $300.

Specifics were what Cingular needed. By July 2006, an exclusive 5-year deal was in place, complete with revenue sharing: a royalty on iTunes Store purchases through phones for Cingular, and $10 per new phone subscriber for Apple. It wasn't the pure MVNO deal Jobs thought he wanted at the onset, but revenue sharing was all Apple really needed.[381]

Extended negotiations were a break for Apple, because they were still nowhere near ready. From a tiny band of UX designers in early 2005, Project Purple swelled. The familiar rounded rectangular outline emerged in an August 2005 mock-up, and by November, serious software and hardware effort began.[382]

The Purple team looked at Linux, but Jobs insisted on modifying Apple code to maintain control. Mac OS X was far too big, over 10 times too much, and Apple had resources tied up in a port to new Intel-based Macs until early 2006. Engineers rotated to Purple and began ripping and stripping code, shaping iOS.[383]

Samsung supplied the S5L8900 processor, labeled APL0098 for Apple. Fabbed in 90nm technology, it packed a 412 MHz ARM1176JZF-S core with an Imagination Technologies PowerVR MBX Lite GPU. One innovation was stacked die, placing two 512Mb SRAM dies on the SoC in a single package. This allowed faster memory transfers, and reduced circuit board size and overall system cost.[384]

Radio technology was new territory. Ive and his team created an elegant brushed aluminum prototype, but Apple's RF experts sent them back to the drawing board. Anechoic chambers were built, human heads were modeled to measure radiation, and millions were spent on cellular network simulation.[385]

Trying to smooth out network qualification, Jobs called de la Vega for their guidelines. Emailed was a 1,000 page document, the first 100 of which explained how keyboards should work. Jobs called back and went nuts. de la Vega laughed, assuring Jobs that didn't apply to Apple. When Cingular's CTO found out an exception was granted, he went nuts. de la Vega said more or less, "trust me."[386]

Everyone from Apple employees to de la Vega was under strict secrecy. Apple teams were signing into Cingular for visits listing their firm as "Infineon". It was a white lie; they were using the Infineon PMB8876 S-Gold 2 multimedia engine – also with an ARM926EJ-S core and a CEVA TEAKlite DSP core inside.[387]

Only about 30 individuals in Apple had a complete picture. Purple staffers were dispersed across campus. Telling a friend about the project at the bar was grounds for dismissal. Hardware engineers had fake software, and software engineers had simulators or fake boards in fake wooden boxes. Chipset vendors had fake schematics, suggesting a next-gen iPod.

On January 7, 2007, at Macworld, thunderous applause erupted when Jobs said he was introducing a revolutionary mobile phone, along with a wide screen iPod with touch controls, and a breakthrough Internet communications device. He repeated that three times, and then revealed they were one device: the iPhone.

Calling out smartphone contemporaries – the BlackBerry Pearl, the Motorola Q, the Nokia E62, and the Palm Treo 650 – as a little smarter than cell phones, he pointed out they were really hard to use. Mocking a thumb-board and stylus, he introduced multi-touch, and told the story of a slimmed-down Mac OS X, iTunes syncing, and advanced built-in sensors. The live demo was a tour de force, all with a Cingular logotype prominently on the display, enabled by an ARM11 core.[388]

What happened next was unprecedented. The 115x61x11.6mm, 135g quad-band GSM/EDGE phone with a luxurious 3.5", 320x480 pixel, 165 pixel per inch display and 2 MP camera went on sale in the US on June 29, 2007. A 4GB model was $499, and an 8GB model was $599. Lines formed waiting for Apple and the just-rebranded AT&T stores to open. 270,000 iPhones sold in the *first 30 hours*. After only 74 days, 1 million units were in customer hands.[389,390,391]

Image 7-2: Apple iPhone

Photo credit: Apple, Inc.

Even with a spectacular debut, Apple was barely a blip on mobile radar in 2007. On 1.1 billion phones shipped worldwide for the year, Nokia still enjoyed a large lead and recovered 3 points to 37.8%. Motorola was second at 14.3%, Samsung third at 13.4%, followed by Sony Ericsson and LG. Siemens had disappeared from mobile entirely, first sold to

BenQ and then bankrupt. A note in a Gartner press release: "The market saw three new entrants into the top ten in the fourth quarter of 2007 ... Research in Motion, ZTE, and Apple."[392]

Faster Networks and Faster Chips

Data monsters required feeding. One of the few complaints with the iPhone was its slow 2G EDGE capability. Moving up to 3G and HSDPA seemed urgent.

There was already big trouble brewing for AT&T. Those questions about how much data iPhone subscribers would use had been answered – 50% more than AT&T projections. Urban hubs like New York and San Francisco experienced the worst service issues. AT&T pointed to iPhone customers consuming 15 times more bandwidth than the "average smartphone customer"; read that as an email user who did occasional web surfing with a primitive mobile browser.[393]

AT&T asked Apple to consider data throttling.

Apple told AT&T to fix their network.

They were both wrong. AT&T claimed it had spent $37B on 3G infrastructure since the iPhone deal, and was preparing to spend another $17B on an HSPA speed upgrade, and billions more on 4G LTE when it was ready to launch. Apple's early baseband code was sloppy, leading to dropped calls and excessive bandwidth usage. Fortunately, Wi-Fi in the iPhone allowed much of the data traffic to be offloaded from the network, heading off an even bigger fiasco.[394]

RF school was back in session. Thinking AT&T might just be the problem, Scott Forstall and his iPhone team paid a visit to Qualcomm in late 2007. What they found was changing carriers, to Verizon for instance, required changing baseband chips. There were physical problems with board layouts, and software problems, but in the end, there was another complex set of carrier qualification issues. The Infineon choice had been super in Europe (their home turf) and OK in the US. A hasty switch from Infineon to Qualcomm solved some issues, but created others, and maybe a Verizon network really wouldn't hold up any better.

Trust was strained, but the Apple-AT&T partnership continued.

Apple quickly spun the iPhone 3G, using the same Samsung S5L8900 processor but enhancing the baseband chip to an Infineon PMB8877 X-Gold 608 with both an ARM926EJ-S and an ARM7TDMI-S inside. GPS was added, and a slightly bigger case available in black or white squeezed in a better battery increasing talk time to 10 hours. iOS 2.0 debuted with the new App Store. The phone went on sale in 22 countries on July 11, 2008 for a much lower price – $199 for an 8GB model, and $299 for 16GB. 1 million units sold in 3 days.[395,396,397]

Gunning for more speed, the iPhone 3GS carried a new chip when it appeared on June 19, 2009. The Samsung S5L8920 processor (later known as the S5PC100), labeled as the Apple APL0298, delivered a 600 MHz ARM Cortex-A8 core with an Imagination PowerVR SGX535 GPU. Its initial versions were in 65nm. The same Infineon PMB8877 baseband processor was used, and a single Broadcom BCM4325 chip replaced separate Marvell Wi-Fi and CSR Bluetooth controllers. A new 3 MP camera was incorporated, and iOS 3.0 was included.[398,399]

During the iPhone introduction, Jobs had quoted Alan Kay, "People who are really serious about software should make their own hardware." Software seriousness was a given at Apple. For the mobile device, the lessons of the iPod and iPhone showed making hardware now meant licensing IP and making SoCs.

A VLSI design team within Apple had done logic designs – for example, a custom ASIC in the Newton – and had been collaborating with IBM on Power Architecture processors and creating larger "northbridge" parts for Macs. There hadn't been a start-to-finish Apple processor design attempt since the Aquarius project two decades earlier. Designing a SoC in RTL using ARM processor IP and Samsung libraries was certainly feasible, but it would have to be much more efficient than desktop designs Apple was accustomed to working with.

Expertise was nearby. Dan Dobberpuhl, of StrongARM fame, formed fabless firm P. A. Semi in 2003 with industry veterans including Jim Keller and Pete Bannon. They embarked on research of Power Architecture, creating the PA6T core and the highly integrated

PWRficient family of processors. PWRficient featured an advanced crossbar interconnect along with aggressive clock gating and power management. Its near-term roadmap had single and dual 2 GHz 64-bit cores. The approach delivered similar performance to an IBM PowerPC 970 – the Apple G5 – at a fraction of the power consumption. This made PWRficient well suited for laptops, or embedded applications.[400]

Timing of PWRficient was inopportune. Before P. A. Semi got its first parts out in early 2007, Apple had switched from PowerPC to Intel architecture. Prior to the changeover, there had certainly been in-depth discussions between Apple and the P. A. Semi design team – but there was no going back for the Mac.

Niche prospects such as defense computing and telecom infrastructure made P. A. Semi viable, and they continued forward. Unexpectedly, Apple bought P. A. Semi and many of its 150 employees in April 2008 for $278M. PWRficient disappeared instantly. The US Department of Defense staged a brief protest over the sudden unavailability. Apple brokered "lifetime" purchases of the processor and a final production run, satisfying both buyers and bureaucrats.[401]

Now Serving Number 4

For months prior to the P. A. Semi acquisition, rumors ran rampant that given Apple switching the Mac to Intel processors, the iPhone would be next with a move to Intel's latest "Silverthorne" Atom processor. Aside from an unnamed source quoted in numerous outlets, this was never more than media speculation.

According to ex-CEO Paul Otellini, Intel had been in discussions about a mobile chip for Apple before the original iPhone design. The cloak of secrecy on the iPhone gave Intel little to go on, and they were skeptical of Apple's volume projections. "There was a chip [Apple was] interested in that they wanted to pay a certain price for and not a nickel more, and that price was below our forecasted cost. I couldn't see it," said Otellini. Intel passed.[402]

Once again, power, cost, and customization favored ARM in mobile.

Samsung did the physical layout, fabbed, packaged, and shipped three SoCs with ARM cores to Apple RTL specifications: the APL0098 for the iPhone, the APL0278 for the 2nd gen iPod Touch, and the APL0298 for the iPhone 3GS. For chip number 4 in the sequence, Apple would take over the complete SoC design from RTL to handoff for fab.

With the P. A. Semi acquisition in place and a VLSI design team bolstered with that new engineering talent, Apple signed a deal with ARM during the second quarter of 2008. ARM was non-specific when discussing its prospects in mobile on its earnings call, referring briefly to "an architecture license with a leading OEM for both current and future ARM technology." The agreement was for multiple years and multiple cores, and an architecture license gave Apple rights to derivative core designs.[403]

Many SoCs were hitting the market with the ARM Cortex-A8 core, and the Samsung S5PC100 was already in the pipeline. Apple wanted to get beyond what was widely available, and get in front of Samsung who was about to launch their own flagship smartphone. Apple was also about to launch an entirely new device, one that would stretch mobile processing power farther than it had been taken.

For a new core, Apple could have asked the P. A. Semi team to develop an ARMv7-compliant design. That would have taken 3 years, or longer. Another Power Architecture refugee was making its name redesigning cores with unique technology – and they were already working on an effort for Samsung.

Intrinsity, formed from the ashes of PowerPC chip designer Exponential Technology, had one of the hottest technologies in SoC design. Their Fast14 methodology combined multi-phase clocking with multi-valued logic using transistor dominos and 1-of-N encoding. The approach left instruction cycle behavior unchanged, but greatly boosted performance while simultaneously lowering power consumption. Their first big success in 2002 was FastMATH, a 2 GHz MIPS-based signal processor chip.[404]

On July 27, 2009, Intrinsity announced "Hummingbird", an implementation of the ARM Cortex-A8 core using Fast14 on a Samsung

45nm LP process reaching 1 GHz. Retaining strict instruction and cycle accuracy meant there were no operating system or application software changes needed. Intrinsity touted that their semi-custom approach could yield a SoC design in as little as four months.[405]

Exactly six months later on January 27, 2010, Apple announced the iPad with a new chip inside – the Apple A4. This powered the tablet's 1024x768 pixel, 9.7" multi-touch display, running the same iOS as the iPhone family and enhanced apps working with the larger screen. A Wi-Fi iPad model with 16GB of memory started at $499, with models including 3G connectivity up to $829. One million units sold in the first 28 days of availability.[406,407]

Image 7-3: Apple iPad

Photo credit: Apple, Inc.

The A4 chip was fabbed at Samsung on its 45nm LP process, featuring a 1 GHz Hummingbird core paired with an Imagination PowerVR SGX535 GPU at 250 MHz. One pundit suggested it "just [wasn't] anything to write home about", other than its cachet as an Apple-only device. Another group of observers termed it evolutionary, not revolutionary. However, its relative speed to market and the associated cycles of learning made it a stepping-stone to bigger things.[408,409]

In March 2010, Apple bought Intrinsity for $121M. Fast14 disappeared – much to the chagrin of AppliedMicro, who was working with Intrinsity on a new Power Architecture core. Apple refunded $5.4M to AppliedMicro in appeasement.[410,411]

The A4 appeared next in the iPhone 4, introduced on June 7, 2010. Even with a lower 800 MHz clock speed, the extra processing power enabled new features such as a 5 MP camera, FaceTime video calling, and an enhanced 3.5", 960x640 pixel, 326ppi "retina" display. Apple proclaimed the iPhone 4 the thinnest smartphone ever at 9.3mm. Two basebands were supported: a CDMA version using a Qualcomm MDM6600, and an HSPA version using the Infineon PMB9801. In the first three days of iPhone 4 sales, Apple racked up 1.7 million units.[412,413]

Mobile phone leadership was in a full-scale shakeup. Closing 2010, the worldwide mobile device market was at 1.6 billion units. Nokia still held first place with 28.9% share. Samsung had taken over second at 17.6%, and LG was in third with 7.1%. Smartphones were no longer "other". Research in Motion held 3.0%, and Apple was fifth on the list with 2.9% and 46.6 million units shipped. Both Sony Ericsson and Motorola had shriveled, with ZTE, HTC, and Huawei on their heels.

Viewed by operating system, the shakeup was even more ominous. Symbian was still first in units but plummeted nearly 10 points in share to 37.6%, and the fall was accelerating. Android was in second and had grown almost 19 points to 22.7%. Blackberry barely hung on to third with 16%, having shrank 4 points. iOS was in fourth with 15.7% and was the only other platform growing. Far behind was a scuffling Microsoft in fifth at 4.2%. A two-horse race was developing.[414]

Namaste, and a "Swift" Response

Alternating volleys of tablets and phones from Apple were in progress. Anxious users expected new SoCs for each subsequent generation. In his last major product introduction, Steve Jobs made an appearance while on medical leave to introduce the iPad 2 on March 2, 2011. It added front and rear cameras and a MEMS gyro, and reduced tablet thickness to 8.8mm.[415]

Its A5 chip held two ARM Cortex-A9 cores on Samsung 45nm. Rumors had Intrinsity working on a Cortex-A9-like core pre-acquisition, but lithography photos revealed the A5 cores were stock ARM IP. Dual 1 GHz Cortex-A9 cores were fast, although not quite "twice as fast" compared to the A4 as Apple suggested. Graphics had improved, with an Imagination PowerVR SGX543MP2 clocked at 250 MHz running apps from three to seven times faster.[416]

Analysts noted the A5 die was huge compared to other dual-core Cortex-A9 parts (122.2mm$^{2)}$). Integrated on the A5 was an image signal processor (ISP) for handling computational photography. It also had noise-reduction technology from Audience, with a DSP managing inputs from multiple microphones.

On October 4, 2011, Tim Cook introduced the iPhone 4S with Siri voice-recognition technology powered by the A5. In the new phone, there was an 8 MP camera with 1080p video and digital stabilization. Qualcomm took over as the sole baseband chip supplier with the MDM6610.[417,418]

The next day, Steve Jobs left this world, quietly and with dignity.

Although nobody could ever replace Jobs, Tim Cook was fully prepared to carry on, having assumed CEO duties with Jobs' recommendation on August 24, 2011. Cook had driven Apple operations since 2007, keeping Apple focused and highly cost competitive even as Jobs' health deteriorated.[419]

Opening the multicore SoC box for tablets had placed Apple in a battle with a relatively new foe – NVIDIA. The Tegra family with its Android support was finding homes in tablets positioned against Apple's iPad. The latest Tegra 3 debuted in November 2011 with quad ARM Cortex-A9 cores along with a low-power companion core and a 12-core GeForce GPU.[420]

A problem developing for Apple was how to give their tablets increased performance without penalizing their phones in cost and power consumption by having to use the same chip. Apple was using advanced dynamic voltage and frequency scaling which helped phones, but there was more headroom available. The solution was bifurcating the SoC family. This explains why Apple went with stock Cortex-A9 cores in the A5: there was a second chip in rapid development.

The first of the tablet-focused chips, the A5X, appeared in the 3rd generation iPad introduced on March 7, 2012. Where press expected a quad-core chipset, what everyone got was another dual Cortex-A9 design. However, Phil Schiller was ready with a quad-core *graphics* story, supporting more pixels on the tablet's 2048x1536, 264ppi retina display.[421]

The A5X held two key improvements: a bigger Imagination PowerVR SGX543MP4 GPU and a 128-bit wide memory subsystem doubling the 64-bit capability in the A5. Freeing up the memory bottleneck delivered results with the A5X beating the Tegra 3 on most graphics benchmarks. While Tegra 3 did outperform on CPU benchmarks, real-world tablet use rarely got that intense.

In the wings, instead of quad-core processing, Apple had a "Swift" response – the custom core everyone had waited for since the ARM architectural license was granted. Two of the new 1.3 GHz custom cores running the ARMv7 instruction set appeared in the A6, fabbed on a Samsung 32nm high-k metal gate (HKMG) low power process that reduced its die size to 97mm^2. With a clear break between lines, the A6 fell back to a 64-bit memory subsystem and a three core PowerVR SGX543MP3 GPU, saving on power and cost for the next phone.[422]

4G LTE highlighted the iPhone 5 with the A6 on September 12, 2012. The redesigned phone was slightly larger for a 4", 1136x640 pixel, 326ppi display. Yet, thanks to an aluminum case, it was thinner and lighter, 123.8x58.6x7.6mm and 112g. The iPhone 5 also featured the new Lightning connector. A Qualcomm MDM9615M broadband chip delivered the 4G LTE capability. 5 million units shipped in the first weekend.[423,424,425]

The A6X came shortly thereafter, cranked up with 1.4 GHz dual "Swift" cores with the quad-core PowerVR SGX554MP4 at 300 MHz and a slightly faster 128-bit memory subsystem, again on Samsung 32nm HKMG LP.[426]

The 4th generation iPad with the A6X was announced on October 23, 2012, immediately replacing the 3rd generation iPad announced just six months earlier. A combination of factors was at work: a nod to how much more competitive the A6X with "Swift" was compared to the A5X with Cortex-A9, moving the user base into Lightning connectors, and creating separation from the new iPad mini with a die-shrunk Samsung 32nm A5 chip inside. More records fell as first weekend sales of the tablet pair topped 3 million units.[427]

"Cyclone" and The 64-bit Question

Qualcomm was both a supplier and competitor for Apple. Increasing acceptance of Snapdragon processors with their custom "Scorpion" core and more advanced "Krait" core on the way meant Apple needed a bigger leap ahead in processor technology.

ARM announced their next innovation in October of 2011, showing off the ARMv8 architecture in all its 64-bit glory. Many analysts saw that as the official move into server space. Companies producing 32-bit ARMv7 multicore server chip suppliers such as Calxeda met with a slow and painful death as opportunities dried up. In an Intel and AMD context, 64-bit multicore was a necessity for servers.[428]

But, for mobile? Analysts giggled. Who needs that much physical memory in a phone? Wouldn't a 64-bit processor take too much power? Where is the mobile operating system for 64-bit, and who is going to rewrite apps to take advantage of it? The consensus was in mobile, 64-bit wouldn't happen quickly, if at all.

Dead wrong. What ARM and Apple sought was not physical memory, but virtual memory – managing multiple applications in a relatively small memory space by swapping them in and out from storage. This capability would be critical in getting one operating system to run on multiple devices. Also in play were benefits of wider registers in the processor, and wider paths between execution units in the SoC and memory, removing bottlenecks and increasing performance.

The rest of the mobile world was pressing for quad-core and octa-core, and leveraging the ARM big.LITTLE concept – octa-core was really two clusters of four processors, one for low power and one for bursts of performance. By October 2012, ARM had announced their first 64-bit ARMv8-A cores, the Cortex-A57 for the big side, and the Cortex-A53 for the LITTLE side. Android had yet to catch up with a 64-bit release, and many SoC vendors stood on the 64-bit sidelines waiting.[429]

Apple was having none of that. Surprising just about everyone, Apple got in front of the 64-bit mobile SoC wave on September 10, 2013. The A7 chip and its dual custom "Cyclone" cores were supported in iOS 7 and inside the new iPhone 5s. Why Jobs pushed so hard to create iOS from Mac OS X was becoming clear.[430,431]

The iPhone 5s carried enhancements in its camera and lens system, along with a new fingerprint sensor. However, the A7 and another ARM-based chip making its first appearance were the biggest developments.

Compliant with the ARMv8 specification, "Cyclone" doubled the number of general-purpose registers to 31, each 64 bits wide, and doubled floating-point registers to 32, each 128 bits wide. The A7 increased cache, with a 64KB data and 64KB instruction L1 for each core, a 1MB L2 shared by both cores, and a 4MB L3 for the CPU, GPU, and other resources. In the iPhone 5s, cores were clocked at 1.3 GHz. Cache latency was half of that seen with "Swift", memory latency was 20% improved, and sustained memory bandwidth was 40 to 50% better.[432,433]

Despite persistent rumors in the media that Apple was plotting to switch suppliers, like its predecessors the A7 was still fabbed by Samsung – correctly predicted by SemiWiki eight months before product release. On a 28nm process, the A7 was compact, with over 1 billion transistors in $102mm^2$. Along with the enhanced CPU cores and cache, it featured the Imagination PowerVR G6430 GPU, a four-cluster engine.[434,435]

Also inside the iPhone 5s was the M7 "motion co-processor", a fancy name for a customized NXP LPC18A1 microcontroller with an ARM

Cortex-M3 core. Its job was sensor fusion, combining readings from the gyroscope, accelerometer, and compass in real-time, offloading those tasks from the main processor. The M7 was the subject of "Sensorgate", with uncorrected accelerometer bias leading to app errors – eventually fixed in an iOS 7.0.3 update.[436,437]

Both the A7 and M7 went to work in the iPad Air and the enhanced iPad with Retina Display beginning October 22, 2013. In the iPad Air, the A7 was upclocked to 1.4 GHz, running iOS 7.0.3. Keeping the same 9.7" display as the 4th generation iPad, the iPad air was 20% thinner at only 7.5mm, and weighed 28% less at 469g. New antenna technology for MIMO enhanced Wi-Fi.[438]

With 64-bit processing and 64-bit memory controller enhancements in the A7, and an iPad refresh complete, Apple passed on an A6X-style enhancement with a 128-bit memory interface for tablets. Whether by planning or coincidence, Apple avoided conflict over the #A7X hashtag with Avenged Sevenfold in social media. (Well played, Apple.)

Nothing circa 2013 in 28nm came close to the "Cyclone" core, especially in mobile space. Compared to 3-wide instruction decode in the ARM Cortex-A57, "Cyclone" issued 6 instructions at a time into a massive 16-deep pipeline. For the next round in 2014, Apple tweaked the core under the name "Typhoon", improving add and multiply latency by one cycle each, and speeding up L3 cache accesses.[439]

The biggest improvement in the A8 was a foundry and process change to a more advanced TSMC 20nm node. Apple bandied a 2 billion transistor count, yet the chip was just 89mm². While not making sweeping microarchitecture changes, Apple teams had gone through the SoC design, optimized performance and power consumption, and adapted it for TSMC processes. A PowerVR GX6450 quad-core GPU gave the A8 some 84 times the graphics power of the original A4, while the dual-core 1.4 GHz processing power had increased 50 times.[440,441,442]

Bigger was the theme for iPhone 6 with the A8 and iOS 8. Two versions debuted on September 9, 2014, one with a 4.7" display and 1334x750 pixels, and the second dubbed "Plus" featuring a 5.5" display with 1920x1080 pixels. A new M8 motion coprocessor, again a customized

NXP LPC18B1 microcontroller, was inside. For the first time Apple incorporated an NFC chip in a phone, the NXP PN548 with an ARM Cortex-M0 core. Qualcomm's MDM9625M provided baseband, including 4G LTE carrier aggregation technology.[443,444]

Bigger it was. A record 10 million iPhone 6 units sold in the first weekend.[445]

For the A8X, Apple planned two new tricks for its tablet refresh. The TSMC 20nm process allowed many more transistors on a chip yet stayed within power limits. Apple started with three enhanced "Typhoon" cores at 1.5 GHz. Next came an Apple-concocted GPU using Imagination IP – essentially bolting two PowerVR GXA6450s together for eight graphics clusters. With an increased 2MB L2 cache and the 128-bit memory subsystem, the result was 3 billion transistors on a $128mm^2$ die.[446]

Slimming down to just 6.1mm thick, the iPad Air 2 launched on October 16, 2014 with the A8X inside. The iPad mini 3 was also announced, staying on the A7 chip. Apple didn't trumpet first weekend shipments – a sign the tablet market was shifting, and faster processors alone would not be the answer.[447]

Calling the Shots in Fabless
For a company that was not in the phone or chip business at the start of 2007, Apple now dominates both the mobile and fabless ecosystems based on design prowess and sheer volumes. Their voyage has gone from buying parts for iPods to feeling their way around a processor specification for the first iPhone to designing highly optimized SoCs with custom 64-bit ARMv8-A processors and multicore GPUs.

1.9 billion mobile phones shipped worldwide in 2014. With all phones taken into account, Samsung leads with 20.9%, followed by Apple with 10.2%, Microsoft (Nokia, assimilated) with 9.9%, and Lenovo (Motorola, expatriated) at 4.5%. Blackberry is now in "other", while half of the top 10 names are Chinese: Lenovo, Huawei, TCL, Xiaomi, and ZTE. Taking just smartphones, the iPhone 6 introduction pushed Apple over Samsung by 1.8 million units in the fourth quarter of 2014.[448]

The iPhone 6s ushered in the Apple A9 chip, along with the 12.9" iPad Pro and its A9X SoC inside, on September 9, 2015. It is intriguing both these devices launched in the same event, a timing change for Apple. Both devices run the latest iOS 9.

Details on the A9 and A9X and their new ARMv8-A "Twister" core are just coming out. Initial reports indicate L2 cache has tripled, from 1MB on Typhoon to 3MB on Twister, and L3 has doubled to 8MB. LPDDR4 memory support has been added doubling bandwidth, and DRAM and cache latency has also been reduced. Branch prediction latency has been cut significantly. These steps, plus an increase to 1.85 GHz and a few other tweaks, means the A9 delivers a 50 to 80% bump in performance over the A8.[449]

Image 7-4

Apple mobile processors

Chip	Device	Year	Cores	Type	Clock	Foundry	Process
APL0098	iPhone	2007	1	ARM1176JZF-S	412 MHz	Samsung	90nm
APL0298	iPhone 3GS	2009	1	ARM Cortex-A8	600 MHz	Samsung	65nm
A4	iPad, iPhone 4	2010	1	"Hummingbird"	1.0 GHz	Samsung	45nm
A5	iPad 2, iPhone	2011	2	ARM Cortex-A9	1.0 GHz	Samsung	45nm
A5X	iPad 3rd gen	2012	2	ARM Cortex-A9	1.0 GHz	Samsung	45nm
A6	iPhone 5	2012	2	"Swift"	1.3 GHz	Samsung	32nm
A6X	iPad 4th gen	2012	2	"Swift"	1.4 GHz	Samsung	32nm
A7	iPhone 5s, iPad Air	2013	2	"Cyclone"	1.3 GHz	TSMC	28nm
A8	iPhone 6	2014	2	"Typhoon"	1.4 GHz	TSMC	20nm
A8X	iPad Air 2	2014	3	"Typhoon"	1.5 GHz	TSMC	20nm
A9	iPhone 6s	2015	2	"Twister"	1.85 GHz	Dual	14/16nm
A9X	iPad Pro	2015	?	"Twister"	details pending at press time		

Incremental improvements in the iPhone 6s include an enhanced 12 MP camera, 23 LTE bands from a Qualcomm MDM9635, 3D Touch for pressure-sensitive "taptic" gesturing, and integration of the motion co-processor on the A9. Once again, even without major new features, the iPhone 6s shattered shipment records, 13M in its first three days.[450]

The iPad Pro goes large, with 5.6 million pixels and a stunning new input device: the Apple Pencil. (Steve Jobs must have rolled over in his grave upon hearing that.)[451,452,453]

Even in a smartphone world that is now 80.7% Android, Apple has an enormous amount of influence because of its iconic status and singular focus, compared to a fragmented pile of vendors. Focusing is about saying no – and that made Apple a $700 billion company based on market capitalization in 2015.[454]

That gives Apple freedom to write very big checks for what they need.

Billions of dollars in foundry business shifted in 2015, as Apple switched some of its orders back to Samsung and a tuned 14nm FinFET LP process for the A9 amid higher volumes of the iPhone 6s. TSMC retained some A9 business (more on the dual sourcing controversy in Chapter 8) and the lower volume A9X business, on its enhanced 16nm FinFET++ process offering higher performance for the iPad Pro. Other TSMC customers, including Qualcomm and MediaTek, may see capacity loosen up as a result.[455]

Demand for Apple mobile devices should continue to be strong. That assumes Tim Cook and his team keep Taylor Swift and millions of Apple Music listeners happy, execute on the IBM MobileFirst for iOS partnership to help tablets, and win with new ideas such as Apple Pay and the Apple Watch. (More ahead in Chapter 10.) The news to watch will be how the foundry business keeps up as Apple and others run into the 10nm process cauldron in 2016 and beyond.

Chapter 8: To Seoul, via Austin

Conglomerates are the antithesis of focus, and Samsung is the quintessential *chaebol*. From humble beginnings in 1938 as a food exporter, Samsung endured the turmoil and aftermath of two major wars while diversifying and expanding. Its early businesses included sugar refining, construction, textiles, insurance, retail, and other lines mostly under the Cheil and Samsung names.[456]

Today, Samsung is a global leader in semiconductors, solid-state drives, mobile devices, computers, TVs, Blu-ray players, audio components, major home appliances, and more. Hardly an overnight success in technology, Samsung went years before discovering the virtues of quality, design, and innovation. The road from follower to leader was long and rocky.

Considering All Aspects

The first Korean consumer electronics firm was not Samsung, but another well-known name with non-electronic roots. GoldStar, the forerunner of LG, was formed in 1958 as a new line of business for the Lucky Chemical Industrial Corporation. They built a tube-based radio in 1959, a portable transistor radio in 1960, and a black and white TV in 1966 – all Korean firsts.[457,458]

On the heels of success in other Asian nations, foreign electronics companies sought to develop the productive, low-cost Korean labor pool. With help from the US, the Korea Institute of Science and Technology (KIST) was chartered in May 1965. The government pushed foreign direct investment via joint ventures. Transistor assembly and test facilities sprang up, starting with Komi in 1965, followed by Fairchild and Signetics in 1966, and Motorola in 1967.[459]

Electronics professor Dr. Kim Wan-Hee from Columbia University visited Korea in August 1967 to provide advice on accelerating domestic capability. His initial observation was an overall lack of clean room technology, indicating a dire need for investment on a much broader scale. Dr. Kim began evangelizing Korean firms to consider joining the electronics push, among them Samsung.[460]

Bidding to industrialize the mostly agricultural South Korea, the government designated electronics as one of six strategic export industries. They passed the Electronics Promotion Act, which took effect in January 1969 with subsidies and export stimulation measures intended to draw in more industry participants.[461]

The time was finally right. Samsung founder and Chairman Lee Byung-Chull gathered his leadership team at the end of December 1968 to decide on a new field of business to enter, and a name. Samsung Electronics Corporation started on January 13, 1969. "Electronics is the most suitable industry for [South Korea's] economic development stage considering all aspects including technology, labor force, added value, domestic demand, and export prospects," said Lee.[462]

Even before officially forming its entity, Samsung had signed a joint venture agreement with Sanyo Electric in November 1968. A second joint venture deal was completed with NEC in September 1969. Based in a new manufacturing facility in Suwon, many of the 137 new Samsung Electronics employees ventured off to locations in Japan to learn the art of TV and vacuum tube production.[463]

By November of 1970, Samsung Electronics produced its first vacuum tubes and 12" black and white TVs, based on the designs of their Japanese partners. Samsung TVs evolved for the next few years, including a 19" transistor-based black and white model in 1973. (At the time, Korean domestic TV broadcasts were in black and white; color TVs were outlawed. Japanese TV imports were blocked – except those made through the joint ventures.) Lines of white goods, including refrigerators, air conditioners, and washing machines debuted in 1974.[464]

From the start, Samsung's strategy in consumer electronics was vertical integration – and a new capability was about to fall into their hands.

Kang Ki-Dong acquired a Ph. D. at The Ohio State University in 1962, and went to work at Motorola in Phoenix, Arizona in one of the largest discrete transistor plants in the world. As a Korean engineer who also spoke Japanese, he gave many plant tours to visiting engineers, building a network. When the time came to open a Motorola facility in

Korea, Kang was sent ahead to perform an initial assessment for land and contacts, including interviewing prospective engineering staff.

After returning to the US and working for another firm, Kang encountered two old friends. The first was Kim Chu-Han, a prominent radio network operator Kang had introduced to ham radio years earlier. The second was a classmate, Harry Cho, an operations manager in semiconductors. Kim had access to financing, Cho could sell, and Kang knew fab technology. Together, the three formulated an idea for a new company: Integrated Circuit International, Incorporated, or ICII.

ICII designed a digital watch chip, and made its first 5 micron CMOS large-scale integration (LSI) parts on a small 3" line in Sunnyvale, California during 1973. Demand was substantial, many times bigger than what ICII could produce, and customers held back volume production orders. Kim's firm was willing to finance expansion, but would only do so if the capital expenditure remained inside Korea.

Kang decided to pivot. He would continue ICII chip design operations in the US, but send the ICII fabrication line to Puchon and expand it there. The new joint venture was Hankook Semiconductor. However, the global oil crisis in 1974 and a litany of import red tape made the relocation much more expensive than planned. The fab finally came up and produced chips, but operating funds dwindled dangerously low within a few months.[465]

There were only so many places to go for major technology financing in Korea. The economic climate was worsening, with oil prices continuing to skyrocket and the Japanese pulling back. Samsung had money. Lee Byung-Chull and his son, Lee Kun-Hee, were convinced they had to enter the semiconductor business, not just buy chips. They tried persuading their management teams that advanced chips such as Hankook was building would be the future. Management balked.

Against such sage advice, on December 6, 1974, the Lees funded a stake in Hankook Semiconductor – using money from their own pockets. By the end of 1977, the operation was fully merged, becoming Samsung Semiconductor.[466,467]

Developing DRAMs

Lee and his son understood one important concept that Kang and their own management team had missed: when it comes to chips, fab cap ex comes first, and if timed correctly, profits follow. Without sufficient fab capacity ready at the moment demand materializes, even the best chip designs cannot succeed. That lesson would repeat itself many times over as Samsung grew.

Happily producing appliances, watches, radios, and TVs, Samsung focused on efficiency. Its assembly plants became more automated, and both Korean consumers and export trading partners were being supplied goods. An indicator of progress: Samsung Electronics America opened in New Jersey in July 1978.

Research on semiconductors in Korea was booming. In 1976, the government-backed Korea Institute of Electronics Technology (KIET) opened a research center in Kumi. Among many activities, they set up a joint venture with VLSI Technology, and created a VLSI wafer fab with capability for 16K DRAMs by 1979.[468]

The government tried to draw the *chaebols* – among them Daewoo, GoldStar, Hyundai, and Samsung – and their talent to Kumi, seeking to create a hub of VLSI fab expertise. Samsung was still focused on LSI technology feeding its own business with linear and digital components, and was fighting allocation battles in procuring those parts from foreign sources. To protect its supply chain, Samsung Electronics integrated Samsung Semiconductors on January 1, 1980.[469]

KIET stopped short of 64K DRAMs for several reasons. The first was the 1981 Long-Term Semiconductor Industry Promotion Plan. Developed by the Korean government with KIET cooperation, it specifically targeted fabrication of memory chips for export. Second, telecommunications assets were being privatized, providing immediate income for the *chaebols* to invest in semiconductors.[470]

Daewoo, GoldStar, and Hyundai were all in on VLSI fab investments, but Samsung had extra incentive. In March 1983, they began producing a PC, the SPC-1000. Vertical integration goals made producing their own DRAM attractive. Samsung went to work. They had to improve processes from 5 to 2.5 micron, increase wafer size to 130mm, and gain key VLSI insight. A yearlong feasibility study began at their new Suwon semiconductor R&D center in January 1982.[471]

With some VLSI knowledge in hand, in early 1983 Samsung set up an "outpost" in Santa Clara, California. Its primary objective was competitive research, seeking a licensor for DRAM technology, and it would serve as a recruiting and training center to add semiconductor talent from the US.

Finding companies to talk to was the easy part. Hitachi, Motorola, NEC, Texas Instruments, and Toshiba all rebuffed Samsung's licensing request. (So much for relying on joint venture partners such as NEC.) The search came down to Micron Technology, who agreed to license its 64K DRAM design in June 1983 after an assembly pilot. Also licensed was a high-speed MOS process from Zytrex.[472,473]

Image 8-1: Samsung 256Kb DRAMs and wafer

Photo credit: Samsung

Samsung went from zero to a 64Kb DRAM in six months, sampling fabbed parts in November 1983. They then fabbed a Micron 256Kb

DRAM design by October 1984. To break free from licensing fees, the Samsung Santa Clara research team designed a 256Kb DRAM through reverse engineering, sampling an all-new part in July 1985. Volume 256Kb DRAM production started in a new facility in Giheung on a 2 micron process.[474,475]

These were the first steps along a path of generational breakthroughs that made Samsung the largest producer of memory chips in the world by 1993 – ten years after sampling their first DRAM part. This set the stage for other advances in VLSI chip fabrication that would be critical for the next consumer device initiative.

Mountains in the Way

Just as the mobile craze started with car phones in most other markets, so was the case in Korea. Korea Mobile Telecommunications Services (KMTS, later to be known as SK Telecom) launched its 0G radio telephone network in April 1984, grabbing 2658 subscribers by the end of the year.[476]

Samsung began dabbling in mobile wireless R&D in 1983 with some forty engineers. Without much to go on except the KMTS 0G network, they spent considerable effort reverse engineering a Toshiba car phone. The resulting design was the Samsung SC-100 car phone produced in 1986. It was rife with quality issues, leading to the R&D team being chopped to just ten members and wondering what to do next. That was probably a blessing, because it inspired team leader Lee Ki-Tae to buy ten Motorola cellular phones for benchmarking.[477]

KMTS was upgrading their network to 1G cellular, with an AMPS infrastructure rollout that would be ready to launch by July 1988 – just in time for the Seoul 1988 Summer Olympic Games. The schedule gave Samsung plenty of time to dissect the Motorola designs and learn about AMPS before having their next phone attempt ready.

Chairman Lee Byung-Chull would not see the Olympic festivities. Lee Kun-Hee assumed control of the firm on December 1, 1987, barely two weeks after his father's passing. At first, it was business as usual – running a large corporation took precedence. The infant cell phone division went mostly unnoticed.

The Samsung SH-100 handheld 1G phone debuted in 1988. It sold fewer than 2000 units, mostly to VIPs, and it too suffered in quality. This cycle repeated several times over the next few years: new Samsung phone, similar lack of quality, and similarly disappointing sales measuring in the few thousands.[478]

Samsung had run head on into the dark art of radio frequency engineering.

Major manufacturing and design issues early on allowed consumer doubt and competition to creep in. Motorola, then the gold standard for quality and mobile phone design, took over half the Korean mobile phone market while Samsung scrapped for mere percentage points in share on their home turf.

When it comes to RF technology, reverse engineering can only tell a team so much. Reproducing a receiver, such as a radio or TV, is an easier but still challenging task. Creating a sophisticated transmit and receive device like an analog 1G AMPS phone, especially with miniaturization techniques applied, is a different matter. Manufacturing quality concerns likely stemmed from a combination of componentry, layout, assembly, and tuning methods.

However, the biggest problem Samsung faced was a serious design flaw. Legend has it that while on a hike in the mountains, a Samsung employee saw another hiker placing a call on a Motorola phone. Sure enough, the Samsung phone the employee was carrying would not connect from that same spot. Whether the anecdote is accurate or slightly embellished, the scenario described held an important clue: two-thirds of Korea's topography is mountainous.

R&D engineers had failed to account for an RF effect called multipath, where a signal reflects off terrain and buildings, and several versions arrive at the receiver at slightly different times in varying strength. Multipath was the root cause of many Samsung call quality issues. Solving the problem meant redesigning handset antennas, improving the physical connection between the antenna and circuit board, and enhancing signal discrimination.

New Management, Fired Up

The struggles of the cell phone operation and growing concern with
Samsung Electronics consumer goods businesses had made it to Lee
Kun-Hee's attention. While visiting Los Angeles in early 1993, Lee
noted the sad state of Samsung products tucked away on back shelves
at an electronics retailer. Unsatisfied with a reputation as a "knockoff"
supplier, Lee began asking questions.[479]

The strategy of low cost, mass production, and reverse engineering that
had served Samsung well in the 1970s and 1980s was limiting
Samsung's competitiveness on a global scale in the 1990s. Developing
Asian nations were entering the fray as even lower cost producers of
electronics. Lee was carefully observing the Japanese response to the
situation, and watching consumer electronics shift from analog to
digital technology.

Sensing the urgency, Lee went outside for help. One of the people he
called on was advisor Tamio Fukuda, who went on to become professor
at the Kyoto Institute of Technology. From a set of inquiries developed
by Lee and his senior staff, Fukuda prepared a comprehensive response
– now known as the Fukuda Report. On June 4, 1993, Fukuda presented
his thoughts.[480]

When asked what design is, Fukuda wrote: "[Design] is not simply
creating a form or color of the product, but rather forming or tapping
cultural activities to create a new kind of user lifestyle by increasing
added value, starting from the study of the convenience of the
product."

It affirmed what Lee had already decided to do. Days later at a larger
gathering of Samsung executives in Frankfurt, Lee rolled out his New
Management initiative. Dislodging employees from ingrained practices
would not be easy. Lee issued workers the famous challenge: "Change
everything except your wife and children." He then detailed a sweeping
set of reforms, including a mandate all workers report two hours early
each day.

Edicts to the cell phone division got very specific. "Produce mobile
phones comparable to Motorola's by 1994 or Samsung will disengage

itself from the mobile phone business." The days of reverse engineering were over. Samsung engineers had a head start on the signal quality problems, and furiously explored every other facet of design from weight to strength.

In November 1993, they presented their product: the SH-700. It was a candy-bar, light at 100g, with an all-new mountain-tested antenna. Lee was given a model to try – and immediately threw it on the ground and stepped on it. He then picked it up, made a call, and to everyone's relief it worked. Designers had placed special pillars into the plastic case and circuit board to withstand typical abuse such as being sat on, or stepped on.

There was more to design than just engineering. A new marketing campaign debuted: "Strong in Korea's unique topography," a reference to the phone actually making calls in the mountains. The SH-700 initially sold 6,000 units a month, and by April 1994 was selling 16,000 units a month. The follow-on SH-770 Anycall was introduced in October 1994, enhancing the brand. By mid-1995, Samsung displaced Motorola as the cell phone market share leader in Korea.[481]

What most consumers didn't see, but Samsung employees felt, was the real quality story. Individual phone screening at the factory reduced problems before shipment, but a massive bone pile of dead phones developed. Lee sent some of the first SH-770s as holiday gifts, getting back reports of some of them not working. Embarrassed by quality escapees, he investigated further – and discovered the bone pile.

In March 1995, Lee visited the Gumi facility where the SH-770 was manufactured. Two thousand employees were invited to a rally in the courtyard, complete with "Quality First" headbands for all. Under a "Quality is My Pride" banner was the bone pile with phones and fax machines from the plant – some say numbering 150,000 units. A handful of workers smashed the defective devices with hammers, threw them into a bonfire, and bulldozed the ashes. Many of those who saw the spectacle wept openly. It was a lesson never forgotten.[482]

Finding Digital Footing

Design teams across Samsung got a message too: get digital capability into products as fast as possible. The push was on three technologies now taken for granted in mobile devices: DRAM, flash, and CDMA.

Samsung had caught the pack in DRAM. With massive fab investments of $500M or more for five consecutive years to get running on 200mm wafers, Samsung vaulted over Toshiba to become global DRAM market share leader in 1993. Heavy R&D was lining up for the next major step, a 256Mb DRAM that would put them ahead of the Japanese technology giants for the first time.[483]

Toshiba had developed a new technology – NAND flash memory – but was losing ground quickly to Intel who was outproducing them on a NOR flash alternative (with different application characteristics). To close the capacity gap, Toshiba licensed its NAND flash design to Samsung in December 1992. Again, it was about a ten-year cycle from licensing to leadership – Samsung shipped its first NAND flash parts in 1994, and by the end of 2002 was the global market share leader at 54% in NAND flash.[484,485]

Digitizing cell phones meant another large investment in new technology. Where Europe forged ahead with its GSM vision, and US carriers waffled between D-AMPS, GSM, and CDMA for 2G, Korea would make a bold move.

Dr. William C. Y. Lee, an integral part of AMPS development at Bell Labs, was deeply involved with a young company developing CDMA technology: Qualcomm. As chief scientist at Pacific Telesis, Lee led several CDMA network trial installations. It was through Lee that Qualcomm was introduced to the Korean government, where the Ministry of Communications (MoC) was seeking a way to help propel Korea onto the world telecom scene.

After rounds of complex negotiation, Qualcomm and Korea's Electronics and Telecommunications Research Institute (ETRI) reached a joint technology development agreement for CDMA infrastructure in May 1991.[486,487]

On the surface, the CDMA choice seemed simple. Among its many technical advantages was better subscriber capacity achieved with fewer cell towers compared to TDMA systems like D-AMPS or GSM, meaning lower infrastructure rollout costs. However, the technology was unproven in a large-scale deployment, and Qualcomm owned it, requiring royalties.

The economic side effects were more compelling. Selecting CDMA would effectively lock out both foreign infrastructure suppliers and handset vendors, buying Koreans time to develop a unique solution with Qualcomm. If CDMA were adopted elsewhere, Korean firms could profit in exports. Four Korean electronics manufacturers – Hyundai, LG, Maxon Electronics, and Samsung – were recruited for the effort, targeting a 1996 launch.[488]

It was a huge win for Qualcomm who would initially provide the chip sets for CDMA phones and infrastructure throughout Korea. In a unique arrangement, Korean manufacturers paid a percentage of their handset selling price as a royalty, and Qualcomm helped fund further joint development effort with ETRI.

SK Telecom IS-95A CDMA service was ready in Seoul in January 1996. Just over a year later, one million subscribers would be using CDMA across Korea.[489]

Among the first CDMA phones in Korea was the Samsung SCH-100, a 175g candy bar handset released in March 1996 with an early Qualcomm MSM chipset. (The beginnings of the Qualcomm MSM family were not ARM-based; Qualcomm didn't have an ARM license until 1998. More ahead in Chapter 9.) Exports of a modified SCH-1011 phone to Sprint in the US started in June 1997.[490,491]

CDMA did gain acceptance in many regions. Samsung quickly garnered 55 percent of the global CDMA handset market by the end of 1997. They were beginning an envelopment strategy in mobile, working on many phone models at once for the home market and for various export markets. Some of the phones appearing in 1998: the SCH-800 CDMA flip phone with SMS messaging, the SPH-4100 PCS phone setting a new lightweight mark of 98g, and the SGH-600 GSM phone that helped European exports.[492]

An Unprecedented ARM License

The pace was also picking up in ASIC design. In May 1994, Samsung paid a substantial sum for an ARM6 and ARM7 license – accompanied with consulting efforts from ARM. One of the first products to receive an ARM-based chip was in a new category: the Samsung DVD-860. Released in November 1996, the DVD player contained four Samsung developed ASICs, beating major firms including Toshiba, Matsushita, and Pioneer to market.[493]

At Hot Chips 1996, Samsung presented what was likely the basis of one of those ASICs: the MSP-1 Multimedia Signal Processor. It combined an ARM7 core with a proprietary 256-bit vector co-processor, used for real-time MPEG video decoding, and 10K of free gates for customization. The MSP-1 was fabbed in 0.5 micron CMOS, came in either a 128-pin package or an extended 256-pin package with a frame buffer memory bus, and consumed 4W.[494]

Extending its ASIC efforts into phones, Samsung licensed the ARM7TDMI core In September 1996. By late 1998, Samsung had a CDMA chipset ready for internal use, appearing first in the Samsung SCH-810 CDMA phone in early 1999 paired with a Conexant Topaz chipset for the CDMA baseband. In February 1999, Samsung took an ARM9TDMI core and ARM920T processor license, preparing parts on a new 0.25 micron process running at over 150 MHz.[495,496]

The first big merchant SoC hit for Samsung came in 2000 with the S3C44B0X, a 66 MHz ARM7TDMI-based part designed into the Danger Hiptop – created by Andy Rubin. That chance encounter between Samsung and Rubin would loom large several years later and prove to be a turning point for the entire mobile industry. The S3C44B0X was fabbed in 0.25 micron, in a 160-pin package.[497]

In July 2002, ARM and Samsung announced a comprehensive long-term licensing agreement. It gave Samsung full access to all current and future ARM IP for the unspecified duration of the agreement – what one industry observer termed the "all-you-can-eat" license. The unprecedented agreement moved Samsung from just another ARM customer into a partner developing the future direction of ARM roadmaps.[498,499]

Image 8-2: Danger Hiptop

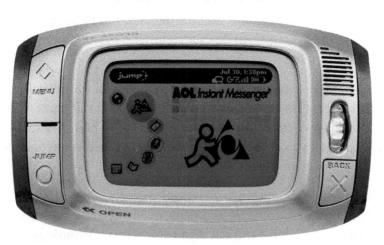

Photo credit: T-Mobile

At the Microprocessor Forum in October 2002, Samsung showcased just how much impact they could have. The stock ARM1020E core shipped from ARM was designed for a 0.13 micron process running at 325 MHz. Using techniques borrowed from the Alpha microprocessor that Samsung had taken over fabbing at the end of its life, Samsung reengineered the ARM1020E into the "Halla" core. Halla was still on 0.13 micron, but ran at up to 1.2 GHz, becoming the first ARM-based design to break the 1 GHz barrier.[500]

Samsung had assembled a stunning array of semiconductor technology for mobile devices: DRAM and flash, ARM processor cores and ASICs, and miniaturized LCD panel capability derived from larger efforts for TVs and monitors – all from its own fab facilities. In what was becoming Samsung modus operandi, they applied their portfolio and expertise in an attempt to envelop two emerging mobile application segments: music players, and the smartphone.

For a Few Flash Chips More

Commodity semiconductors are a tricky business. Insufficient capacity means competitors win sockets with better pricing and shorter lead times. Too much capacity leads to a drag on costs as expensive equipment sits idle, or worse yet layoffs occur and facilities close. Once major new fab capacity comes on line, demand has to be stimulated to fill it. Many times, long-term deals are cut with customers to lock in forecasts and pricing.

The vertical integration strategy Samsung deployed was initially a response to being on the tail end of the supply chain. If parts were scarce, production lines for consumer goods could halt. Paying too much for parts hurt competitiveness. Samsung's own semiconductor fabs assured electronics factories kept running.

As Samsung's DRAM offerings improved, exports boomed. Profits were plowed back into fab capacity and R&D, even in economic downturns, to increase market share and outpace competitive technology advances. Flash memory was an extension of the success, another way to utilize wafer starts.

Lee Kun-Hee was operating in a very different competitive environment from what his father experienced. His passion for quality, branding, and design stemmed from understanding that success in electronics would mean opening new markets and then creating new and exciting application segments. Competing in both semiconductor technology and finished consumer goods meant competing with Samsung's own customers – or suppliers – in many cases.

With the DVD player off and running, Samsung was again looking for a new consumer application segment for digital technology. 1998 brought the flash-based MP3 player, with the SaeHan MPMan and the Diamond Multimedia Rio PMP300 hitting the market. The Rio PMP300 came with 32 MB of internal flash and a more aggressive $200 price tag, and sold well – too well. It drew the wrath of the RIAA as the mobile device, along with Napster, that was enabling copyright infringement on a mass scale.[501]

Samsung smelled flash sales and dove in anyway. At CES 1999, they introduced the Yepp brand of flash-based MP3 player. There was an ominous footnote in the press release indicating they were seeking "official approval from the RIAA," with agreement to participate in the SDMI initiative. Yepp would become a sprawling MP3 product line with many models and variants. After 2003, the Yepp brand was retired outside Korea, but new models continued under Samsung branding until 2013.[502]

A few months after the Yepp introduction came another category-breaker in August 1999. The Samsung SPH-M2100 was a PCS phone with an integrated MP3 player and 16 or 32MB of flash – the first phone with an MP3 player. (The Samsung Uproar, or SPH-M100 introduced later in November 2000, usually gets that credit; it was exported to Sprint and got far more visibility.)[503,504]

Curiously, Samsung went with a non-ARM architecture for early MP3 players. Most players had an 8-bit MCU for the user interface, a DSP for the MP3 decoding, flash to store the MP3 files, and a USB chip for connecting to a PC. In August 2001, Samsung announced a new chipset called the CalmRISC Portable Audio Device (C-PAD) for MP3 player OEMs and use in its Yepp lines. The single chip S3FB42F combined a CalmRISC 8-bit MCU with a 24-bit DSP.[505,506]

On October 23, 2001, Apple changed almost everything about music players. Given the timing, the Samsung S3FB42F was probably not one of the nine MP3 chips Apple evaluated for the iPod. Once word got out about the PortalPlayer PP5002 being in the iPod, the S3FB42F and 8-bit chips like it were old news.

New companies flowed in to MP3 players, including iriver formed by ex-Samsung personnel. A big barrier fell when SDMI went on indefinite hiatus, killed by a combination of concerns from sound quality to a controversial cracking of their encryption mechanism. Even Samsung eventually turned to PortalPlayer; the PP5020 appeared inside the YH-820 at CES 2005.

Coincidentally, January 2005 was the same time Apple decided to get into flash-based players with the iPod Shuffle. That threw more demand for NAND flash into a tight market – and there was a lot more demand coming shortly, if someone could assure Apple of supply.

It sounds odd to characterize a $20B market as "tight", but indeed flash producers were having trouble keeping up in 2005. After the 2001 dot-com downturn, the overall flash market – NAND plus NOR – doubled in three years. Like other DRAM producers, Samsung was shifting capacity toward flash to capture higher selling prices and margins while filling demand. They moved so much to the flash side, flash average selling prices (ASPs) fell under DRAM ASPs for the first time, and it was looking like 2006 might be an overcapacity year.[507]

The wildcard was Apple. Samsung controlled nearly a third of the flash market, and could boost its share and expand further. Apple was preparing to launch the iPod nano in September 2005, with up to 4GB of flash in each unit. One analyst estimated the nano introduction, *by itself*, could increase the worldwide flash market some 22%.

To win the Apple business, Samsung pledged 40% of its NAND flash fab capacity at a 30% discount. Apple covered its bases, saying they had supply agreements with Hynix, Intel, Micron, Samsung, and Toshiba for five years of NAND flash. The bulk of their supply came from Samsung.[508,509]

When elephants make deals, it is the grass that suffers. Flash was finally cheap, if one could get it. Apple got all it wanted, but hundreds of smaller MP3 flash-based player manufacturers worldwide suddenly found themselves with enormous lead times for flash – or no allocation at all. Many of these firms simply disappeared, unable to ship product to meet increasing demand.

Capacity would catch up, but it would take a few years. Samsung immediately kicked off expansion at their Hwaseong complex for more DRAM and FLASH capacity in a seven-year, $33B cap ex program. Another expansion was coming soon, deep in the heart of Texas, and it would lead to even bigger deals.[510]

Smartphone Sampler

Meanwhile, Samsung started pumping out smartphones everywhere, in a myriad of styles and configurations, hot on the trail of competitors. Nokia was firmly behind Symbian, for better or worse. Research in Motion was on its own operating system platform, and Apple would develop their own as well.

At the other end of the spectrum, Motorola at one point had 20 different phone operating systems in various stages of development. Similarly, Samsung spent the period from 2001 to mid-2009 wandering between several operating system options. A quick look at some of their more significant efforts during this period shows just how broad their smartphone – or "mobile intelligent terminal" as they called it in the beginning – portfolio became.

The darling of the early smartphone era was Palm OS, and for a while, Sprint was very enamored with it. The Samsung SPH-i300 released in late 2001 ran Palm OS 3.5 on a 33 MHz Motorola DragonBall 68328 processor. In 2003, the SPH-i500 introduced a sleeker clamshell design running Palm OS 4.1 on a 66 MHz DragonBall 68328. The updated SPH-i550 had Palm OS 5.2, featuring a 200 MHz Motorola DragonBall MX1 and its ARM920T core. After delays, it was finally ready in early 2005, but Samsung was suddenly jilted right before shipping. Sprint cancelled the phone, going with the Palm Treo 650 instead. With Palm about to lose all momentum, Samsung shifted resources and the Palm OS phase was over.[511,512,513]

Next up was Microsoft Windows Mobile. In November 2003, Samsung and Verizon teamed up on the SCH-i600. It was in almost the same clamshell exterior as its Palm-based counterpart the SPH-i500. Inside was an Intel XScale PXA255 at 200 MHz supporting Windows Mobile 2003. June 2005 brought the all-new SCH-i730 with a slider physical keyboard design, and a much faster Intel XScale PXA272 running at 520 MHz.[514,515]

The Motorola Q was announced a month later with Windows Mobile 5.0. The nearly yearlong FCC delays in shipping the Q gave Samsung an opportunity to catch up. The controversial new phone introduced in late 2006 was the Samsung SGH-i607, better known as the BlackJack –

drawing a swift legal response from Research In Motion for camping near their name. Both the Q and the BlackJack featured a thumb-board layout eerily similar to RIM phones. Samsung's processor choice was the TI OMAP1710, a 220 MHz ARM926EJ-S core. Alongside was the Qualcomm MSM6275 baseband chip with another ARM926EJ-S core.[516]

Windows Mobile 6.1 moved to an all-touchscreen metaphor for its user interface, typified by the Samsung i900 Omnia in June 2008. Most of its variants had the Marvell PXA312 with an ARM920T core at 624 MHz. By this time, users were comparing any smartphone against the Apple iPhone. Creating a distinct look and feel, Samsung introduced the TouchWiz UI on the i900 Omnia, but its integration with apps was questionable in many cases. Samsung has continued efforts into Windows Phone 7 and beyond under the Omnia brand.[517]

Then, there was Symbian. Samsung tested the waters with the SGH-D700, a Symbian flip phone sporting an unusual camcorder-style rotating screen and lens, demonstrated at a special event in September 2003 but never launched. The first Symbian phone released by Samsung was the SGH-D710 in May 2004. It was small, 51x101x24mm and 110g, and its 192 MHz TI OMAP5910 with an ARM925 core ran Symbian OS 7.0s. That chipset served several years through the Samsung SGH-Z600 flip phone with Symbian OS 8.1 in March 2006.[518,519,520]

For Symbian OS 9.2, Samsung went to the TI OMAP2430, with an ARM1136 core at 330 MHz. The slider SGH-i520 was the first Samsung release in April 2007, followed by the SGH-i550 that borrowed the BlackJack look in May 2008, and the GT-i8510 large screen slider in October 2008. The last of the Samsung Symbian phones was the GT-i8910, with two variants running Symbian OS 9.4 released in mid-2009. These ran on a 600 MHz TI OMAP3430 and its Cortex-A8 processor core.[521,522,523]

During this period, Samsung had seven phones that sold over 10 million units each. None ran on these three operating systems – instead, it was a homebrew J2ME platform doing most of the selling.[524]

Your Loss is Our Foundry

Perhaps Samsung-branded smartphones hadn't done all that well early on, but Samsung was definitely a lynchpin in launching the smartphone revolution. Apple's immediate smash hit with the iPhone was a direct result of a buildup of fab capability at Samsung over nearly ten years. Prudent investment in multiple areas was about to pay off in a big way.

The first fab Samsung established outside of Korea was in Austin, Texas. With an opening investment of $1.3B, the 200mm Fab 1 began sampling memory chips in 1997, moving to full-scale production in 1998. Part of the fab costs were offset with an equity investment from Intel, widely believed to be 10%, in return for guaranteed allocation of memory products.[525]

Logic products were also growing. After licensing ARM9 cores in 1999, Samsung scored big wins in 2003. A Samsung chip was powering pocket PCs including the HP iPAQ H1940, the Everex E500, and later the Acer n30, all running Microsoft Windows Mobile. Inside was the S3C2410, a 266 MHz ARM920T processor fabbed on 0.18 micron, in a 272-pin BGA. The S3C2410 even showed up in the HP49g+ graphing calculator, underclocked to save power. Another important part in this family was the S3C2443 in 2007, running at 533 MHz on 0.13 micron in a 400-pin package, which found design wins in portable navigation devices like the Asus R300 and the LG LN800.[526,527,528]

Pushing its process further, Samsung opened its 300mm S1 line in Giheung in mid-2005, establishing production of DRAM on a 90nm process by the end of the year. To develop the next 65nm process node, estimated to cost $5B or more, Samsung allied with Chartered Semiconductor and IBM in the Common Platform initiative. IBM piloted a 65nm process at its Fishkill, New York facility and Samsung was preparing to roll it out at Giheung in early 2006.[529,530]

With advanced fab capacity in the works, Samsung quietly began socializing its foundry capability – supporting fabless semiconductor firms with fabrication services. In November 2005, they announced their first major foundry customer: Qualcomm. In March 2006, they added industry veteran Ana Molnar Hunter (fresh off experience at

Chartered) to run the foundry business. In April 2006, Samsung announced plans for Fab A2 at its Austin complex, adding a 300mm line in a new larger building.[531,532,533,534]

Samsung VP Jon Kang then walked into the SEMI Strategic Business Conference in Napa, California on April 26, 2006 and spouted, "I knew PortalPlayer would take a dive." His bravado stemmed from a new SoC, the Samsung S5L8701, slated for future Apple iPod designs. The new chip carried an ARM940T processor and a DSP core on a conservative 0.18 micron process. Perhaps most importantly it integrated a flash controller as well as LCD and USB controllers, reducing power consumption and cost.[535,536,537,538]

That was where PortalPlayer lost. True, Samsung had created a higher performance, low power ARM9 chip for Apple. Using its fab might, Samsung then bundled everything together – SoC, DRAM, and flash – and applied forward pricing plus allocation commitments. PortalPlayer was late to update its chip leaving them vulnerable. Realistically, they never stood a chance at Apple in the face of a combined supply chain and system design onslaught.

An erroneous analyst report in late 2006 had NVIDIA with its new PortalPlayer acquisition winning back iPod designs and perhaps the rumored Apple phone. That never happened. Apple moved beyond simply buying SoCs into specifying RTL designs, with the Samsung foundry doing the rest. Starting the sequence, the 90nm S5L8900 with its ARM11 core shipped in the original iPhone in June 2007 and the iPod Touch in September 2007.[539]

What appeared as a sudden disruptive change in Samsung's favor was in fact the result of nearly a decade of planning and a wide-ranging chain of events. Samsung was about to stretch the limits of its complex ecosystem even further.

On Second Thought, Android Works
The late 2004 meeting between Andy Rubin and Samsung executives in Seoul was no random event. Rubin had been a Samsung customer with some success at Danger. Samsung was working with the three most prominent smartphone operating systems of the day, so they were

a logical place to seek venture capital for another operating system, what would become Android. At that point, Samsung had no idea that most of their existing operating system choices would turn sour.

Rubin threw everything he had at the room, and got silence back. From Samsung's perspective, it was all risk: How many people do you have working on this operating system? Six. How many phones have shipped with it? None. How many OEMs are committed as customers? None. Thanks for coming.

Things started to change while Samsung executed its original three-pronged software strategy. Google bought Android. Palm OS sank. Research in Motion didn't share its code with anyone, for any price. Nokia wore its Symbian albatross. Microsoft Windows Mobile had significant traction until Apple showed up with the iPhone and iOS.

Open source teaming arrangements, especially in contrast to Apple's closed environment, became more and more interesting – and far less risky. In January 2007, the LiMo Foundation set up an effort for Linux-based mobile devices, with members including Motorola, NEC, NTT DoCoMo, Panasonic, and Samsung. In November 2007, the Open Handset Alliance unveiled its plans for Android phones, backed by Google, HTC, LG, Motorola, Qualcomm, and Samsung.[540,541]

Motorola hired Sanjay Jha away from Qualcomm in August 2008, giving him the co-CEO title and oversight of the mobile device operation. Jha promptly ended the nonsense of far too many mobile operating systems. His strategy for mainstream Motorola smartphones was Android with a bit of Windows Mobile and the proprietary J2ME P2K mixed in the portfolio.[542]

By 2009, Samsung also set its sights on Android and Windows Mobile, along with LiMo and the homegrown 'bada' operating system– later merged into Tizen.[543,544]

The Samsung Galaxy GT-i7500 launched in June 2009. It measured 115x56x11.9mm and weighed 114g, with a 3.2" OLED touchscreen at 320x480 pixels. Running Android 1.5 was the Qualcomm MSM7200A, a 528 MHz part in 65nm. Highly integrated, a single chip had an ARM1136J-S processor, a Qualcomm DSP core for applications, and an

ARM926 core running the baseband with another smaller Qualcomm DSP core.[545,546]

That was just the beginning of what Dan Rowinski of ReadWrite called the Samsung "spray and pray" strategy. The approach launched many smartphone models under Galaxy and Omnia umbrellas and other sub-branding, tailored for different carrier requirements (sometimes changing out SoCs or baseband chips), in every market Samsung could qualify in across the globe. Some sold well, some didn't, but new models were always on the way shortly. This was key to enveloping Apple, who essentially launched one hugely successful phone per year until the iPhone 5s and iPhone 5c and the iPhone 6 and iPhone 6 Plus duos.[547]

Quickly heading for their own chips, Samsung launched many models on its S3C6410 SoC starting in 2009. This 65nm, 424-pin part ran at 800 MHz with an ARM1176JZF-S core and Samsung's own FIMG-3DSE GPU core. In the Samsung GT-i5700 Galaxy Spica with Android 1.5 that shipped in November 2009, the S3C6410 was alongside the Qualcomm MSM6246 HSDPA baseband chip. The S3C6410 was also in the Samsung GT-i8000 Omnia II with Windows Mobile 6.1 that shipped in August 2009, with a slightly larger 3.7", 480x800 pixel touchscreen display.[548,549,550,551]

Exynos Takes Over the Galaxy

The flagship Samsung Galaxy S (GT-i9000) began shipping in June 2010 on Android 2.2, and within seven months became the first smartphone in the Samsung 10-million-seller club. Inside was the S5PC110 chip – rebranded as Exynos 3110, and later known as the Exynos 3 Single.[552,553]

At a block diagram level, the overall similarity of the Exynos 3 Single to the Apple A4 (shipped in the iPhone 4 beginning the same month) is hard to overlook. Inside was the same 1 GHz Intrinsity Hummingbird core and a PowerVR SGX540 GPU at 200 MHz. It was fabbed in Samsung 45nm LP, and came in a 598-pin BGA. Matching Apple's tablet move earlier in the year, Samsung announced the 7" Galaxy Tab (GT-P1000) in September 2010 using the same chip.[554,555]

Image 8-3: Samsung Galaxy S

Photo credit: Samsung

With the next step, Samsung beat Apple to the line. The Exynos 4 Dual debuted as the Exynos 4210 on February 15, 2011, fabbed in a Samsung 45nm LP process. The dual 1.2 GHz ARM Cortex-A9 cores gave a 20% processing edge. At that moment, the ARM Mali-400 MP4 GPU at 266 MHz put Samsung briefly ahead in smartphone graphics.[556,557]

For May 2011, the Samsung Galaxy S II (GT-i9100) was ready to ship using the Exynos 4210, running Android 2.3. Its claim to fame was its thinness, checking in at only 8.49mm. The Exynos 4210 also powered the first of the Samsung "phablets", the larger Galaxy Note (GT-N7000) measuring 147x83x9.65mm, and the Galaxy Tab 7.0 (GT-P7560), both launched in October 2011.[558,559,560]

Also in October 2011, the Exynos 4212 got a bump to a new 32nm HKMG process – brought up and running at Austin Fab A2 – reducing power and increasing clock speed to 1.5 GHz.[561,562]

First sampled in November 2011 was the Exynos 5 Dual, with two new ARM Cortex-A15 cores at 2.0 GHz, also on 32nm HKMG. The Exynos 5250 doubled memory bandwidth to 12.8 GB/sec, and used the ARM Mali-T604 MP4 GPU clocked at 533 MHz. It would appear in the

Samsung XE303C12 Chromebook, and the Google Nexus 10 tablet.[563,564,565,566]

Another new part showed up in 2011: a Samsung LTE baseband chip. First spotted in the Samsung Droid Charge for Verizon, the CMC220 provided the 4G Cat 3 connectivity. An enhanced CMC221 also appeared in the Galaxy Nexus.[567,568]

Following in April 2012 was the Exynos 4 Quad, a 1.4 GHz Cortex-A9 quad core again in 32nm HKMG. To help with power consumption, the Exynos 4412 used power gating and per-core frequency and voltage scaling on all four cores. The same Mali-400 MP4 GPU from the dual version was clocked at 400 MHz. This processor and its slightly faster "Prime" version appeared in several versions of the Galaxy S III (GT-i9300) with Android 4.0 as well as the Galaxy Note II (GT-N7100). One of the more interesting attempts with this part was the EK-GC100 Galaxy Camera.[569,570,571,572]

2013 marked the move to 28nm. Samsung chose the ARM big.LITTLE path, previewing the Exynos 5 Octa at CES 2013. The Exynos 5410 had four Cortex-A15 cores at 1.6 GHz paired with four Cortex-A7 cores at 1.2 GHz. In an unusual move, it used the Imagination PowerVR SGX544MP3 GPU running at up to 533 MHz in some cases, but often throttled back to 480 MHz to prevent overheating.[573]

The Exynos 5410 powered the Galaxy S4 (GT-i9500) with Android 4.2 in April 2013 – labeled as "life companion", with an even bigger 5" Super AMOLED display with 441ppi as its most prominent feature. In its first month, the Galaxy S4 shipped over 10 million units, becoming Samsung's fastest selling phone. Most of that success came on a different S4 configuration in the US with a 1.9 GHz Qualcomm Snapdragon 600 inside. (More ahead in Chapter 9.)[574,575]

Reverting to an ARM Mali-T628 MP6 GPU for the next iteration, Samsung enhanced the big.LITTLE configuration in the Exynos 5420. Core speeds were upped to 1.9 GHz for the Cortex-A15s and 1.3 GHz for the Cortex-A7s. They repaired a serious CCI-400 cache coherency bug, and added support for global task scheduling (GTS) to improve performance and power consumption. The beneficiaries of the new chip were the Galaxy Note 3 and the Galaxy Tab S.[576,577]

At Mobile World Congress 2014, Samsung rolled out the Exynos 5422. Still in 28nm and 113mm^2, clock speeds were bumped up to 2.1 GHz for the Cortex-A15s and 1.5 GHz for the Cortex-A7s, with the same Mali-T628 MP6 GPU. Added was HMP, or heterogeneous multi-processing, enabling all eight cores to be active concurrently for the first time. With a 16 MP rear camera and computational photography features such as high dynamic range (HDR), the Galaxy S5 again had both Exynos 5422 and Qualcomm Snapdragon 801 variants.[578,579,580]

 A brief stop in 20nm was next for the Galaxy Note 4 and the Galaxy Tab S2 in September 2014. Caught in between nomenclature, the Exynos 5433 was originally part of the Exynos 5 Octa family. However, its new 64-bit configuration of four Cortex-A57 cores at 1.9 GHz plus four Cortex-A53 cores at 1.3 GHz, plus a Mali-T760 MP6 GPU at 700 MHz, earned it Exynos 7 Octa branding.[581,582]

Avoiding the Zero-Sum Game

Vertical integration and design innovation have brought Samsung mobile devices on par with any in the world with just under 21% market share closing 2014. Moving from dubious quality and threatened capitulation in 1994 to leadership in mobile devices 20 years later is an amazing story. Despite legal challenges from Apple over who may have had an idea for a smartphone feature first, Samsung's record shows how innovation in design and heavy investment in fab technology recreated the brand and reshaped the mobile industry.

Continued expansion in Texas has kept Samsung fabs at the cutting edge, and kept much of the mobile industry running. The latest 14nm FinFET process in Austin is home to the Apple A9 and the Samsung Exynos 7420, the real Exynos 7 Octa. It may also become home to the Qualcomm Snapdragon 820.[583,584]

That would be an interesting twist given the drama surrounding the launch of the Samsung Galaxy S6 on March 1, 2015. Most observers expected a version using the Qualcomm Snapdragon 810. Weeks earlier, Qualcomm reported loss of "a major customer" in its quarterly earnings call.

Image 8-4: Inside Samsung's foundry

Photo credit: Samsung

Numerous reports surfaced that the Snapdragon 810 was experiencing overheating issues, denied but never quite disproven by Qualcomm. The Galaxy S6 debuted with the Exynos 7420, a tiny 78mm² die with four 2.1 GHz Cortex-A57s and four 1.5 GHz Cortex-A53s, plus a Mali-T760 MP8 at 772 MHz. Found with the Exynos 7420 in the S6 was the Samsung "Shannon" Exynos Modem 333 for 4G LTE baseband, along with Samsung-designed RF and PMIC parts.[585,586]

More than likely, Samsung has just decided it is ready to move to its own parts. The baseband program has been several years in the making, tracing back to 2011 when their LTE basebands were first spotted. In addition to Shannon stand-alone baseband chips, ModAP is the brand integrating baseband controllers with application processors as part of a custom ASIC business.[587]

Two lessons should be obvious. Samsung will use their own chips, if they have them, to improve availability and margins. They will use somebody else's chips if that is the most expedient way to qualify and release a device in a particular market – until they can design and build equivalent parts. Qualcomm likely has some content in some Galaxy S6 versions somewhere, but if the Exynos 7420 ships in the US versions of the S6, that would be a significant change.

Questions continue to circulate as to whether Samsung has enough capacity to service all three sources of demand – Apple, Qualcomm, and themselves. It's a legitimate concern. Samsung has cross fab flexibility with the Giheung complex and a partnership with GLOBALFOUNDRIES, which helps. An early S6 teardown indicated Exynos 7420 parts came from Albany, pointing to GF as an alternate foundry for some of the first chips produced.[588,589]

Speaking of alternate foundries, Samsung and TSMC are pitted against each other in the Apple iPhone 6s, each supplying a version of the A9 chip in an undisclosed split. Labeled as "Batterygate", viral reports surfaced of a significant power consumption difference between phones using either part, anywhere from 10 to 33% difference in favor of TSMC. Some social media suggested any phones with Samsung parts were defective and should be returned immediately.

Test conditions for those reports were suspect at best. Apple later issued statements saying they were observing only a 2 or 3% difference. TSMC proponents jumped on the advantages of their 16nm process, particularly its reduced leakage power. Samsung supporters point out that the 14nm part with its smaller die size is likely cheaper for Apple and that dual-sourcing means higher volumes and fewer shortages.[590]

The fact is both A9 parts started from the same Apple high-level design but there are variations between more than the processes. Libraries vary between Samsung and TSMC. Dynamic voltage and frequency scaling (DVFS) makes it difficult to say what a complex processor is doing with precision. Power and clock domain differences likely exist. In other words, the two parts are the "same", but different.

Most consumers don't care what chip is in a phone, right? The uproar seems to have died down, in spite of third-party apps to check what chip is inside an iPhone 6s. Just as Apple solved "Sensorgate" with an iOS update, ultimately any major differences between Samsung and

TSMC A9 chips may disappear with an iOS 9 update soon. What Apple does for the iPhone 7 and if dual-sourcing continues is worth watching.

The smartphone market is changing. IDC reports annual growth has slowed to around 11%. Slowing growth in smartphones makes competition between Apple, Qualcomm, and Samsung closer to a zero-sum game – when one wins, the other two lose, at least from a high-end application processor view.[591]

Image 8-5

Samsung mobile processor highlights

Chip	Flagship Device	Year	Cores	Type	Clock	Process
S3C44B0X	Danger Hiptop	2000	1	ARM7TDMI	66 MHz	250nm
S3C2410	HP iPAQ H1940	2003	1	ARM920T	266 MHz	180nm
S5L8701	Apple iPod nano 2nd gen	2006	1	ARM940T	200 MHz	180nm
S3C2443	Asus R300	2007	1	ARM920T	400 MHz	130nm
S5L8900	Apple iPhone	2007	1	ARM1176JZF-S	412 MHz	90nm
S3C6410	Samsung Galaxy Spica	2009	1	ARM1176JZF-S	800 MHz	65nm
Exynos 3110	Samsung Galaxy S	2010	1	"Hummingbird"	1.0 GHz	45nm
Exynos 4210	Samsung Galaxy S II	2011	2	ARM Cortex-A9	1.2 GHz	45nm
Exynos 5250	Google Nexus 10	2011	2	ARM Cortex-A15	2.0 GHz	32nm
Exynos 4412	Samsung Galaxy S III	2012	4	ARM Cortex-A9	1.4 GHz	32nm
Exynos 5410	Samsung Galaxy S4	2013	8	ARM Cortex-A15 ARM Cortex-A7	1.6 GHz 1.2 GHz	28nm
Exynos 5420	Samsung Galaxy Note 3	2013	8	ARM Cortex-A15 ARM Cortex-A7	1.9 GHz 1.3 GHz	28nm
Exynos 5422	Samsung Galaxy S5	2014	8	ARM Cortex-A15 ARM Cortex-A7	2.1 GHz 1.5 GHz	28nm
Exynos 5 Octa 5433	Samsung Galaxy Note 4	2014	8	ARM Cortex-A57 ARM Cortex-A53	1.9 GHz 1.3 GHz	20nm
Exynos 7 Octa 7420	Samsung Galaxy S6	2015	8	ARM Cortex-A57 ARM Cortex-A53	2.1 GHz 1.5 GHz	14nm
Exynos 8 Octa 8890		2015	8	Exynos M1 ARM Cortex-A53		14nm

Samsung is responding by trying to differentiate its application processors. With both Apple and Qualcomm already having ARMv8-A custom cores, Samsung has chimed in with its own core design codenamed "Mongoose" and recently introduced as Exynos M1.[592,593]

The Exynos 8 Octa 8890 is the first high-end Samsung part to combine an application processor cluster with a baseband modem on a single chip. The application processor side pairs four Exynos M1 cores with four ARM Cortex-A53 cores in big.LITTLE, fabbed in 14nm FinFET.[594]

Where the Exynos M1 core lands against Qualcomm's "Kryo" core in performance will be interesting. Initial benchmark results put the Exynos 8 Octa 8890 ahead of the Snapdragon 820 – however, judging Qualcomm on pre-release silicon may be premature. We will know a lot more when the Samsung Galaxy S7 and competing phones with the Qualcomm Snapdragon 820 release in 2016.

A bigger question is how Samsung, and others, continue to innovate in smartphones beyond just more advanced SoCs. There are also other areas of growth, such as smartwatches and the IoT, where Samsung is determined to play. There are me-too features, such as Samsung Pay, and new ideas like wireless charging and curved displays. (More ahead in Chapter 10.)

How this unfolds, with Samsung both supplier and competitor in an era of consolidation for the mobile and semiconductor industries, depends on adapting the strategy. Innovations in RF, battery, and display technology will be highly sought after. Software capability is already taking on much more importance. As Chinese firms improve their SoC capability, the foundry business may undergo dramatic changes – and the center of influence may shift again.

History says Samsung invests in semiconductor fab technology and capacity during down cycles preparing for the next upturn. Heavy investments in 3D V-NAND flash, the SoC foundry business, and advanced processes such as 10nm FinFET and beyond are likely to accelerate, and competition with TSMC and other foundries will intensify as fab expenses climb.

Chapter 9: Press 'Q' to Connect

Unlike peer firms who started in other electronics segments and moved into communications devices later, Qualcomm has always focused on wireless technology to connect data between destinations reliably. Its CDMA technology was a leap ahead for mobile devices – if it could be made small enough, and if carriers could be persuaded to change from D-AMPS and GSM.

Qualcomm's roots trace to some of the brightest minds in academia at the foremost technology universities in the US, first brought together working on the US space program as young engineers. A depth of technical expertise gained through serving demanding clients with digital communication systems established a foundation from which patents, chips, and devices grew.

Actual Rocket Scientists

The seminal article "A Mathematical Theory of Communication" published by Claude Shannon of Bell Labs in 1948 established information theory. Along with the invention of the transistor and advances in digital coding and computing, Shannon's theorem and his tenure at the Massachusetts Institute of Technology (MIT) inspired an entire generation of mathematicians and scientists.

In June 1957, Andrew Viterbi, a graduate from MIT with a master's degree in electrical engineering, joined the staff at the Jet Propulsion Laboratory (JPL) in Pasadena, California. At the time, JPL was owned by the California Institute of Technology, but worked under the auspices and funding of the US Army Ballistic Missile Command.

Viterbi was in JPL's Communications Section 331, led by Solomon Golomb. They were developing telemetry payloads for missile and satellite programs. Golomb pioneered shift-register sequence theory, used to encode digital messages for reliability in high background noise. Viterbi was working on phase locked loops, a critical element in synchronizing a digital radio receiver with a transmitter so a stream of information can be decoded.[595]

Image 9-1: NASA Jet Propulsion Laboratory, Pasadena, CA

Photo credit: NASA

On October 4, 1957, the Russians launched Sputnik I. The next day, the Millstone Hill Radar at MIT Lincoln Labs (MITLL) – where researcher Irving Reed, best known for Reed-Solomon codes, was on staff – detected Sputnik in low-earth orbit. A young Ph. D. candidate at Purdue University, William Lindsey, used a ham radio to monitor a signal broadcast by Sputnik that rose and faded every 96 minutes as the satellite orbited.

The Space Race was officially underway. The US Navy rushed its Vanguard program to respond. On December 6, 1957, Test Vehicle 3 launched with a 1.3kg satellite. It flew an embarrassing 1.2m, crashing back to its pad just after liftoff and exploding. Its payload landed nearby in the Cape Canaveral underbrush, still transmitting. "And that was our competition," said Golomb.[596]

On January 31, 1958, JPL's Project Deal – known to the outside world as Explorer I – achieved orbit. *Life* magazine featured a photo of Golomb and Viterbi in the JPL control room during the flight. On July 29, 1958, President Eisenhower signed the National Aeronautics and Space Act, creating NASA. JPL requested and received a move into the NASA organization in December 1958.[597,598]

Viterbi enrolled at the University of Southern California (USC) to pursue his Ph. D., the only school that would allow him to continue working full time at JPL. He finished in 1962 and went to teach at the University of California, Los Angeles (UCLA). He recommended

Golomb join the USC faculty in 1963. That started an influx of digital communications talent to USC that included Reed (who had moved to the Rand Corporation in Santa Monica in 1960), Lindsey (who joined JPL in 1962), Eberhardt Rechtin, Lloyd Welch, and others.[599]

Lindsey would quip years later, "I think God made this group." Rechtin would say that together, this group achieved more in digital communications than any of them could have done alone. They influenced countless others. (Personal note: that includes a co-author of this book who studied under Lindsey and Reed for an MSEE in the Distance Education Network at USC.)

Linked to San Diego

At the 1963 National Electronics Conference in Chicago, best paper awards went to Viterbi and Irwin Jacobs, a professor at MIT whose office was a few doors down from that of Claude Shannon. Jacobs and Viterbi had crossed paths briefly in 1959 while Jacobs visited JPL for an interview, and they knew of each other's work from ties between JPL and MIT.[600, 601]

Reacquainted at the 1963 conference, Jacobs suggested to Viterbi that he had a sabbatical coming up, and asked if JPL was a good place to work. Viterbi said that indeed it was. Jacobs' application was rejected, but Viterbi interceded with division chief Rechtin, and Jacobs was finally hired as a research fellow and headed for Pasadena. Viterbi was teaching at UCLA and consulting at JPL, and the two became friends in the 1964-65 academic year Jacobs spent working there.

After publishing the landmark text "Principles of Communication Engineering" with John Wozencraft in 1965, Jacobs migrated to the West in 1966. He was lured by one of his professors at Cornell, Henry Booker, to join the faculty in a new engineering department at the University of California, San Diego (UCSD). Professors were valuable, and digital communication consultants were also in high demand. One day in early 1967, Jacobs took a trip to NASA's Ames Research Center for a conference. He found himself on a plane ride home with Viterbi and another MIT alumnus, Len Kleinrock, who had joined the UCLA faculty in 1963 and became friends with Viterbi. The three started chatting, with Jacobs casually mentioning he had more consulting work than he could handle himself.[602]

Viterbi was finishing his masterpiece. He sought a simplification to the theory of decoding faint digital signals from strong noise, one that his UCLA students could grasp more easily than the complex curriculum in place. Arriving at a concept in March 1966, he refined the idea for a year before publication. In April 1967, Viterbi described his approach in an article in the IEEE Transactions on Information Theory under the title "Error bounds for convolutional codes and an asymptotically optimum decoding algorithm."[603]

The Viterbi Algorithm leverages "soft" decisions. A hard decision on a binary 0 or 1 can be made by observing each noisy received bit (or group of bits encoded into a symbol), with significant chance of error. Viterbi considered probabilistic information contained in possible state transitions known from how symbols are encoded at the transmitter. Analyzing a sequence of received symbols and state transitions with an add-compare-select (ACS) operation identifies a path of maximum likelihood, more accurately matching the transmitted sequence.[604]

It was just theory, or so Viterbi thought at first. The algorithm reduced computations and error compared to alternatives, but was still intense to execute in real-time, and thought to require "several thousand registers" to produce low error rates. Several other researchers picked up the work, notably Jim Massey, David Forney, and Jim Omura. They were convinced it was optimum. Jerry Heller, one of Jacobs' doctoral students at MIT who had come with him to San Diego, was working at JPL. He decided to run some simulations during 1968 and 1969 and found Viterbi had been too pessimistic; 64 registers yielded a significant coding gain. That was still a rather large rack of computing equipment at the time.[605]

The entrepreneurial thought Jacobs planted for a consulting firm had stuck. With an investment of $1500 (each man contributing $500) Linkabit was born in October 1968 with an address of Kleinrock's home in Brentwood. Soon, offices moved to a building in Westwood near UCLA. At first, it was a day-a-week effort for Jacobs, Kleinrock, and Viterbi, who all kept their day jobs as professors.

There was even more business than anticipated. Linkabit's first new-hire engineer in September 1969 was Jerry Heller, soon followed by engineers Andrew Cohen, Klein Gilhousen, and Jim Dunn.

Len Kleinrock stepped aside for a few months to pursue his dream project, installing the first endpoints of the ARPANET and sending its first message in October 1969. According to him, when he tried returning to Linkabit he was promptly dismissed, receiving a percentage of the firm as severance. With Kleinrock out and Viterbi not ready to relocate for several more years, Jacobs moved the Linkabit office to Sorrento Valley – the tip of San Diego's "Golden Triangle" – in 1970. His next hire was office manager Dee Coffman (née Turpie), fresh out of high school.[606,607]

Programming the Modem

"Coding is dead." That was the punchline for several speakers at the IEEE Communication Theory Workshop in 1970 in St. Petersburg, Florida. Irwin Jacobs stood up in the back of the room, holding a 14-pin dual-in-line package – a simple 4-bit shift register, probably a 7495 in TTL families. "This is where it's at. This new digital technology out there is going to let us build all this stuff."

Early on, Linkabit was a research think tank, not a hardware company. Its first customers were NASA Ames Research Center and JPL, along with the Naval Electronics Laboratory in Point Loma, and DARPA. Linkabit studies around Viterbi decoding eventually formed the basis of deep space communications links used in JPL's Voyager and other programs. However, compact hardware implementations of Viterbi decoders and other signal processing would soon make Linkabit and its successor firm legendary.

Heller and Jacobs disclosed a 2 Mbps, 64 state, constraint length 7, rate ½ Viterbi decoder in October 1971. It was based on a commercial unit built for the US Army Satellite Communications Agency. The Linkabit Model 7026, or LV7026, used about 360 TTL chips on 12 boards in a 19 inch rackmount, 4.5U (7.9") high, 22" deep enclosure. Compared to refrigerator-sized racks of equipment previously needed for the Viterbi Algorithm, it was a breakthrough.[608,609]

Speed was also a concern. Viterbi tells of an early Linkabit attempt to integrate one ACS state of the decoder on a chip of only 100 gates – medium scale integration, or MSI. In his words, the effort "almost bankrupted the company" through a string of several supplier failures.

Almost bankrupt? It sounds like an exaggeration until considering the available alternatives to TTL. From hints in a 1971 Linkabit report and a 1974 Magnavox document, Linkabit was playing with fast but finicky emitter-coupled logic (ECL) in attempts to increase clock speeds in critical areas. Many companies failed trying things with ECL. Viterbi omitted names to protect the guilty, but the ECL fab suspects would be Fairchild, IBM, Motorola, and Signetics.[610,611,612,613]

A different direction led to more success. Klein Gilhousen started tinkering with a concept for a Linkabit Microprocessor (LMP), a microcoded architecture for all the functions of a satellite modem. Gilhousen, Sheffie Worboys, and Franklin Antonio completed a breadboard of the LMP using mostly TTL chips with some higher performance MSI and LSI commercial parts in May 1974. It ran at 3 MIPS. There were 32 instructions and four software stacks, three for processing and one for control. It was part RISC (before there was such a thing), part DSP.[614,615]

Jacobs began writing code and socializing the LMP, giving lectures at MITLL and several other facilities about the ideas behind digital signal processing for a satellite modem. The US Air Force invited Linkabit to demonstrate their technology for the experimental LES-8/9 satellites. TRW had a multi-year head start on the spread spectrum modem within the AN/ASC-22 K-Band SATCOM system, but their solution was expensive and huge.

Linkabit stunned the MITLL team by setting up their relatively small system of several 19" rackmount boxes and acquiring full uplink in about an hour, a task the lab staff was sure would take several days just to get a basic mode running. In about three more hours, they found an error in the MITLL design specifications, fixed the error through reprogramming, and had the downlink working. Despite TRW's certification and production readiness, the USAF general in charge of the program funded Linkabit – a company that had never built production hardware in volumes for a defense program – to complete its modem development.[616,617]

Besides the fact that the LMP worked so well, the reason for the intense USAF interest became clear in 1978. The real requirement was for a dual modem on airborne command platforms such as the Boeing EC-135 and Strategic Air Command aircraft including the Boeing B-52. The solution evolved into the Command Post Modem/Processor (CPM/P), using several LMPs to implement dual full-duplex modems and red/black messaging and control, ultimately reduced to three rugged ½ ATR boxes.[618]

Linkabit was growing at 60% a year. Needing further capital to expand, they considered going public before being approached by another firm with expertise in RF technology, M/A-COM. In August 1980, the acquisition was completed. It radically altered the Linkabit culture from a freewheeling exchange of thoughts across the organization to a control-oriented, hierarchical structure.

It didn't stop innovation. Several significant commercial products debuted. One was Very Small Aperture Terminal (VSAT), a small satellite communications system using a 4 to 8 foot dish for businesses. Its major adopters included 7-11, Holiday Inn, Schlumberger, and Wal-Mart. Another was VideoCipher, the satellite TV encryption system that went to work at HBO and other broadcasters. Jerry Heller oversaw VideoCipher through its life as the technology grew.[619]

Jacobs and Viterbi had negotiated the acquisition with M/A-COM CEO Larry Gould. As Jacobs put it, "We got along very well, but [Gould] went through a mid-life crisis." Gould wanted to make management changes, or merge with other firms – none of it making a lot of sense. The M/A-COM board of directors instead replaced Gould (officially, "retired") as CEO in 1982.

Jacobs was an M/A-COM board member but was travelling in Europe and was unable to have the input he wanted in the decision or the new organizational structure. He subsequently tried to split the firm and take the Linkabit pieces back, going as far as vetting the deal with investment bankers. At the last moment, the M/A-COM board got cold feet and reneged on allowing Linkabit to separate.

After finishing the three chips for the consumer version of the VideoCipher II descrambler, Jacobs abruptly "retired" on April 1, 1985. Within a week Viterbi left M/A-COM as well and others quickly followed suit.[620]

"Let's Do It Again"

Retirement is far from all it's cracked up to be. For someone who hadn't wanted to run Linkabit day-to-day, Irwin Jacobs had done a solid job running it. Shortly after his M/A-COM departure, one of his associates asked, "Hey, why don't we try doing this again?" Jacobs took his family, who he had promised to spend more time with, on a car tour of Europe to think about it.

On July 1, 1985, six people reconvened in Jacobs' den – all freshly ex-Linkabit. Besides Jacobs, there was Franklin Antonio, Dee Coffman, Andrew Cohen, Klein Gilhousen, and Harvey White. Tribal legend says there were seven present; Andrew Viterbi was there in spirit, though actually on a cruise in Europe until mid-July, having agreed on a direction with Jacobs before departing. This core team picked the name Qualcomm, shorthand for quality communications, for a new company. They would combine elements of digital communications theory with practical design knowledge into refining code division multiple access, or CDMA.[621]

In his channel capacity theorem, Shannon illustrated spread spectrum techniques could reliably transmit more digital data in a wider bandwidth with lower signal-to-noise ratios. CDMA uses a pseudo-random digital code to spread a given data transmission across the allocated bandwidth.

Different code assignments allow creation of multiple CDMA data channels sharing the same overall bandwidth. To any single channel, its neighbors operating on a different code look like they are speaking another language and do not interfere with the conversation. To outsiders without the codes, the whole thing is difficult to interpret and looks like background noise. This makes CDMA far more secure from eavesdropping or jamming compared to the primitive ideas of frequency hopping postulated by Nikola Tesla and later patented in 1942 by actress and inventor Hedy Lamarr and her composer friend George Antheil.

Unlike a TDMA system using fixed channels determining exactly how many simultaneous conversations a base station can carry in an allocated bandwidth, CDMA opens up capacity substantially. With sophisticated encoding and decoding techniques – enter Reed-Solomon codes and Viterbi decoding – a CDMA system can handle many more users up to an acceptable limit of bit error probability and cross-channel interference. In fact, CDMA reuses capacity during pauses in conversations, an ideal characteristic for mobile voice traffic.

Coding techniques also gave rise to a solution for multipath in spread spectrum applications. The RAKE receiver, developed by Bob Price and Paul Green of MITLL originally for radar applications, used multiple correlators like fingers in a rake that could synchronize to different versions of a signal and statistically combine the results. RAKE receivers made CDMA practically impervious to noise between channels.[622]

USAF SATCOM planners were the first to fall in love with CDMA for all its advantages, but it required intense digital compute resources to keep up with data in real-time. Jacobs and Viterbi realized they had some very valuable technology, proven with the digital signal processing capability of the LMP and the dual modem that had handled CDMA for satellite communications reliably. Could Qualcomm serve commercial needs?

Two things were obvious right from the beginning: cost becomes a much bigger issue in commercial products, and regulators like the FCC enter the picture for non-defense communication networks. So Qualcomm found itself picking up right where they left off at Linkabit – working government communication projects, trying to make solutions smaller and faster.

Those government projects spawned a single-chip Viterbi decoder. Finally, CMOS ASIC technology had caught up, ending the need for hundreds of TTL chips and exotic measures like ECL. Qualcomm had its first chip design ready in September 1987: the Q1401, a 17 Mbps, 80 state, K=7, rate ½ decoder. It was fabbed by LSI Logic in 1.5 micron, estimated to be a 169mm^2 die in a 155 pin ceramic PGA. It was available in both commercial and military grades, slightly downgraded in speed at the wider military temperatures.[623,624]

Space Truckin'

Just before Qualcomm opened for business, Viterbi received an interesting phone call. It was Allen Salmasi – who left JPL to start OmniNet in 1984 – asking if his firm could work with Qualcomm on a new location system for trucks.

The FCC allocated frequencies for RDSS (radiodetermination satellite service) in 1984. OmniNet held one RDSS license, competitor Geostar the other. Geostar's concept had position reporting and messaging from a truck to an L-band satellite, relayed to the trucking company. If OmniNet could deliver RDSS with a link from the trucking company back to the truck, it could be a huge opportunity.

Qualcomm wasn't too sure. Salmasi gave them $10,000 to study the situation – he had no customers, no venture capital (nobody believed it would work, not even Geostar who refused a partnership offer), and only "family and friends" money. OmniNet had to commercialize to survive, and Qualcomm was the best hope.

L-band satellites were scarce and expensive, partly because they used a processing payload that had to be mission customized. Ku-band satellites used for VSATs and other applications were ample, less expensive, allowed for ground signal processing, and could provide both uplink and downlink capability, but there was a catch. The FCC had licensed Ku-band for fixed terminals, with large ground parabolic dish antennae that had to be pointed within a degree or two. Secondary use permitted mobile if and only if it did not interfere with primary uses. A smaller ground dish antenna, especially one on a moving truck, would have both pointing and aperture issues almost certain to cause interference.[625]

Then Klein Gilhousen said, "We're using CDMA."

In theory CDMA and spread spectrum would solve any interference issues on the transmit side, and if antennae pointing were accurate enough, the receive side would work. Now the FCC were the ones not so sure. Qualcomm convinced the FCC to grant an experimental license, one that would cover 600 trucks. Jacobs and his teams created a unique directional antenna system that was compact at 10" in diameter and 6" tall, but highly accurate. A Communication Unit measuring 4"x8"x9" did the processing, and a Display Unit had a 40 character by four line readout with a small keyboard and indicators for the driver. By January 1988, the system began limited operational testing on a cross-country drive.[626]

Still without a customer, Salmasi was out of capital – so Qualcomm bought him, his company, and the entire system, launching it as OmniTRACS in August 1988. With zero reports of interference, the FCC granted broader operating authority for the system. By October, Qualcomm had their first major customer in Schneider with about 10,000 trucks. OmniTRACS was on its way, with some 1.5 million trucks using the system today. This first important win provided income for Qualcomm to contemplate the next big market for CDMA.

Just Keep Talking

Gilhousen bent both Jacobs' and Viterbi's ears with the suggestion that Qualcomm go into cellular phones with CDMA. Viterbi found the idea familiar, having presented it in a 1982 paper on spread spectrum. Moving from defense satellite networks for several hundred B-52s and EC-135s to private satellite networks with 10,000 trucks and more had been straightforward, but a public cellular network presented a well-known problem.

While CDMA signals reduced interference between digital channels, there were still RF characteristics to consider with many transmitters talking to one terrestrial base station simultaneously. For satellite communication systems, every terminal on the Earth is relatively far away and should have roughly the same signal strength under normal operating conditions.

In a cellular grid with low power handsets, distance matters and the near-far problem becomes significant. Near-far relates to the dynamic range of a base station receiver. If all handsets transmit at the same power, the closest one captures the receiver and swamps handsets transmitting farther away from the cell tower making them inaudible in the noise.

Viterbi, Jacobs, Gilhousen, and Butch Weaver set off to figure out the details. While they ran CDMA simulations, the Telecommunications Industry Association (TIA) met in January 1989 and chose TDMA in D-AMPS as the 2G standard for the US. D-AMPS was evolutionary to AMPS, and some say there was a nationalistic agenda to adopt an alternative to the European-dominated GSM despite its head start. FDMA was seen as a lower-risk approach (favored by Motorola, AT&T, and others), but TDMA had already shown its technical superiority in GSM evaluations.

Few in the industry took CDMA seriously. The Cellular Telecommunication Industry Association (CTIA) pushed for user performance recommendations in a 2G standard with at least 10 times the capacity of AMPS, but also wanted a smooth transition path. D-AMPS did not meet the UPR capacity goals, but was regarded as the fastest path to 2G.[627]

Capacity concerns gave Qualcomm its opening. Jacobs reached out to the CTIA to present the CDMA findings and after an initial rebuff got an audience at a membership meeting in Chicago in June 1989. He waited for the assembled experts to shoot his presentation full of holes. It didn't happen.[628]

One reason their presentation went so well was that they had been test driving it with PacTel Cellular since February 1989. After the TIA vote, Jacobs and Viterbi started asking for meetings with regional carriers. "All of a sudden, one day, Irwin Jacobs and Andy Viterbi showed up in my office. Honestly, I don't even know how they got there," said PacTel Cellular CEO Jeff Hultman.[629]

However, William C. Y. Lee, PacTel Cellular chief scientist, knew why they had come. PacTel Cellular was experiencing rapid subscriber growth in its Los Angeles market, and was about to experience a capacity shortfall. Lee had been studying digital spread spectrum efficiency and capacity issues for years, comparing FDMA and TDMA. What he saw with CDMA – with perhaps 20 times improvement over analog systems – and the risks in developing TDMA were enough to justify a $1M bet on research funding for Qualcomm. Lee, like many others, needed to see a working solution for the near-far problem and other issues.[630]

Just under six months later on November 7, 1989, Qualcomm had a prototype system. A CDMA "phone" – actually 30 pounds of equipment – was stuffed in the back of a van ready to drive around San Diego. There were two "base stations" set up so call handoff could be demonstrated.

Image 9-2: Qualcomm team including Andrew Viterbi (left), Irwin Jacobs (center), Butch Weaver, and Klein Gilhousen (right) with CDMA van, circa 1989

Photo credit: Qualcomm

Before a gathering of cellular industry executives, at least 150 and by some reports as many as 300, William C. Y. Lee made a presentation, Jacobs made his presentation, and Gilhousen described what visitors were about to see. Just before dismissing the group for the demonstration, Jacobs noticed Butch Weaver waving frantically. A GPS glitch took out base station synchronization. Jacobs improvised, and kept talking about CDMA for some 45 minutes until Weaver and the team got the system working.[631]

Many attendees at the demonstration were thrilled at what they had seen. The critics said CDMA would never work, that the theory would not hold up under full-scale deployment and real-world conditions, and it "violated the laws of physics" according to one pundit. Additionally, there was the small problem of getting it to fit in a handset – a problem Qualcomm was prepared to deal with.

Beyond a need for miniaturization and the basics of direct sequence spread spectrum and channelization, Qualcomm was developing solutions to three major CDMA issues.

First was the near-far problem. Dynamic power control changes power levels to maintain adequate signal-to-noise. CDMA handsets closer to base stations typically use less transmit power, and ones farther away use more. The result is all signals arrive at the base station at about the same signal-to-noise ratio. Lower transmit power also lowered interference and saved handset battery power. Qualcomm used aggressive open loop and closed loop power control making adjustments at 800 times per second (later increased to 1500), compared to just a handful of times per second in GSM.

Second was soft handoffs. In a TDMA system, dropped calls often happened when users transitioned from one base station to another due to a hard handoff. CDMA cells establish a connection at the next base station while still connected to the current one.

Third was a variable rate vocoder. Instead of on-off encoding used in GSM, a variable rate encoder adapts rapidly as speech naturally pauses and resumes, reducing the number of bits transmitted by handsets and effectively increasing overall capacity at the base station. This feature was not present in TDMA, since channels are fixed and unsharable.[632]

Get In and Hang On

If CDMA could be productized, Hultman had promised PacTel Cellular's support but other deals would be needed to reach critical mass. PacTel helped introduce Qualcomm to higher-level executives at the other Baby Bells and the major cellular infrastructure vendors, looking for markets where CDMA would be welcome. Qualcomm leadership also made a fateful decision on their business model: instead of building all the equipment themselves, they would license their CDMA intellectual property to manufacturers.[633]

Another cellular market with looming capacity headaches was New York, home to NYNEX. Qualcomm carted its CDMA prototypes to Manhattan for field trials during February 1990. NYNEX already had AT&T looking at next-generation infrastructure specifics, and by early July, AT&T and Qualcomm had a license agreement for CDMA base station technology. On July 31, 1990, Qualcomm published the first version of the CDMA specifications for industry comments – the Common Air Interface. On August 2, NYNEX announced it would spend $100M to build "a second cellular telephone network" in Manhattan by the end of 1991, mostly to provide time for frequency allocation and base station construction. $3M would go to Qualcomm to produce CDMA phones.[634]

Others held back. The two largest cellular infrastructure vendors, Ericsson and Motorola, had plans for TDMA networks. Motorola hedged its bet in a September 1990 CDMA infrastructure cross-licensing agreement with Qualcomm, but publicly expressed technical concerns. Carriers like McCaw Cellular (the forerunner of AT&T Wireless) and Ameritech were trying to postpone any major commitments to CDMA. Internationally, Europe was all in on GSM based on TDMA, and Japan was developing its own TDMA-based cellular network.[635]

In the uncommitted column was Korea, without a digital solution. Salmasi leveraged introductions from PacTel's Lee in August 1990 into rounds of discussion culminating in the May 1991 ETRI CDMA joint development agreement (see Chapter 8 for more). Although a major funding commitment with a lucrative future royalty stream, the program would take five years to unfold.

Even with these wins, Qualcomm was hanging on the financial edge. Every dollar of income was plowed back into more employees – numbering about 600 at the close of 1991 – and CDMA R&D.

PacTel continued with its CDMA plans, leading to the CAP I capacity trial in November 1991 – using commercial-ready Qualcomm CDMA chipsets. Five ASICs were designed in a two-year program. Three were for a CDMA phone: a modulator, a demodulator, and an enhanced Viterbi decoder. Two more were created for a base station, also used with the Viterbi decoder. These chipsets interfaced with an external microprocessor. The trials proved CDMA technology was viable on a larger scale, and could produce the capacity gains projected.

Image 9-3: Qualcomm CDMA chipset circa 1991

Photo credit: Qualcomm

On the heels of disclosing the CAP I trial success and the ASICs at a CTIA technology forum, Qualcomm proceeded with its initial public offering of 4 million shares, raising $68M in December 1991. PacTel bought a block of shares on the open market, and kicked in an additional $2.2M to buy warrants for 390,000 more shares, assuring CDMA R&D would continue uninterrupted.[636,637]

Along with the Korean ETRI joint development deal, four manufacturers were onboard with Qualcomm and CDMA entering 1992: AT&T, Motorola, Oki, and Nortel Networks. Licensee number five in April 1992 was none other than Nokia, the climax of a year and a half of negotiations directly between Jacobs and Jorma Ollila. Nokia had been observing the PacTel trials with keen interest, and had set up their own R&D center in San Diego to be close to the action with CDMA. One of the sticking points was the royalty: Nokia is thought to have paid around 3% of handset ASPs under its first 15-year agreement.[638]

On March 2, 1993, Qualcomm introduced the CD-7000, a dual-mode CDMA/AMPS handheld phone powered by a single chip baseband: the Mobile Station Modem (MSM). The phone was a typical candy bar, 178x57x25mm weighing a bit over 340g. The first customer was US West, with a commitment for at least 36,000 phones.

Also in March 1993, plans for CDMA phones and infrastructure in Korea were announced with four manufacturers: Goldstar, Hyundai, Maxon, and Samsung.[639]

Qualcomm provided details of the new MSM baseband chip at HotChips in August 1993. The three basic CDMA functions of modulator, demodulator, and Viterbi decoder were on a single 0.8 micron, 114mm^2 chip. It had 450,000 transistors and consumed 300mW, still requiring an external processor and RF circuitry to complete a handset. Qualcomm indicated a multi-foundry strategy, but didn't disclose suppliers – later reports named IBM as the source.[640]

The TIA finally relented, endorsing CDMA with first publication of the IS-95 specification in July 1993, known commercially as cdmaOne. Cellular markets now had their choice of 2G digital standards in CDMA, D-AMPS, and GSM.[641]

Roadblock at Six Million

Inside the CD-7000 phone with the MSM chip was an Intel 80C186 processor. The logical next step was to integrate the two, except ... Intel was not in the intellectual property business. Intel denied Qualcomm's advances at first. Under persistent nagging from its San Diego sales office, Intel's embedded operation in Chandler, AZ learned all about Qualcomm, CDMA technology, and market opportunities before agreeing to provide an 80C186 core.

Converting the 80C186 design from Intel-ese to a more industry-standard design flow proved difficult. Qualcomm had designed the MSM with high-level hardware description language (HDL) techniques that could be resynthesized on different libraries quickly, along with a simulation database and test vectors. It quickly became obvious that it was easier to move the Qualcomm MSM IP into the Intel design flow, and have Intel fab the entire chip. Qualcomm agreed. Intel was about to enter both the mobile business and the foundry business.[642]

On February 1, 1995, Qualcomm announced the Q5257 MSM2 with its Q186 core in a 176-pin QFP, along with the Q5312 integrated Analog Baseband Processor (BBA2) replacing 17 discrete chips in an 80-pin QFP. Those two chips formed most of a CDMA phone – such as the QCP-800 announced the next day. Gearing up for larger volumes, Qualcomm formed a joint venture with Sony to produce the new dual-mode phone that more than doubled battery life to a five-hour talk time. Also announced was the single chip Q5160 Cell Site Modem (CSM) for CDMA base stations, without an integrated processor.[643,644]

The Q5270 MSM2.2 was introduced in June 1996. Its major enhancement was the 13 Kbps PureVoice vocoder using QCELP, providing higher voice quality without sacrificing power consumption. It was offered in both a 176-pin QFP for production use and a larger 208-pin QFP for enhanced in-circuit debugging.[645]

Reducing power was the objective of the MSM2300, announced in March 1997. Its searcher engine, using a hardwired DSP, ran up to eight times faster than the MSM2.2, reducing the amount of time the microprocessor spent acquiring signals. Its 176-pin QFP was pin compatible, allowing direct upgrades.[646,647]

Chipset volumes exploded as CDMA deployed around the world. Qualcomm claimed combined shipments of MSM variants – mostly the MSM2 and MSM2.2 fabbed by Intel – reached six million units in June 1997. Intel had also driven its lower power 386EX embedded processors into handheld designs at Nokia and Research in Motion. What could possibly go wrong?[648]

That was probably what Qualcomm asked when Intel balked on providing a roadmap update for an embedded core. In fairness, the degree of difficulty in fabbing a 386EX was substantially higher, and there was more Qualcomm IP to put next to it. Intel probably saw risk in both design and yield that even six million units did not justify.

Qualcomm forced the issue with an RFQ and got a rather perfunctory response without major improvements in CPU performance. (Intel was likely in the midst of settling Alpha litigation with DEC when this request arrived. Had the Qualcomm need for a new core been just a bit later, and if Intel had figured out an IP or foundry business model for StrongARM, the outcome for Intel in mobile may have been very different.) While existing parts still shipped, the Intel phase for next-generation parts at Qualcomm was over.

Detour for Better Cores

It was a short search for a higher performance CPU core. Many Qualcomm CDMA licensees, particularly LSI Logic, Lucent Technologies (spun out from AT&T), Samsung, and VLSI Technology, were ARM proponents. Officially, Qualcomm announced its first ARM license in July 1998.[649]

Chipset launches accelerated – quickly making Qualcomm one of the more prolific ARM-based chip suppliers used extensively in thousands of mobile devices. What follows is primarily a chip discussion with only highlights of key releases.

Already in progress when the ARM deal became public, the MSM3000 was announced in February 1998 with a core change to ARM7TDMI. It had other enhancements including the SuperFinger demodulator for faster data transfers up to 64 Kbps, and enhanced sleep modes. It was fabricated in a 0.35 micron process. For the first time, Qualcomm parts were coming from TSMC. To avoid confusion since all-new software was required, the same 176-pin QFP had a vastly different pinout.[650,651]

Another core was also being productized. DSP was a feature of the product line for some time, and in February 1999 the MSM3100 was introduced with both an ARM7TDMI core and a homegrown, programmable QDSP2000 core. The 40-bit execution unit in the

QDSP2000 featured a five-deep pipeline with optimized instructions for EVRC and other needs such as echo cancellation.[652]

3G technology made its debut in the MSM5000 supporting the updated cdma2000 specification. Announced in May 1999, and still running on the ARM7TDMI core, the new chip achieved data rates of 153.6 Kbps and further improved searching capabilities. The MSM5000 supported the field trials of cdma2000 the following year and its High Data Rate (HDR) technology would evolve into 1xEV-DO.[653,654]

A flirtation with Palm and the pdQ CDMA phone in September 1998 led to investigation into smartphone operating systems. In September 1999, Qualcomm tipped plans for iMSM chips targeting Microsoft Windows CE and Symbian, including the dual core iMSM4100 with two ARM720T processors, one for baseband and one for the operating system. With StrongARM and other solutions appearing, the iMSM4100 was ahead in integration but behind in performance when it launched. Qualcomm knew its baseband business, but had much more to learn about application processors.[655,656]

Image 9-4

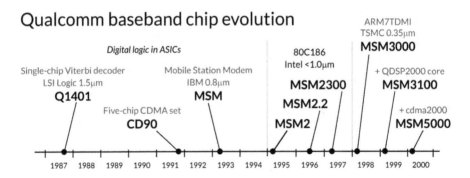

By mid-2000, three different families of chips were in development: 2G cdmaOne baseband, 3G cdma2000 baseband, and notional application processors such as the MSP1000 (essentially an iMSM with just one ARM720T processor). With numerous OEMs producing CDMA phones, Qualcomm exited the handset business, selling to Kyocera in February 2000. After years of visionary thinking, Andrew Viterbi announced his retirement in March. In May, Qualcomm announced its cumulative MSM chipset shipments surpassed 100 million.[657,658,659]

In February 2001, Qualcomm laid out an ambitious plan. The roadmap for the MSM6xxx family offered a wide range of products, starting at the entry-level MSM6000 on the ARM7TDMI supporting only 3G cdma2000. The Launchpad application suite, on top of the new BREW API, helped OEMs produce software more efficiently. Also added were radioOne for more efficient Zero Intermediate Frequency conversion, and gpsOne for enhanced location services.[660]

At the high end would be the MSM6500 on the ARM926EJ-S with two QDSP4000 cores, supporting 3G cdma2000 1xEV-DO and GSM/GPRS plus AMPS, all on one chip. The MSM6500 finally sampled nearly two years later, fabbed in 0.13 micron, packaged in a 409-pin CSP.[661,662]

2003 marked the start of leadership change. In January, Don Schrock announced plans to retire as president of Qualcomm CDMA Technologies (QCT), succeeded by Sanjay Jha who had led MSM development teams.[663]

The MSM7xxx family was next on the roadmap, previewed in May 2003 with a similar broad plan for variants from entry-level to high-end. The 90nm version of the MSM7600 would carry an ARM1136J-S at 400 MHz and a QDSP5000 for applications, plus a 274 MHz ARM926EJ-S and a QDSP4000 for multimode baseband. Also on chip was the Q3Dimension GPU from a licensing agreement for IMAGEON with ATI. The MSM7600A would shrink to 65nm in 2006 with a 528 MHz clock. While still under the MSM banner, the MSM7600 and its stable mates indicated the direction for future Qualcomm application processors.[664,665,666]

In September 2003, Qualcomm reached the 1 billion-chip milestone for MSM shipments – nine years after its commercial introduction.[667]

"Scorpion", "Hexagon", and Gobi

"[Qualcomm has] always been in the semiconductor business," opened Klein Gilhousen in his presentation at Telecosm 2004. "We have always recognized that the key to feasibility of CDMA was VERY aggressive custom chip design." Qualcomm's next moves would test how aggressive they could get.[668]

Irwin Jacobs stepped down as CEO of Qualcomm on July 1, 2005 – the 20th anniversary of its founding – moving into the role of Chairman. His successor was his son, Paul Jacobs, who had been behind development of speech compression algorithms and the launch of the pdQ smartphone as well as BREW and other projects. Steven Altman, who had overseen Qualcomm Technology Licensing, took over as president for the retiring Tony Thornley. Overall, the strategy remained unchanged.[669]

Image 9-5: Paul Jacobs and Irwin Jacobs, circa 2009

Photo credit: Qualcomm

Many ARM licensees expressed immediate support for the new ARM Cortex-A8 core when it launched in October 2005. Rather than go off-the-shelf, Sanjay Jha took out the first ARMv7 architectural license granted by ARM and unveiled a roadmap for the "Scorpion" processor core in November 2005. Media headlines blaring that it was the first 1 GHz ARM core were slightly overstated; Samsung pushed the ARM10 "Halla" design to 1.2 GHz three years earlier.[670]

Nonetheless, Qualcomm pushed Scorpion beyond the competition such as the TI OMAP 3 using a tuned Cortex-A8, and beat Intrinsity's

"Hummingbird" core design to market by a bit more than two years. Their advantage stemmed from a little-known acquisition of Xcella in August 2003, a North Carolina firm started by ex-IBMers including Ron Tessitore and Tom Collopy, bring a wealth of processor design experience.[671]

Scorpion used a similar 13-stage load/store pipeline as Cortex-A8, but added two integer processing pipelines, one 10 stages for simple arithmetic, and one 12 stages for multiply/accumulate. SIMD operations in its VeNum multimedia engine were deeply pipelined and data width doubled to 128 bits. "Clock-do-Mania" clock gating, an enhanced completion buffer, and other power consumption tweaks for TSMC's 65nm LP process yielded about 40 percent less power compared to the Cortex-A8.[672,673]

DSP capability received an enhancement as well. The "Hexagon" DSP core, also referred to as QDSP6, was also moving to 65nm. Started in the fall of 2004, Hexagon applied three techniques to deliver performance at low power: Very Long Instruction Word (VLIW), multi-threading to reduce L2 cache miss penalties, and a new instruction set to maximize work per packet. Dual 64-bit vector execution units handled up to eight simultaneous 16-bit multiply-accumulate operations in a single cycle. Three threads could launch four instructions every cycle, two on the dual vector execution units, and two on dual load/store units.[674]

Both new cores were bound for the new application processor brand: Snapdragon. On November 14, 2007, Qualcomm showed off the new QSD8250 supporting HSPA and the dual mode QSD8650 with CDMA2000 1xEV-DO and HSPA. Each carried a 1 GHz Scorpion processor core and a 600 MHz Hexagon V1 DSP core on the application side. Also on chip was the Adreno 200 GPU (renamed after Qualcomm purchased the ATI mobile graphics assets from AMD in 2009) running at 133 MHz. The multimode baseband core combination of the ARM926EJ-S with a QDSP4000 continued.[675, 676]

Qualcomm was benefitting from the "netbook" craze, and was finding itself more and more in competition with Intel and its Atom processor. WiMAX was Intel's anointed standard for broadband access from laptops, but required an all-new infrastructure rollout. Taking the opening, Qualcomm introduced the first Gobi chipset in October 2007, with the 65nm MDM1000 for connecting netbooks and similar non-phone devices to the Internet using EV-DO or HSPA over existing 3G cellular networks.[677]

Selling into PC and netbook opportunities made Gobi an immediate hit, where Snapdragon was on a slower build-up. Resources poured into Gobi. The roadmap for the MDM9x00 family announced in February 2008 bumped parts to 45nm and enhanced the modem for LTE support, later found to be ARM Cortex-A5 based.[678]

After Sanjay Jha departed for Motorola in August 2008, Qualcomm promoted Steve Mollenkopf to head of QCT to keep the overall strategy rolling forward.

A big change was about to occur in mobile operating systems that would help Snapdragon. In September 2008, the T-Mobile G1, built by HTC, was the first phone released running Android – on a Qualcomm MSM7201A chip. LG and Samsung were both working on Android phones with Qualcomm chips for 2009 release, and Sony Ericsson was not far behind.[679]

Snapdragon moved forward with a second generation introduced on 45nm in November 2009. The MSM7x30 parts aimed to reduce cost and power, falling back to an 800 MHz Scorpion core with a QDSP5000 at 256 MHz and a shrunk Adreno 205 GPU.[680, 681]

Preparing for dual core, the 45nm version of Scorpion received debug features borrowed from the ARM Cortex-A9 and enhancements in L2 cache. In June 2010, the third-generation Snapdragon MSM8260 and MSM8660 featured two Scorpions running at 1.2 GHz paired with the Hexagon V3 at 400 MHz, plus a higher performance Adreno 220 GPU. Packages were getting larger; the MSM8x60 came in a 976-pin, 14x14mm nanoscale package (NSP).[682,683,684]

"Krait", Tiers, and an A/B Strategy
The Qualcomm modus operandi for major introductions is generally to tip the news in a roadmap preview early, followed by product one, two,

sometimes three years later. When Mobile World Congress (MWC) convened in February 2011, Qualcomm had two major moves up its sleeve for announcement.

In its first move, Gobi was headed for 28nm in the form of the MDM9x25. The enhancement added support for Category 4 downlink speeds up to 150 Mbps on both LTE FDD and LTE TDD, and support for HSPA+ Release 9. These third-generation parts sampled at the end of 2012.[685]

Its second move had been previewed in part, twice. Two MWCs earlier, Qualcomm had mentioned the MSM8960, a new Snapdragon variant planned for multimode operation including LTE. At an analyst briefing in November 2010, the part was identified as moving to 28nm with a next-generation processor core on a new microarchitecture, along with a faster Adreno GPU. At MWC 2011, the first ARM processor core to be on 28nm had a name: "Krait".[686,687,688]

Krait was announced as the core inside three different chips. At the low end was the dual-core 1.2 GHz Krait MSM8930, with the Adreno 305 GPU. Mid-range was the MSM8960, a dual-core 1.5 GHz Krait with the faster Adreno 225 GPU. High end was the APQ 8064 with a quad-core 1.5 GHz Krait with the Adreno 320 GPU.

With cores independent in voltage and frequency, Krait allowed significant power savings of 25-40% compared to on-off SMP approaches such as big.LITTLE with the ARM Cortex-A15, depending on workload. Performance gains came in part from 3-wide instruction decode compared to 2-wide in Scorpion, along with out-of-order execution, 7 execution ports compared to 3, and doubled L2 cache to 1 MB. This raised Krait to 3.3 DMIPS/MHz.[689]

Attempting to sort out the pile they had created, Qualcomm set up tiered branding for Snapdragon parts at its analyst meeting in November 2011. The new Krait based parts in 28nm were Snapdragon S4, separated into S4 Play, S4 Plus, and S4 Pro. The 65nm Scorpion parts were labeled Snapdragon S1, the 45nm single-core Scorpion parts Snapdragon S2, and the 45nm dual-core parts Snapdragon S3.[690]

Sometimes, marketers can get a little too clever; tiering is good, obscure nomenclature that doesn't translate well outside of English, not so much. The second try at CES 2013 set up today's Snapdragon number-driven branding.

The flagship Snapdragon 800 for high end phones was announced with quad-core Krait 400 CPUs at 2.3 GHz plus the Hexagon V5 at 600 MHz and an Adreno 330 at 450 MHz, and the LTE "world mode" modem. The Snapdragon 600 had quad Krait 300 CPUs at 1.9 GHz with a Hexagon V4 at 500 MHz an Adreno 320 GPU at 400 MHz, omitting the modem for cost reasons.

Subsequent launches since CES 2013 fit into the Snapdragon 200 entry level tier for phones, Snapdragon 400 volume tier for phones and tablets, Snapdragon 600 mid-tier, and Snapdragon 800 high-end devices. The Snapdragon 200 lines adopted the ARM Cortex-A7 core to keep costs low.[691]

There was more not-so-clever marketing. Shortly after the unexpected launch of the Apple A7 chip with 64-bit support in September 2013, Qualcomm's chief marketer Anand Chandrasekher sounded a dismissive tone questioning its actual value to users. After further review (and probably some testy phone calls from ARM), Chandrasekher was placed in the executive penalty box and his statements officially characterized as "inaccurate" a week later.[692]

Crisis was averted but unanswered. At its November 2013 analyst meeting Qualcomm showed the fourth-generation Gobi roadmap moving to 20nm with the 9x35, supporting LTE Category 6 and carrier aggregation. The hasty December 2013 introduction of a quad ARM Cortex-A53 core in the Snapdragon 410 got Qualcomm back in the 64-bit application processor arena.[693,694]

It might have been coincidental timing, but a few days after the Snapdragon 410 announcement, a major management turnover occurred. Paul Jacobs announced he would step aside as Qualcomm CEO, remaining Chairman, and Steve Mollenkopf was promoted to CEO-elect on December 12, 2013 pending stockholder approval the following March.[695]

Image 9-6: Steve Mollenkopf

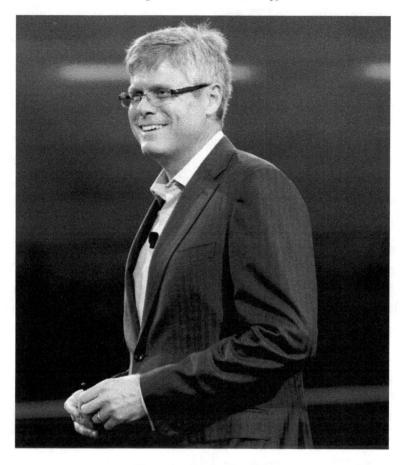

Photo credit: Qualcomm

April 2014 saw the preview of the Snapdragon 810 on TSMC 20nm. Its octa-core big.LITTLE setup featured four ARM Cortex-A57 cores at 2 GHz with four Cortex-A53 cores at 1.5 GHz. Also inside was a retuned Hexagon V5 and its dynamic multi-threading at 800 MHz, an Adreno 430 GPU at 600 MHz, and new support for LPDDR4 memory. It also packed a Cat 9 LTE modem, full support for 4K Ultra HD video, and two Image Signal Processors for computational photography. Its sibling, the Snapdragon 808, used two ARM Cortex-A57 cores instead of four, downsized the GPU to an Adreno 418, and supported only LPDDR3.[696,697]

Fifth-generation Gobi 20nm parts were the main subject of analyst day in November 2014, with LTE Advanced Category 10 support in the Gobi 9x45. These offered download speeds of 450 Mbps using LTE carrier aggregation.[698]

What appears to have developed on the Qualcomm roadmap is an A/B strategy – take ARM's IP where it exists for expedience, follow it with internally developed cores, and repeat the cycle. This is the only feasible way to compete on a broad swath of four tiers from entry-level to super-high-end. The Snapdragon 200 series is facing a flood of ARM Cortex-A5 based parts from Taiwan and China, while the Snapdragon 800 series and Gobi are up against the behemoths including Apple, Intel, Samsung, and many others.

What Comes After Phones?

The relentless pursuit of better chip designs at Qualcomm took CDMA and Android to astounding levels of success. In a maturing cell phone market settling in with around 11% growth and some 80% market share for Android, Qualcomm faces new challenges unlike any seen before.

Instead of celebrating its 30-year anniversary, Qualcomm announced a 15 percent workforce reduction in July 2015. Pundits hung that sad news on the notion that the 64-bit wave started by Apple caught Qualcomm off guard, followed by the Snapdragon 810 overheating scandal at LG and Samsung.[699]

Qualcomm VP of marketing Tim McDonough has his version of the Snapdragon 810 overheating story, saying phone decisions get made 18 months before the public sees them happen – and as we have seen, major chip roadmap decisions get made 18 months before that. The latter is under Qualcomm control. The former may be getting shorter than Qualcomm would like. There are hints in source code that LG may have executed a switch from the Snapdragon 810 to the scaled down Snapdragon 808 – with the same LTE broadband implementation – just a few months before the LG G4 production release.

McDonough contended the issues seen were with pre-release Snapdragon 810 silicon (since updated, and reports of overheating are gone), and that vendors adopting the Snapdragon 808 did so because they didn't need the full end-to-end 4K video experience. The long pole in the tent is carrier qualification of the LTE modem, and it was well along in the process. This would make a switchover – if it did indeed happen at LG – seem quick and less painful. Samsung may have had its own ax to grind in pointing out the problem, with its flagship Exynos 8 Octa launch pending at the time.[700]

Image 9-7

Qualcomm mobile processor highlights

Chip	Year	CPU cores	DSP cores	Process
MSM6500	2003	1 ARM926EJ-S 150 MHz	1 QDSP4000 75 MHz	130nm
MSM7600	2005	1 ARM1136J-S 400 MHz	1 QDSP5000	90nm
Snapdragon S1 QSD8250	2007	1 "Scorpion" 1.0 GHz	1 Hexagon V1 600 MHz	65nm
Snapdragon S2 MSM7630	2009	1 "Scorpion" 800 MHz	1 QDSP5000 256 MHz	45nm
Snapdragon S3 MSM8660	2010	2 "Scorpion" 1.2 GHz	1 Hexagon V3 400 MHz	45nm
Snapdragon S4 MSM8960	2011	2 "Krait" 1.2 GHz	1 Hexagon V3 500 MHz	28nm
Snapdragon 600	2013	4 "Krait" 300 1.9 GHz	1 Hexagon V4 500 MHz	28nm
Snapdragon 800	2013	4 "Krait" 400 2.3 GHz	1 Hexagon V5 600 MHz	28nm
Snapdragon 410	2013	4 ARM Cortex-A53 1.2 GHz	1 Hexagon V5	28nm
Snapdragon 808	2014	2 ARM Cortex-A57 2.0 GHz 4 ARM Cortex-A53 1.5 GHz	1 Hexagon V56 800 MHz	20nm
Snapdragon 810	2014	4 ARM Cortex-A57 2.0 GHz 4 ARM Cortex-A53 1.5 GHz	1 Hexagon V56 800 MHz	20nm
Snapdragon 820	2015	4 "Kryo" 2.2 GHz	1 Hexagon V6 1.0 GHz	14nm

Note: Additional ARM cores and DSP cores exist on the baseband side of these integrated parts. Qualcomm typically does not specify these cores in their publicly available information.

Perhaps recent events are leading to more caution in disclosing roadmaps for public consumption. At MWC 2015 in March, the big reveal was the Snapdragon 820 with "Kryo", Qualcomm's new 64-bit

ARMv8-A CPU core design. Details are trickling out with a quad-core clock speed of 2.2 GHz (with rumors of even faster speeds) and a new fab partner in Samsung with their 14nm FinFET process. In August, plans for the Adreno 530 GPU and a new Spectra ISP bound for the Snapdragon 820 were shown and a new Hexagon 680 DSP is also in the works. [701, 702, 703]

Qualcomm used its media day on November 10, 2015 to reiterate the Snapdragon 820 consumes 30 percent less power than the Snapdragon 810, They also explored system-level support, with Cat 12 LTE, 802.11ad Wi-Fi, and malware-fighting machine learning technology. Their marketing is moving away from pure IP specsmanship and toward use cases for features, a welcome change. [704]

Kryo creates a possible entry point into the nascent 64-bit ARM server market. Competing with Intel and AMD on their turf could be an adventure. Qualcomm is also chasing the IoT, with technology from acquisitions of Atheros and CSR, plus software development in AllJoyn.

How Qualcomm shifts its business model based on licensing sophisticated communication algorithms to what comes next will determine if they remain a leader in fabless semiconductors. Can they develop intellectual property supporting a new application segment, such as drones? (More ahead in Chapter 10.) Is there more work to be done in the 4G LTE cellular arena and will 5G technology coalesce sooner rather than later?

The clamoring from investors to split the firm into an IP licensing business and a chip business seems poorly conceived. While the IP licensing side of the business has a built-in legacy revenue stream from CDMA, the chip operation has thrived from lockstep operation as specifications advanced. Without that synergy, what drives the chip business and prevents it from commoditization?

As long as mobile devices connect wirelessly, Qualcomm should be there. Hard strategy questions lie ahead near term, and that could have a significant ripple effect on foundry strategy and competition in application segments depending on how they proceed.

Chapter 10: An Industry in Transition

The mobile device industry is showing definite signs of maturity. Leadership has concentrated in four firms we just examined – Apple, Samsung, Qualcomm, and by direct association with all three, ARM. They capitalized on shifts in technology, economic conditions, consumer trends, and strategy to rise from the back of the pack to the front, creating markets as they went forward.

What happened to the former leaders? Who else is in the running? How could emerging trends further disrupt an already disrupted mobile space? Finally, what does all this mean for ARM and designers looking to use its technology? A quick walk through recent history leads to thoughts on what might be ahead.

Early Exits for Big Names

Near extinction after selling its PalmSource software operations to ACCESS in 2005, CEO Ed Colligan mounted a comeback attempt. For its "Nova" project, Palm secured a royalty-free license for Palm OS Garnet source code in December 2006.

The next-generation user interface in Nova proved non-trivial. Paul Mercer of Pixo fame tried, then Matias Duarte tried harder, but even simple tasks like centering text were difficult, and gesture code was slow and complex. Third party developers took one look at a Nova preview in early 2008 and revolted. In a desperate weekend, Greg Simon and Andy Grignon (both ex-Pixo) came up with a wild idea: use open source WebKit code as the rendering engine.

A beta version of webOS running on the TI OMAP3430 worked well enough to demonstrate the Palm Pre at CES 2009. By June, Pre shipped exclusively on Sprint – a deal negotiated by the un-retired Jon Rubinstein. The first month of sales went well, but a bizarre advertising campaign raised doubts. Verizon signed as a second carrier promising better marketing. When the Motorola Droid showed up in November 2009 and became an instant hit, Verizon dialed its commitments to the Pre way back. Palm was broken beyond recovery.[705]

HP stepped in as the suitor, buying Palm in April 2010 for its tablet plans. The HP TouchPad with the latest webOS 3.0 was announced in February 2011. Soon, a scandal-ridden CEO transition from Palm advocate Mark Hurd to the enterprise software-centric Leo Apotheker exposed the project to scrutiny.[706]

On July 1, 2011, the TouchPad went on sale with a Qualcomm Snapdragon S3 APQ8060 processor inside. It ran straight into the Apple iPad 2 buzzsaw. The new operating system lacked applications, and pricing was uncompetitive due in large part to display shortages caused by Apple. By August 16, Best Buy halted all TouchPad payments to HP with inventory and customer returns piling up.[707]

Two days later, after only 49 days of consumer availability, an impatient Apotheker cancelled the TouchPad. About a month later, the HP board abruptly discontinued Apotheker. After open sourcing webOS and eventually spinning it off to LG in early 2013, CEO Meg Whitman pushed for a reentry into tablets. The HP Slate 7 debuted in May 2013 with Android and a relatively obscure Chinese SoC supplier – whose name CNET botched in first reports.[708]

Another tablet failure was developing. The BlackBerry PlayBook released in April 2011 carried a TI OMAP4430 and a tablet version of the QNX operating system, popular in embedded yet new to mobile devices. RIM embarked on an aggressive developer ecosystem program to gain applications for the new device. It got a lukewarm reception mostly for lacking an email client but was otherwise likable.[709]

A new merged operating system for the PlayBook and phones was being developed. First called BBX, then after a legal challenge BlackBerry 10 the project ran into delay after delay and missed promise dates. Highly publicized BlackBerry service outages compounded problems. Sales of existing products shrank, layoffs and defections set in, and investors clamored for leadership changes. In January 2012, co-CEOs Jim Balsillie and Mike Lazardis stepped aside.[710]

New BlackBerry CEO Thorsten Heins, an engineering insider chosen to get development teams back on track, sealed the fate of the PlayBook with curious comments in April 2013. "In five years I don't think there will be a reason to have a tablet anymore. Maybe a big screen in your workplace, but not a tablet as such. Tablets themselves are not a good business model." Heins withdrew the promised BB10 update for the PlayBook, akin to pulling the life support plug and letting the market take its course. BlackBerry pulled the plug on Heins as CEO a few months later, replacing him with John Chen.[711,712]

The Motorola brand was back on the map thanks to the Droid, and not a moment too soon. The path of unlocking shareholder value started with the Freescale spinoff. Consumer businesses – phones and set-top boxes – separated into Motorola Mobility on January 5, 2011. Sanjay Jha's teams had become the lead implementers for new versions of Android. Soon, Andy Rubin had Google crawling through Motorola's patent portfolio. Google decided to purchase the entire company on August 15, 2011, for a whopping $12.5B.[713]

Chipmakers were also starting to feel the heat. Infineon sold its baseband SoC business to Intel for $1.4B in August 2010. The WiMAX play was not going as well as hoped, with most of its opportunity usurped by LTE. Intel surmised that combining its wireless operation with Infineon, whose customer list included Apple, would reinforce its mobile strategy.[714]

Image 10-1: Intel acquires Infineon baseband SoC business

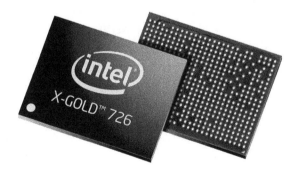

Photo credit: Intel

In January 2011, Qualcomm made a similar play, buying Atheros for $3.1B. This put Qualcomm into Wi-Fi to augment its 3G/4G cellular technology, and pitted them against Broadcom and Intel in PC connectivity. This was perhaps the clearest signal things were changing structurally – Qualcomm was the undisputed leader among mobile semiconductor suppliers, and growing. If they recognized a need for change, things were becoming dire indeed.[715]

Break Glass in Case of Fire

At Nokia, the warning signs were also growing. Stephen Elop left Microsoft to become Nokia's CEO in September 2010, greeted immediately by strategy and financial challenges. After open sourcing much of its code earlier in the year, Symbian support waned when Sony Ericsson pulled out, fleeing for Android. Nokia was exploring MeeGo, an open source operating system project merging Nokia's Maemo with Intel's Moblin, but products and ecosystems were still far away.

Elop fired off his infamous "Burning Platform" internal memo about a week before MWC 2011 would open. He likened Nokia's predicament to a man standing on a burning oil-drilling rig in the North Sea. They could perish in flames, or jump into dark water. It was a confession that Nokia was losing rapidly. Apple had taken the high-end. Android was pushing down to mid-range. An emerging threat, MediaTek, was enabling the low-end across Asia. Symbian was "non-competitive" and MeeGo was unfolding far too slowly.[716]

A few days later, on the Friday prior to MWC 2011, came the formal announcement: all Nokia smartphone efforts would shift to Microsoft Windows Phone 7. The premise behind the move was Nokia needed a strong ecosystem, but it also needed differentiation to survive. That ruled out Android, and the closed environments of Apple and BlackBerry, making Microsoft the best choice for an alliance. It set off a chain reaction of events.[717]

Qualcomm enjoyed a brief monopoly supporting Windows Phone 7 phones with Snapdragon chips. Nokia disclosed they were using the NovaThor platform from the ST-Ericsson joint venture. Also unveiled at MWC 2011, NovaThor combined Nova application processors and Thor baseband modems into a single part. The NovaThor U9500 featured dual ARM Cortex-A9 cores at 1 GHz with an ARM Mali-400 GPU and integrated the functions of the M5730 HSPA+ modem.[718]

The same man who helped put TI in Nokia with an integrated processor plus 2G baseband chip – ST-Ericsson CEO Gilles Delfassy – was now helping take TI out of Nokia with an integrated processor plus 4G baseband chip.

Analysts chanted that integrated basebands were essential for SoC vendor survival, especially at the low end where BOM costs dominated. Qualcomm owned nearly half of the baseband market, integrated or not. Intel by acquisition of Infineon was a significant chunk, and MediaTek broke into the top five riding the low-end, passing TI and ST-Ericsson. Fear of missing out sent NVIDIA scurrying off to buy their own baseband capability, acquiring Icera in May 2011.[719,720]

Where was TI's baseband strategy? We need to give TI credit for having foresight – after all, they practically *invented* the mobile SoC and brought ARM to the party. As with any strategy in tech, there is the capability to do something, weighed against the potential to make money doing it on an ongoing basis.

TI ratcheted down its baseband efforts in 2008, reduced to custom efforts for select customers like Nokia. At the high-end integration was less important, and the development pace of multimedia application processors and baseband modems were very different. Qualcomm Gobi and Snapdragon timelines confirm that. Apple consistently used external basebands, sometimes splitting business for different markets. Samsung also routinely swapped out processors and modems in different phone SKUs targeting different carrier requirements.[721,722]

Legacy customers were also becoming a problem. TI was an incumbent at places like BlackBerry, Motorola, Nokia, and Palm – all in trouble, even considering the Motorola Droid. Another indicator: Nokia had gotten out of Nokia, selling its own baseband modem efforts to Renesas in July 2010.[723]

Nonetheless, TI was increasingly vulnerable. Two prized Android tablet design wins, the French firm Archos and the Amazon Kindle Fire, succeeded where the iPad stampede trampled others. There were few

Archos and Amazons out there, however – the Barnes & Noble Nook paled by comparison. Qualcomm was setting up Snapdragon tiering and a flock of vendors headed for the low-end business. In response, TI had OMAP 5 with dual ARM Cortex-A15 cores coming with a lead port of Android 4.0 demonstrated at CES 2012. There was also the potential for the much-ballyhooed version of Microsoft Windows on ARM coming soon.[724]

TI measured their mobile prospects, stepped back, looked at their total opportunity space and their strengths, and made their own leap. On a September 25, 2012 conference call with investors, TI said they would shift out of the smartphone and tablet segments altogether. They were not killing the product lines; OMAP would continue as a platform for multimedia applications in embedded segments, particularly automotive.[725]

For Nokia, the outcome of a major strategy change was uncertain. For TI, it was just a return to embedded business as usual. As we will see shortly, the long-term future for ARM may also depend less on mobile and more on embedded.

Pounding the Tablet

After the launch of the Apple iPad in January 2010, the Android community needed a response. A gaggle of Android tablets – from at least 29 vendors, led by the Samsung Galaxy Tab, the BlackBerry Playbook, and the Motorola Xoom – showed up at CES 2011. Very few of those devices would survive on the market for long, but three things became evident.[726]

The first observation was the aggregate weight of the Android ecosystem, with dozens of vendors launching devices at the same time, could outweigh Apple's advantages – much as the Gang of Nine had tackled IBM in the PC days. With Apple pursuing its design-centric premium strategy, there was lots of room in the mid-range and low-end for Android tablets.

There was also room for new chipsets in tablets. Smartphones require vast amounts of functionality and performance packed into a tiny space. Heat removal can be a problem, and battery-draining power consumption is a bigger problem. In a tablet, with a bigger display, there is more room to spread out. Parts can consume slightly more power and dissipate heat over a wider area. Bigger frames hold bigger batteries, and power is not as limited a commodity. A less aggressive chip design could do the job in a tablet, for a little more power consumption.

Cost was also a looming consideration. At the high-end, tablets are essentially scaled-up smartphones. In the mid-range and low-end, not all tablets needed 3G/4G as a base option, and Wi-Fi was sufficient – also meaning a data plan from a carrier was not required. Low-end tablets, particularly in Asia, were being given as gifts, an inexpensive alternative to a laptop. To serve these basic needs, some companies minimized Android costs, pre-loading a set of applications and forgoing the cost of licensing what is now the Google Play Store.

These effects brought intense new competition among SoC vendors.

Inside the Motorola Xoom and Android tablets from Acer, ASUS, Dell, Notion Ink, Velocity Micro, and others was the NVIDIA Tegra 2. NVIDIA's SoC efforts were an outgrowth of the PortalPlayer acquisition years earlier, with the first big win inside the Microsoft Zune media player. Tegra also powered the Microsoft KIN social media phone, the Windows CE-powered evolution of the Danger Hiptop (whom Microsoft acquired in 2008).[727,728]

NVIDIA repositioned its graphics capability front and center for the tablet market. Announced at the previous CES 2010, Tegra 2 was fabbed in TSMC 40nm with dual ARM Cortex-A9 cores and an ultra-low power version of the GeForce GPU. Gamers were viewed as a core audience for tablets, and a bigger screen with more graphics power could draw both enthusiasts and game titles.[729]

Freescale had exited phones and was refocusing efforts on tablets, building on a win in the Amazon Kindle 2 e-reader in 2009. The i.MX3 and i.MX5 families shifted away from smartphones and toward tablets, winning designs in many white-box Chinese tablet vendors. Freescale brought its latest i.MX6 to CES 2011, in single, dual, and quad ARM

Cortex-A9 configurations with a Vivante GC2000 GPU on the larger parts.[730]

Marvell was also using Vivante GPUs, with a family connection – sister Weili Dai co-founder of Marvell, and brother Weijin Dai CEO of Vivante. Marvell SoCs powered many models in the BlackBerry Curve and Bold families, as well as some popular Samsung phones. Their latest innovation in September 2010 was the ARMADA 628, a tri-core PJ4 design running two cores at up to 1.5 GHz and one at 624 MHz. Their Moby tablet design demonstrated at CES 2011 targeted a $99 textbook replacement for schools, falling back to the less expensive and lower power ARMADA 168 processor.[731,732]

Asian ARM Fusion

Suddenly, a flood of Asian SoC firms made their intentions known in the Android mobile device space. Lesser recognized outside of their region, most of these firms were not brand-new startups. Many had been designing multimedia chips for PCs and other consumer electronics.

Nufront was among the first Chinese names to appear. The NuSmart 2816 launched in September 2010 delivered a dual-core ARM Cortex-A9 at up to 2 GHz with an ARM Mali-400MP GPU in TSMC 40nm. Clocked down to 1.6 GHz, the part consumed less than 2 W of power. Nufront was also tinkering with a $250 Linux desktop, perhaps a laptop as well, and preparing an Android tablet product line.[733,734]

Allwinner Technology was next, signing an ARM license in April 2011 for the ARM Cortex-A8 processor and the Mali-400MP GPU. Allwinner was closer to a startup, founded in 2007 around expertise in HD video decoding for set-top boxes and TVs. The Allwinner A10 would be first in a rapidly growing family of parts.[735]

Leadcore Technology also licensed ARM technology in April 2011. Leadcore was a Datang affiliate (an ARM licensee since 2003) focused on TD-SCDMA, the Chinese effort to create a 3G alternative to W-CDMA. The Leadcore LC1810 was their first smartphone chip, a dual mode TD-HSPA+ and GSM design on a dual-core ARM Cortex-A9 at 1.2 GHz.[736,737]

HiSilicon, the ASIC arm of Huawei, held a previously undisclosed ARM Cortex-A9 license, and signed on for the ARM Cortex-A15 core in August 2011. Huawei first licensed ARM in 2004, and set up HiSilicon to focus its chip efforts the same year. The ARM Cortex-A9 core appeared in the HiSilicon K3V2, a quad-core 1.5 GHz SoC with a Vivante GC4000 GPU. It launched in February 2012 in the Huawei Ascend D quad smartphone and the Huawei MediaPad 10 FHD tablet.[738,739,740]

Rockchip (the firm whose name CNET flubbed in their HP Slate 7 review) was the nickname for Fuzhou Rockchip Electronics, formed in 2001. Aptly named, Rockchip's first efforts were SoCs for MP3 players. By 2010, the RK2818 pushed an ARM926EJ-S and an accompanying DSP core to 622 MHz (not, as some outlets claimed, 1 GHz) running Android 2.1 for low-end Chinese tablets. In February 2012, Rockchip revealed an ARM Cortex-A9 license for its dual-core RK30xx family. The 1.6 GHz RK3066 SoC was in HP and many other tablets.[741,742]

Then there was MediaTek, the Taiwanese firm that had everyone talking. Formed out of a lab at the foundry UMC in 1997, MediaTek began life making controller chips for CD and DVD drives. In July 2002, MediaTek was already one of the top 10 fabless chip firms in the world before taking out their first ARM license.

MediaTek's plan was to create a single-chip design with ported software for GSM phones (a reference platform). This would enable hundreds of primarily Chinese manufacturers with electronic assembly capability but little design expertise to produce a feature phone quickly and cheaply. According to its datasheet, the MT6205B was ready in October 2003, with a 26 MHz ARM7TDMI core for control and a DSP core handling the GSM channel and speech coding. Fabbed in 0.18 micron, it was in a 181-pin 12x12mm BGA.[743]

In 2004, the MT6205B shipped 3 million units. Extensions to the MT62xx family powered MediaTek to 300 million mobile chipsets by 2009. All this was done mostly without a major cellphone manufacturer (except LG) adopting the solution. While many analysts and even Nokia's CFO debated the legitimacy of grey market phones, "shanzhai" counterfeiters, and over or under counting, the fact was MediaTek chips were shipping in large numbers.[744,745]

Until 2009, all MediaTek success was on 2G. They and Leadcore had been working together to develop TD-SCDMA specifications for China, then quietly went separate ways to produce products. MediaTek had also licensed Qualcomm W-CDMA for other markets such as Brazil and India. They launched a wide range of chips in the MT65xx family for 3G. In February 2012, they moved up to 40nm with the MT6575 and its 1 GHz ARM Cortex-A9 processor, Imagination PowerVR SGX531 GPU, CEVA DSP core, and Android 4.0 support.[746,747]

Spreadtrum formed in 2001 and licensed ARM technology in 2003, trying to create a reference design model similar to MediaTek. The SC6600B baseband chip launched with ARM7TDMI and CEVA DSP in January 2003. Their success was not quite equivalent, and by early 2009, Spreadtrum was caught in a financial crisis compounded by product quality issues. Barely surviving regulatory scrutiny and securing stop-gap funding, the company recovered and launched the 40nm multi-mode SC8800G baseband for TD-SCDMA in January 2011. One derivative, the SC8802G, powered the Samsung Galaxy S II for China Mobile.[748,749,750,751,752]

Plunder and Pillage

Disruption in the mobile supply chain was about to take on entirely new dimensions, introducing one major new player and rebranding two others. All three cases pointed to new motives that would leave weaker mobile chip suppliers exploring their strategic options.

Jeff Bezos revealed his new device on September 28, 2011: the Amazon Kindle Fire tablet. Instead of heading for Android 3.0 as most others had, Amazon forked an earlier Android 2.3 release and built its own user interface and its own app store. The reasons were obvious. With a huge online catalog of books, movies, and MP3s, Amazon was entering the mobile content delivery business. Its new tablet was a shopping cart for all kinds of digital goods.[753,754]

The Kindle Fire Tablet scored with users, cutting into Apple's iPad lead and rocketing past Samsung and Motorola taking over 50% share in

Android tablets. One reason was a lighter price tag at $199. Another reason was the 7" size (forcing Apple to respond later with the iPad Mini). Amazon gave only a vague "1 million per week" sales figure for all Kindle devices during December, while analysts estimated 4Q 2011 shipments between 3.9 million and 6 million units. It reflected strong consumer demand for content, not just tablet hardware.[755,756,757]

Microsoft was executing a long and difficult straddle. Their Windows 8 announcement at CES 2011, with a new version for ARM chips from NVIDIA, Qualcomm, and TI, created a stir. Big features were the "Metro" tiled user interface, first seen in Windows Phone 7, and a new Windows Store for apps.[758]

In theory, ARM-based Windows 8 devices could offer longer battery life and smaller physical size through lower SoC power consumption. On October 26, 2012, Windows RT shipped on the ASUS VivoTab RT and the Microsoft Surface tablets, both on the 1.3 GHz NVIDIA Tegra 3. In the following months, Dell and Lenovo also released Windows RT tablets.[759]

Sales were tepid. Users quickly discovered that Windows RT was not Windows 8 when it came to applications, despite a version of Microsoft Office 2013 ported to the platform. Long-held expectations that a "Windows" machine should be able to run most "Windows" legacy applications proved to be a terminal disease. Samsung withdrew its Windows RT offering before it arrived in the US.

The fatal blow may have been self-inflicted. Two versions of the Surface had been previewed in June, one on an ARM processor, and the other on an Intel processor. The Intel-based version named Surface Pro was over 220g heavier and 4.2mm thicker, but small enough to be innovative.[760]

On February 9, 2013, the Surface Pro shipped with a 1.7 GHz dual-core Intel Core i5 processor, fully compatible with all Windows 8 software. (Note the parallel to the Motorola ROKR V1 and Apple iPod nano episode.) Surface Pro got off to a moderate start, but thrived with generational improvements and relentless advertising. Microsoft would do one more version of Windows RT on Surface 2 with an NVIDIA Tegra 4 before converting Surface 3 to Intel parts.[761]

The endgame for Microsoft was clear. Eventually, all devices – phones, tablets, and desktop PCs – were to run the same user interface and the same applications, delivering a seamless user experience. Saying that and achieving that were two different things. Microsoft's huge code base and software ecosystem were like a battleship in a flank speed turn, and Windows 8 was only Step 1.

Step 2 was Windows Phone 8, announced on October 29, 2012, three days after the Surface debut. The release updated the architecture from Windows CE to the same Windows NT kernel in Windows 8 and added support for multicore processors, over-the-air updating, and NFC among other features. Nokia launched its new Lumia 920, HTC the Windows Phone 8X, and Samsung the ATIV S – all three phones running on a dual-core 1.5 GHz Qualcomm Snapdragon S4.[762]

Step 3 was a return to Microsoft hardware. On September 3, 2013, Microsoft announced they would buy the devices and services business of Nokia, plus licenses for their sizable patent portfolio. Cries of "Trojan horse" and "Plan B" went up across Finland, but if Windows Phone was to live, this was the best option. With Windows 10 development for mobile nearing release, we will soon know if this strategy pays off.[763]

Image 10-2: Microsoft's Windows 10 unification strategy

Photo credit: Microsoft

Similarly, Google's acquisition of Motorola was all about assembling a patent portfolio in defense of Android. To get the patents, Sanjay Jha forced Google to take all of Motorola Mobility (already separated from its infrastructure business). In a very different situation from Microsoft, Google tired quickly of hearing a steady torrent of complaints of competing with its Android customers, with Motorola enjoying a perceived unfair advantage.

Lenovo purchased Motorola Mobility for $2.91B on January 29, 2014. The bargain basement price included the Motorola brand and products, but not most of the patent portfolio Google had coveted. It wasn't a random choice. Motorola had run high-profile consumer branding campaigns in China since 1998, and the ROKR concept had been aimed in large part at Chinese consumers.[764,765,766]

It would be a challenge to merge the Lenovo brand and its phone and tablet activities, which included the IBM PC business it acquired in 2005, with Motorola and its more powerful global brand. There were other ramifications since Lenovo was one of a handful of users of another mobile chipset architecture.

Many of those other mobile chipsets fell like dominos. The ST-Ericsson run with NovaThor was cut short, perhaps a direct result of losing Windows Phone 8 business to Qualcomm. In March 2013, Ericsson and STMicro parted amicably. The application processors went to ST, and the LTE baseband parts went to Ericsson. ST was now effectively back in the embedded business.[767]

LTE baseband development was becoming an expensive undertaking. Broadcom announced it was out in June 2014. CEO Scott McGregor said they were losing $2M per day and losing customers to Qualcomm, Intel, and MediaTek. Focus would be on Wi-Fi and combo connectivity parts.[768,769]

Retracing its steps, NVIDIA also exited LTE baseband in May 2015, winding down the Icera acquisition. NVIDIA's strategy had shifted to automotive, with a flagship win for Tegra 3 SoCs in the 17" center console and the instrument cluster of the Tesla Model S. There was also a gaming focus, with the SHIELD tablet running on the Tegra K1.

(SHIELD hasn't gone so well; 88,000 units were recalled in July 2015 for battery overheating issues.)[770,771,772,773]

The Atom Contra Affair

The one company that could have mounted significant resistance – Intel – was mostly watching the smartphone world go by after StrongARM left. They were also seeing PCs start to change as consumers opted for mobile devices.

Their first attempt to jump on the bandwagon was the ultra-mobile PC (UMPC) and Project Origami with Microsoft in 2006. UMPCs typically had a small touch display and external keyboard and ran full-up Windows on X86 processors. ASUS grabbed the idea for its EeePC 701 in 2007. They put the keyboard back in a netbook making it half way between a UMPC or subnotebook and a full-sized notebook. It was a hit, small enough to be light and yet large enough to type on somewhat comfortably, and many PC makers hopped on.[774,775]

For years, Intel misunderstood the words "low power" pretending 5 W from an underclocked Celeron processor was awesome in contrast to 35 W for their normal fare. Compared to ARM processors, it wasn't close to mobile needs, and AMD and VIA also had lower power options. To push the power-performance curve, Intel created the Atom processor family in 2008.[776]

Open sourcers in Taiwan initiated the Android-X86 project in July 2009, porting code on an EeePC 900a with an Intel Atom processor. Intel launched the "Moorestown" platform in 45nm, hoping to target smartphones and Android tablets, but it was not until the "Medfield" platform arrived in 32nm with official Intel Android support in 2011 that some progress was made. The big wins were, coincidentally, at Lenovo (K800) and Motorola (Razr i). The other "wins" at Indian firm XOLO (X900) and Orange in France and the UK (San Diego) were private labeled for those firms, produced by Taiwanese firm Gigabyte for Intel.[777,778,779]

Combining a few Atom converts with the just-acquired Infineon baseband business and a roadmap to the 64-bit "Merrifield" on 22nm FinFET, Intel finally thought it had a decent mobile strategy.

The same tactic Intel used to fend off PC processor competitors – a roadmap with a blizzard of releases at various price and performance points versus a "coming soon" box with a next-generation savior – worked against them in mobile processors. Merrifield was dual-core, ARM roadmaps were for quad-core and beyond. Integrated baseband was nowhere in Intel's plan, with Infineon parts on a separate fab track at TSMC. Merrifield was Osborned (orphaned by self-infliction) at launch, with a roadmap to the quad-core "Moorefield" slid across the table in the same press release.[780]

However, this is Intel we are talking about with billions of dollars to spend and gargantuan fabs to fill, and they don't like to take 'no' for an answer once they make up their mind to do something.

On the tablet trail – with "Clover Trail" in 32nm, and "Bay Trail" on the 22nm roadmap for later in 2013 – Intel was having more success. The Intelerati again pointed to superiority in technology and manufacturing scale that was going to overwhelm the rest of the mobile world. The Windows 8 tablet business was growing, essentially zero in 2012 and on radar at 4.3% market share at the close of 2013. Bay Trail announced in September 2013 added Android support.[781,782]

Things were going according to plan until the Taiwanese rumor mill broke a story in November 2013 claiming Intel was offering $1B to subsidize tablet makers to take their processors. The credibility of the report was in some doubt.[783]

Such Intel marketing measures were not unprecedented. For years, every time TV viewers heard the five-tone sound mark and saw the "Intel Inside" logo on one of many PC vendor commercials, an ad agency got its check. The practice is known as co-op advertising, where a manufacturer makes advertising funds available for their OEM customers based on a percentage of their chip purchases in exchange for a prominent logo display.

The rumor fit with what people were seeing on Intel's financial statements – massive bleeding from the mobile business. New platforms, tons of R&D, advanced process nodes, $5B fabs, blah-blah-blah. Intel is not famous for its transparency.

When touting forecasts for 2014 tablet shipments, CEO Brian Krzanich said out loud what many had wondered: "I'd say the majority of the [tablet] projects that we have in 2014 use some level of contra-revenue." Intel spokespeople were quick to say Intel was not giving away chips, and contra-revenue was not a subsidy. It was a combination of marketing support, engineering support, and moral support to "bridge that gap" between Intel chips and ARM chips.[784]

Contra-revenue was also real money. With the unit losing over $3B in 2014, Chairman Andy Bryant finally demanded action. "We will not continue to accept a business with multi-billion dollar losses. But this [reorganization] is the price you pay to get back in and we will get back in." The reorganization, combining Intel's mobile and PC groups, allegedly provides better customer engagement.[785]

Intel's mobile roadmap launched at MWC 2015 got a complete makeover, rebranding Atom into x3 – also known as SoFIA – and x5 and x7 lines, the latter two based on 14nm "Cherry Trail". Rockchip is designing one member of the Atom x3 lineup, a quad-core with integrated 3G modem in 28nm. Atom x3 has also swapped GPUs, moving to ARM Mali variants.[786,787,788]

Maybe Intel got the message, and the contra-revenue era is ending.

Restocking the Shelves

The ARM Cortex-A8 (circa 2005) and Cortex-A9 (circa 2007) cores hit the mainstream and are still in broad use, but by no means did ARM stand pat on its success. Only the largest vendors can afford and execute on architectural licenses. Many companies in the ecosystem depend on ARM to continue its innovation. New ARM cores began arriving annually, extending the performance range and providing migration paths – both crucial product roadmap elements for success.

October 2009 saw the debut of the ARM Cortex-A5 processor, highly optimized for the TSMC 40nm process. It excelled in single core designs replacing older ARM926EJ-S and ARM1176JZ-S processors with a similar footprint and power profile to the ARM926EJ-S but higher performance than the ARM1176JZ-S. It also supported up to quad-core implementations, ready to support Android and other software for the Cortex-A series.[789]

Raising the bar on out-of-order execution and deep pipelining, the ARM Cortex-A15 went for raw performance in October 2010. Cortex-A1x series cores decode three instructions per clock. The Cortex-A15 pipeline was 15 to 24 stages long, varying with queues behind eight different execution ports. It also carried Large Physical Address Extensions (LPAE) for 40-bit physical addressing, and support for hardware virtualization. Vendors quickly pushed designs from 28nm to 20nm processes.[790,791]

Moving back to the energy efficiency side for 28nm, the ARM Cortex-A7 launched in October 2011. Power savings resulted from falling back to in-order execution and a simpler 8 to 10 stage pipeline with less parallelism. The Cortex-A7 was one-fifth the size of the Cortex-A8 and five times more energy efficient. A Cortex-A7 cluster could pair with a Cortex-A15 cluster in a big.LITTLE model or Cortex-A7 cores could be used individually up to quad-core.[792]

In October 2012, the ARM Cortex-A5x series was introduced, the premiere of stock 64-bit ARMv8-A cores. In the big.LITTLE model the Cortex-A57 was the performance side with out-of-order execution and deep pipelining, and the Cortex-A53 the power efficient side with in-order simplifications. Each could be used individually up to quad-core. Both cores were eventually taped out in TSMC 16nm FinFET and Samsung 14nm FinFET.[793]

Back to the mid-range and 28nm, the ARM Cortex-A12 appeared in June 2013, bringing many of the enhancements from the Cortex-A15 into a core targeting an upgrade path for Cortex-A9 developers. Compared to the Cortex-A9, the Cortex-A12 used 40% less power and offered virtualization features.[794]

The Cortex-A12 was a good idea but might have missed the target just slightly. ARM enhanced the design and released it as the ARM Cortex-A17 in February 2014, this time with complete support for big.LITTLE. Power consumption improved to be 60% better than a Cortex-A9.[795,796]

Most of our focus throughout this book has been on the Cortex-A family as the primary application core for mobile devices. One of the newer Cortex-M cores, the ARM Cortex-M7 introduced in September 2014, is significant for several reasons. First, it brings performance enhancements similar to those found in Cortex-A parts (such as a six-stage superscalar pipeline) down into microcontroller lines. Second, with the increase in sensor processing, we expect to see more co-processors in smartphones and tablets.[797]

Additionally, since the Cortex-M7 sits in between the existing Cortex-M and Cortex-A lines, we anticipate a new class of core is forming on the ARM roadmap specifically targeting wearables and the Internet of Things (IoT) – more on the roadmap possibilities in our Epilogue.

Image 10-3

ARM Cortex-A processor cores

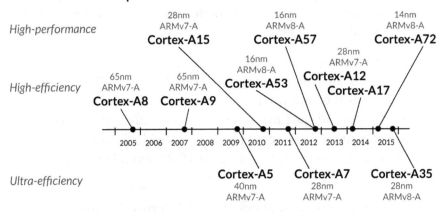

In February 2015, the ARM Cortex-A72 arrived, again in both TSMC 16nm FinFET+ and Samsung 14nm. Its job is to compete with the bevy of self-designed ARMv8-A cores from Apple, AppliedMicro, Broadcom, Cavium, NVIDIA, Qualcomm, and Samsung. Many of those cores are targeting server-class parts while ARM is servicing both the high-end of the mobile device market and its server aspirations.

To improve performance and power efficiency, ARM went back into the details of branch prediction, instruction decode, and dispatch for the Cortex-A72, reoptimizing most of the Cortex-A57 logical blocks. In a telling sign, the first wave of endorsements for the Cortex-A72 came from HiSilicon, MediaTek, and Rockchip.[798,799]

Reigniting Mobile Innovation

Even with all these ARM cores to choose from, providing flexibility to design precisely the chips needed, the industry faces a minor crisis: breakthrough innovation in mobile devices is becoming harder to accomplish.

Over its first 30 years, the mobile industry created the conditions for innovation with generational advances. First was the novelty and productivity factor for 1G. Then came smaller devices with better roaming, improved voice quality, and text messaging in 2G. Smartphones and Internet access appeared with 3G, and the streaming data and social media wave has powered 4G. Each transition point saw bigger, faster chips inside the latest phones.

There was also innovation in form factors. Phones evolved through bag, "brick", candy bar, flip, slider, thumb board, and touchscreen. As each of these shapes appeared, there was a burst of activity as competitors responded with their version. The race was often about achieving smaller and lighter phones.

With 5G cellular infrastructure still years away, and the basic shape of a smartphone defined, what innovations kept people buying in 2015? Following are just some examples of attempts to reignite interest in new hardware.

Smartphones with touchscreens and icons reversed a long-standing trend. People want *bigger* phones: phablets, with screen sizes 5.5" and up. Samsung has squeezed a 5.7" QHD Super AMOLED display, 2560x1440 pixels at 518ppi, into the Samsung Galaxy Note 5 with an Exynos 7420. Once committed to a larger display, a larger battery is possible, in turn enabling a higher performance SoC. Of course, premium sized phablets are premium priced, and may be just too large for some users to handle. The trend has its limits, since 7" devices become tablets.[800]

A different attempt at bigger is the BlackBerry Passport, with a Qualcomm Snapdragon 801 running BB10. This phone has an unusual 4.5" square display at 1440x1440 pixels and 453ppi, with a physical keyboard. Many people panned the unit as oddly wide at 90.5mm, while diehard BlackBerry users generally see it as a productivity tool for enhanced email – not entertainment. The launch of a new Android phone with a vertical sliding keyboard, the BlackBerry PRIV, may keep BlackBerry in the game a bit longer.[801,802,803]

Curved displays sound like a quirky idea, until we see what they do. The LG G Flex 2 – and yes, it runs a Qualcomm Snapdragon 810, updated to V2.1 – is concave along its length at a 700mm radius. One claim is the curve fits the user's face, placing the microphone nearer the mouth for less background noise. Another is the display is more immersive; CNET said it feels like users are "more drawn in". The phone can actually be flattened by pushing on its back (or sitting on it), and flexes back to its normal shape instinctively.[804,805]

The Samsung Galaxy S6 Edge+ takes the curve in a different direction, wrapping the touch display over the long edges and providing access to applications, contacts, and notifications. A nice feature is a color-coded alert for an incoming call or text from one of five favorite contacts.

Another feature showing up in the latest Samsung devices is wireless charging. Three specifications are out there: Qi and PMA for inductive, and A4WP for magnetic resonance. Qi is so far the best adopted, and Starbucks is backing PMA with Powermat stations. The Samsung Galaxy S6 supports both Qi and PMA today. The trade organizations behind A4WP and PMA have recently combined, with their technologies anticipated to combine into a multi-mode system.[806]

With everyone taking pictures, the smartphone has replaced the digital camera for all but high-end professional usage. Computational photography is a natural fit for SoCs with DSP or GPU cores. The LG G4 with its Qualcomm Snapdragon 808 and f/1.8 lens has placed well in DxOMark ratings, slightly ahead of the Apple iPhone 6 in still photos. The G4's 16 MP rear camera has a range of manual image controls, and shoots 4K Ultra HD video.[807]

Embedded vision – processing, recognizing, and tracking objects in a scene – is also becoming important. One now-failed attempt in embedded vision was the Amazon Fire Phone with Firefly technology that could pull up information about many things by pointing the camera and pushing a button. Other uses for embedded vision, such as facial passwords, mHealth, and emotional reaction measurement hold more promise. New technology such as Intel RealSense and Google Project Tango may soon turn the 3D camera fad into a useful feature.

In many use cases, a keyboard is just unacceptable. Apple set the high bar for voice activation with Siri, and in the iPhone 6 it is "always-on" (listening without a button push) when the phone is plugged into a charger. "OK Google" and Microsoft Cortana bring similar capability to Android and Windows 10 respectively. Consumers are becoming more comfortable with voice technology as a way to interface with more devices like TVs, set-top boxes, and an emerging category we will look at shortly.

NFC has also become must-have after Apple, who already held numerous patents, finally adopted the technology in the iPhone 6 and the Apple Watch. This compelled Google into a complete redesign of Google Wallet to Android Pay, and Samsung to create Samsung Pay. (Talk about "me too" product naming.) The battle for credit card payments flowing through mobile devices is going to be epic.

Another epic battle is shaping up in the car. With many SoC vendors such as Altera, Freescale, NVIDIA, Renesas, and TI and operating system vendors like QNX shifting energy to automotive, a spurt of innovation has followed. Advanced driver assistance systems (ADAS) combine embedded vision with other sensing technologies to enhance collision avoidance.

Both Apple and Google want in. While the in-dash electronics can provide many features for the connected car, the infotainment experience many consumers want is already on their preferred smartphone environment. Forcing a consumer to switch can be a deal-breaker. Each has announced a smartphone integration strategy, Apple CarPlay and Android Auto, giving consumers control over the user interface and (with any luck) reducing distracted driving.

Wearables and the IoT

With global mobile device penetration now around 51% at over 3.6 billion devices, it is time to look beyond phones and tablets. Where does a new billion-device market come from?[808]

The buzz across the tech industry in 2015 revolves around two topics: wearables, and the Internet of Things (IoT). Each is leveraging the advances in semiconductor technology created for mobile devices. Both are looking for the use case that catapults them from phenomenon to mainstream.

Wearables are nothing new for chip vendors. In 1970, Seiko introduced a CMOS chip to the 36SQC quartz watch. Hamilton shipped its Pulsar digital watch with an RCA chip in 1972, replacing 44 discrete chips in its prototypes. Samsung's semiconductor heritage began with digital watch chips in 1973. In 1974, Intel produced the 5810 digital watch chip with 1850 transistors for their Microma subsidiary. Dozens of vendors climbed on, most notably TI in September 1975 who quickly took market share with single-chip watches under $40.[809,810,811]

The 1970s digital watch craze came and went, but the precedent for digital wearable technology was set. The emergence of Bluetooth connectivity chips, inexpensive MEMS sensors, and low-cost, lower-power SoCs – many with ARM cores inside – enabled a new generation of wearables 40 years later.

Image 10-4: Fitbit Surge smartwatch

Photo credit: Fitbit

Activity trackers had a head start in the wearables category and three of those vendors remain in the list of top wearable devices in mid-2015: Fitbit, Xiaomi, and Garmin.[812]

The Apple Watch is already challenging Fitbit for the top wearables spot, taking 75% share among smartwatches in its first few months of availability. Apple's S1 multi-chip module contains a processor labeled APL0778, fabbed by Samsung in 28nm. Some clever timing analysis by the folks at AnandTech shows it is likely an ARM Cortex-A7 core or derivative at 520 MHz.[813,814]

Samsung is the other top five wearables vendor. The Samsung Gear S2 runs Tizen on an Exynos 3250, a dual-core 1 GHz ARM Cortex-A7. Most other smartwatches have opted for Android Wear, including the Moto 360 running on a TI OMAP3630. Also running Android Wear are offerings from ASUS, Huawei, LG, and Sony, while Pebble is running FreeRTOS.[815,816]

There are also many devices targeted at specific niches, such as the UnaliWear Kanega for seniors, and the Filip 2 for child tracking and contact. The Intel purchase of Basis and their fascination with the will.i.am Puls – which got some of the worst reviews ever published – remain inexplicable. Google Glass was an interesting experiment in social media, and with Glass 2 coming Google may have studied the Apple Newton focus group anecdote we shared in Chapter 4.

Even more fragmented are devices for the IoT. First, we should point out that there is a huge difference between the industrial IoT and the consumer IoT. Industrial IoT applications are the traditional embedded fare: bigger, more complex problems; long design-in cycles and lifetimes; tiered architecture with sensors, gateways, private or hybrid application clouds; and strict requirements for connectivity, real-time behavior, security, provisioning, and more. While these applications may aid enterprises in providing customer services, most consumers will never see the inner workings.

For consumers, the on-ramp to IoT applications is either a smartphone or tablet with Bluetooth and Wi-Fi, backed by a Wi-Fi home router or connectivity in a car. A personalized cluster of wireless devices forms around the user providing services augmented by cloud-based applications.

The allure for chipmakers is there are potentially a lot more IoT devices than there are people, and the basics of connectivity and processing already exist. The problem for designers are use cases and utility. The consumer IoT is laden with some very cool things that makers and technologists appreciate, but the average person may not absolutely need just yet. The operative word is "yet".

One of the more visible consumer IoT successes is Google Nest, the learning home thermostat. Its value proposition is energy savings and simplicity. The 2nd generation Nest used a TI Sitara AM3703 on an ARM Cortex-A8 in 45nm. A 3rd generation unit has recently released, with an improved display and a predictive feature for possible furnace issues – no word on an updated processor yet.[817,818]

Image 10-5: Nest thermostat

Photo credit: Nest

Google is providing an entire set of consumer IoT tools: Thread, a low-level lightweight protocol for connecting devices, also backed by ARM and Samsung; Weave, a framework for interoperability between phones, devices, and the cloud; and Brillo, a reduced version of Android for embedded use.

Qualcomm is pushing another interoperability solution primarily for Wi-Fi devices in AllJoyn. An interesting development is support for AllJoyn from Microsoft in Windows 10. Microsoft has also joined the Thread Group, and may be the force to unify those two communities. Some unification would be a welcome development, because there are far too many IoT protocols and interoperability specifications currently. Samsung is trying to gain consumer IoT market presence by acquiring SmartThings, makers of a multi-protocol hub. Apple's HomeKit is rolling out slowly, requiring customized silicon until recently only Broadcom, Marvell, and TI were making. Both Dialog Semiconductor and MediaTek have weighed in with HomeKit support, which could ignite its adoption.[819]

One of the cooler, more useful IoT applications is beacons – small Bluetooth devices that broadcast information a smartphone equipped with the right application can decipher. When a consumer approaches a beacon, the app can go to the cloud to get further information. Beacons are gaining popularity in retail locations, airports, and sports venues as a way to engage consumers in their immediate surroundings. A leading beacon supplier is Gimbal, started inside of Qualcomm and now a spun-off firm.

ARM is very active in IoT circles, dating back to its support for the Weightless initiative, a longer-range wireless protocol for distances up to 10 km. ARM has also acquired several IoT firms, notably Sensinode for the CoAP protocol and Offspark for lighter weight SSL. The learning is going into mbed OS, an open-source operating system tailored for IoT devices.

On the hardware IP side, ARM Cortex-M cores are already widely adopted in IoT applications. ARM has created the Cordio radio core IP (developed by a team at the ARM-incubated Sunrise Micro Devices including some ex-Motorolans) using subthreshold logic and other techniques to achieve extremely low power. To support IoT designs through TSMC, ARM has created an optimized subsystem for TSMC 55nm ULP. Many IoT parts are implemented in more mature process nodes, with integrated mixed signal capability.

A long list of MCU vendors – Atmel, Cypress, Freescale, Infineon, NXP, Silicon Labs, STMicro, TI, and others – are obviously deeply involved in wearables and the IoT. The trend of interest is that the mobile SoC vendors are joining in.

MediaTek announced LinkIt with the "Aster" MT2502A SoC in June 2014. Aster is a blast from the past with an ARM7EJ-S core, a 2G GSM baseband for those parts of the world still using it, and a Bluetooth 4.0 interface.[820,821]

Qualcomm has just launched Snapdragon Flight, a reference platform for drone and robotic makers. The small 58x40mm board carries a Snapdragon 801 with the ability to integrate Sony IMX cameras and Omnivision OV7251 computer vision sensors, along with a variety of inertial measurement units. The compute capability plus 4G connectivity could bring a new aspect to drone design.[822,823]

Samsung has previewed ARTIK, a set of small form factor modules with what appears to be a new family of integrated SoCs. ARTIK 5 is 29x25mm and based on dual ARM Cortex-A7 cores at 1 GHz, with Wi-Fi, Bluetooth 4.0, ZigBee, and Thread. ARTIK 10 is 39x29mm with an octa-core ARM Cortex-A15 and Cortex-A7 configuration and similar connectivity.[824,825]

Changing the World with One Chip

If there is one constant in technology, it is change. When one chip was created by the team that imagined ARM architecture, its intentions were to change the fortunes of one tiny computer company, making something exciting in the process. As that chip was refined, an unanticipated need emerged in mobile devices. Through skill, creativity, luck, determination, and the unfolding of many overlapping events, those ideas turned into 60 billion chips.

ARM is in capable hands, with Simon Segars having assumed the reins as CEO on July 1, 2013. With $1.3B in annual revenue and just under 3300 employees, ARM is now widely regarded as one the world's most innovative companies.[826,827]

2015 has seen tremendous upheaval in semiconductor firms. Freescale was purchased by NXP in March, Broadcom bought by Avago Technologies in May, and Atmel bought by Dialog Semiconductor in September. Rumors have Marvell selling off its mobile chip operations. We wait for possible moves at Qualcomm.

The mobile device industry is also very different. Nokia has disappeared from shelves, replaced by Microsoft branding. Motorola now calls China home, and other Chinese device vendors such as Xiaomi have stepped on the world stage. The popular theory that Apple, Qualcomm, and Samsung have "taken all the money" in mobile is almost certain to be tested soon.

ARM and its technology have weathered change. The post-PC era is upon us. Mobile devices are part of daily life for over half the world's population, and are very likely to stay that way. Connected cars are here. Are wearables and the IoT, and other embedded applications the next major phase? Will 64-bit ARM servers become a significant part of cloud infrastructure? Left to the ARM ecosystem, the answer is likely to involve a combination of all the above.

That is exactly what makes ARM so special. Most other major chip vendors offer essentially a "we-built-it-and-you'll-like-it" approach. ARM offers canvas and paint through which designers large and small can express their vision of how things with a chip inside should work – the very essence of what makers do.

The next chip that changes the world may come from any number of places, but there is a good chance it will run on ARM technology.

Epilogue

When ARM celebrated its 25th anniversary in November 2015 we expected a big product splash from the company at ARM TechCon. What happened instead was a pronounced shift in ARM strategy, perhaps ultimately as important as the Cortex strategy revealed in the Warren East keynote 11 years prior.

The blogosphere whispered rumors about an all-new ARM roadmap. The obligatory core introduction pre-show was the ARM Cortex-A35 moving ARMv8-A into a mainstream of lower-end smartphone devices. This should erase any doubt about the viability of 64-bit processing in mobile devices. ARM and Gartner believe this segment will top 1B units in 2020, in all likelihood powered mainly by the Asian firms we introduced earlier. ARMv8-A now stretches across three tiers – high-performance, high-efficiency, and ultra-efficiency – to keep mobile devices running well into the future.

Image E-1: Simon Segars delivering keynote at ARM TechCon 2015

Photo credit: ARM

At prior TechCons, a major new core probably would have been the lead topic for the CEO keynote. Not on November 11, 2015 when Simon Segars devoted his remarks entirely to the Internet of Things (IoT). ARM clearly intends to become a systems enabler, not just a device enabler. Three themes interconnect in ARM's IoT strategy: two technological, and one cultural.

End-to-end security starts with trust. ARM's pre-show announcement that ARM TrustZone is moving down to ARMv8-M, the microcontroller profile, is a play to secure the three-tier IoT from the edge through the gateway into the infrastructure. ARM has engineering activity where Cortex-M sits today but made no specific product announcement. It isn't hard to see where this is headed: chips designed for the IoT solving the end-to-end security problem with more than just wishful thinking. Carrying TrustZone from the smallest microcontroller to the largest multicore server chip, and everything in between, could be a huge development in plugging a lot of security holes.

Software will also play a huge role and much of ARM's ecosystem at TechCon was telling an IoT software story. ARM itself placed huge emphasis on mbed and its IoT Device Platform while a flurry of partners launched both competing and complimentary products. We ran into several backroom conversations at the show around Thread, now natively supported in the mbed OS Technology Preview release. mbed Device Connector is enabling prototyping of up to 100 devices with cloud connectivity, supporting another trend we heard at the show of customers looking to pilot IoT projects on a smaller scale before a massive rollout.

The third theme, a deeply rooted belief in ARM culture, may be the most important in enabling IoT systems. Segars had a great line saying the hard thing on the IoT may not be a thing at all – it may be "getting industries who haven't collaborated before to collaborate."

Going all the way back to Sir Robin Saxby's original mantra as he took the reins, creating a business around the ARM architecture meant becoming the global embedded standard. The only way to accomplish that was to get people to collaborate, both internally and externally. Since its formation ARM has embraced collaboration at every step of the way, allowing employees, partners, and customers across the ecosystem to have a say in almost every outcome.

Shifting into the post-PC era is more than creating fantastic mobile devices – we are eight years into post-PC, and still counting. It is about breaking the stranglehold of a few vendors who have dictated terms of design and use of computing technology for over 34 years, providing the motivation that sparked Furber and Wilson to do something remarkable at the beginning of this story.

ARM is borrowing heavily from the open source playbook for the IoT while still developing a flow of high-value intellectual property for many others to build upon in creating valuable mobile, consumer, and embedded systems. The success within the ecosystem is a direct result of a collaborative ARM culture.

Image E-2: ARM partner pavilion at ARM TechCon 2015

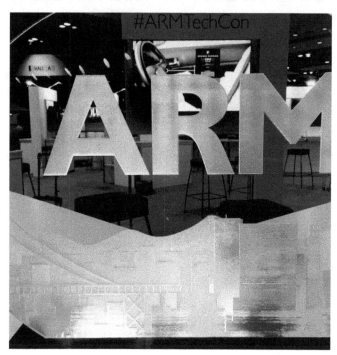

Photo credit: ARM

Who is in a better position to lead the IoT than ARM and their ecosystem? Segars may not have the quasi-religious following of others who ushered in sweeping changes in mobile. What he and ARM have is the benefit of seeing all these changes unfold – after all, cycles tend to repeat in the technology industry.

The IoT combines everything preceding it in computing and semiconductors, plus new cycles of learning as expansive system and social design principles take hold. It will be a fitting legacy if the man who built Thumb extends ARM's reach from billions of chips to trillions, plus software for the IoT.

This ends our book but it is, of course, far from the end of the ARM saga as Sir Robin alluded to in his foreword. The next 25 years of ARM may be even more exciting than the first 25 that we have tried to capture in sampling and sorting through a complex timeline of interactions bringing us to this point. We'll be following this journey, wherever it goes, along with all of you.

Endnotes

Prologue

[1] "ARM Creators Sophie Wilson and Steve Furber", Part Two: the accidental chip, Chris Bidmead, The Register, May 3, 2012,
http://www.theregister.co.uk/2012/05/03/unsung_heroes_of_tech_arm_creators_sophie_wilson_and_steve_furber/
[2] "The Next 100 Billion Chips", ARM, http://www.next100billionchips.com/

Chapter 1

[3] "The First Cellphone Went on Sale 30 Years Ago for $4,000", Stewart Wolpin, Mashable, March 13, 2014,
http://mashable.com/2014/03/13/first-cellphone-on-sale/
[4] Intel Corporation Annual Report, 1984, http://www.intel.com/content/dam/doc/report/history-1984-annual-report.pdf
[5] "IBM is Licensed to Make Intel Chip", David E. Sanger, The New York Times, March 10, 1984,
http://www.nytimes.com/1984/03/10/business/ibm-is-licensed-to-makeintel-chip.html
[6] "The BBC Micro", Chris Garcia, Computer History Museum, http://www.computerhistory.org/atchm/the-bbc-micro/
[7] "MOS – The Rise of MOS Technology & the 6502", Ian Matthews, Commodore.ca,
http://www.commodore.ca/commodore-history/the-rise-of-mos-technology-the-6502/
[8] Tube Application Note, Chris's Acorns, http://chrisacorns.computinghistory.org.uk/docs/Acorn/AN/004.pdf
[9] "Back From the Brink", Carol Atack, Acorn User, December 1988, http://www.stairwaytohell.com/articles/AU-AcornHistory.html
[10] "Design and Implementation of RISC-I", Carlo Sequin and David Patterson, University of California Berkeley, July 1982,
http://www.eecs.berkeley.edu/Pubs/TechRpts/1982/CSD-82-106.pdf
[11] "An Interview with Steve Furber", Jason Fitzpatrick, Communications of the ACM, Vol. 54, No. 5, May 2011,
http://cacm.acm.org/magazines/2011/5/107684-an-interview-with-steve-furber/fulltext
[12] "Oral History of Sophie Wilson", interview by Douglas Fairbairn, Computer History Museum, January 31, 2012,
http://archive.computerhistory.org/resources/access/text/2012/06/102746190-05-01-acc.pdf
[13] Email comments from Chris Shore of ARM to Daniel Nenni, August 2015.

Chapter 2

[14] "Olivetti to rescue Acorn with heavy rights issue", Christopher Sims, The Glasgow Herald, February 21, 1985, p. 13.
[15] "How Olivetti stitched up Acorn", Ellee Seymour, February 24, 2012, http://elleeseymour.com/2012/02/24/how-olivetti-stitched-up-acorn/
[16] "AT&T's Talks With Olivetti Break Down", Reuters, April 12, 1988, http://articles.latimes.com/1988-04-12/business/fi-1023_1_olivetti-stake
[17] "A Short History of OS/2", David Both, OS/2 VOICE, July 1997, updated 1999, http://www.databook.bz/?page_id=223
[18] "John Sculley Just Gave His Most Detailed Account Ever of How Steve Jobs Got Fired from Apple", Randall Lane,
Forbes, September 9, 2013, http://www.forbes.com/sites/randalllane/2013/09/09/john-sculley-just-gave-his-most-detailed-account-ever-of-how-steve-jobs-got-fired-from-apple/
[19] "The birth of the web", CERN, http://home.web.cern.ch/topics/birth-web
[20] "The IBM RT PC ROMP processor and memory management unit architecture", R. Simpson and P. Hester, IBM
Systems Journal, Volume 26, Issue 4, 1987, pp. 346-360,
http://ieeexplore.ieee.org/xpl/login.jsp?tp=&arnumber=5387644
[21] TS-1 and NS-1 entries, OpenPA.net, http://www.openpa.net/pa-risc_processor_pa-early.html#ts-1
[22] "MIPS Computer Systems jumps into OEM mart with RISC-based products", James Connolly, Computerworld, May 12, 1986, p. 34.
[23] "The Mouse and WIMP", Artie Kuhn, Armstrong Institute for Interactive Media Studies, Miami University, October 27, 2011, http://aims.muohio.edu/2011/10/27/the-mouse-an d-wimp/
[24] ARM2 entry on Everything2 by alisdair, http://everything2.com/title/ARM2
[25] "Back From the Brink", Carol Atack, Acorn User, December 1988, http://www.stairwaytohell.com/articles/AU-AcornHistory.html
[26] Email comments from Chris Shore of ARM to Daniel Nenni, August 2015.
[27] "Micro Channel Bus Technical Summary", TechFest, http://www.techfest.com/hardware/bus/mc.htm

[28] "Open: How Compaq Ended IBM's PC Domination and Helped Invent Modern Computing", Rod Canion, BenBella Books Inc., Oct 15, 2013, pp. 126-128, http://www.thecompaqstory.com/

[29] "9 Clonemakers Unite to Take On the Industry Giant", Michael Bane, Chicago Tribune, November 20, 1988, http://articles.chicagotribune.com/1988-11-20/business/8802180783_1_extended-industry-standard-architecture-ibm-compaq-computer-corp

[30] "Continuity and change in a spin-off venture: the process of reimprinting", Simone Ferriani, Elizabeth Garnsey, and Gianni Lorenzoni, Oxford Journals, Industrial and Corporate Change, March 8, 2012, http://icc.oxfordjournals.org/content/21/4/1011.full

[31] ARM3 entry on Everything2 by alisdair, http://everything2.com/title/ARM3

Chapter 3

[32] Personal website of Tom Pittard, http://www.tompittard.com/page4.html

[33] "The RISC For the Rest of Us", Art Sobel, http://www.advanced-risc.com/art1stor.htm

[34] General Information Systems Ltd. website, Company history, http://www.gis.co.uk/history.shtml

[35] "Technology entrepreneur and venture capitalist Hermann Hauser", Stephen Harris, The Engineer, March 11, 2013, http://www.theengineer.co.uk/more-sectors/electronics/in-depth/technology-entrepreneur-and-venture-capitalist-hermann-hauser/1015726.article

[36] Andy Hopper's Home Page, http://www.cl.cam.ac.uk/~ah12/

[37] "An Interview with Steve Furber", Fitzpatrick.

[38] "Brief History of GSM & the GSMA", GSMA, http://www.gsma.com/aboutus/history/

[39] "Steve Jobs: Can He Do it Again?", Katherine Hafner and Richard Brandt, BusinessWeek, October 24, 1988, http://www.businessweek.com/1989-94/pre88/b30761.htm

[40] "Can Steve Jobs Do it Again?", Andrew Pollack, New York Times, November 8, 1987, http://www.nytimes.com/1987/11/08/business/can-steve-jobs-do-it-again.html

[41] "Growing Apple with the Macintosh: The Sculley Years", Tom Hormby, Low End Mac, February 22, 2006, http://lowendmac.com/2006/growing-apple-with-the-macintosh-the-sculley-years/

[42] "How the Knowledge Navigator Video Came About", Bud Colligan, Dubberly Design Office, November 20, 2011, http://www.dubberly.com/articles/how-the-knowledge-navigator-video-came-about.html

[43] "Apple Confidential 2.0: The Definitive History of the World's Most Colorful Company", Owen Linzmayer, No Starch Press, January 1, 2004, pp. 183-184, http://www.nostarch.com/apple2.htm

[44] "Transmeta's Big Gamble", Justin Hibbard, Red Herring, February 29, 2000, http://www.investorvillage.com/mbthread.asp?mb=329&tid=2870071&showall=1

[45] "Oral History of Sophie Wilson", Fairbairn.

[46] "Tales Of Optimism Inside Olivetti's Brave New Labs", Angola Bono, The Scientist, December 12, 1988, http://www.the-scientist.com/?articles.view/articleNo/10014/title/Tales-Of-Optimism-Inside-Olivetti-s-Brave-New-Labs/

[47] "Active Book Prototype Circuit Boards", The Centre for Computing History, http://www.computinghistory.org.uk/det/21617/Active-Book-Prototype-Circuit-Boards/

[48] ARM3 entry on Everything2 by alisdair, http://everything2.com/title/ARM3

[49] Larry Tesler's website, "The Fallen Apple Corrections", http://www.nomodes.com/LinzmayerBook.html

[50] Tom Pittard entry on Facebook, https://www.facebook.com/permalink.php?id=328925453809613&story_fbid=370284416345553

[51] "The Long View: Macintosh Common Lisp", http://basalgangster.macgui.com/RetroMacComputing/The_Long_View/Entries/2013/2/17_Macintosh_Common_Lisp.html

[52] "Oral History of Lawrence G. 'Larry' Tesler", interview by Al Kossow, Computer History Museum, February 12, 2013, http://archive.computerhistory.org/resources/access/text/2014/08/102746675-05-01-acc.pdf

[53] "A Brief History of ARM, and What it Taught Me About Business", Lee Smith, presentation to Cambridge University Entrepreneurs, February 9, 2008, http://vision.ouc.edu.cn/~zhenghaiyong/courses/dsd/20122/materials/Brief_History_of_ARM-LeeSmith.pdf

[54] "Oral History of Sir Robin Saxby", interview by Dane Elliot and Doug Fairbairn et al, Computer History Museum, October 16, 2012, http://archive.computerhistory.org/resources/access/text/2013/04/102746578-05-01-acc.pdf

[55] "Chip Maker Without a Country", Steven Greenhouse, New York Times, August 1, 1988, http://www.nytimes.com/1988/08/01/business/chip-maker-without-a-country.html

[56] "Oral History of Sir Robin Saxby", Elliot and Fairbairn.

[57] Email comments from Chris Shore of ARM to Daniel Nenni, August 2015.

[58] ARM Holdings plc Annual Report and Accounts 1998, http://media.corporate-ir.net/media_files/irol/19/197211/ar/ar98.pdf

[59] "'Advanced RISC Machines Ltd' Launched to attack RISC business", archived in eunet.micro.acorn in Google Groups, https://groups.google.com/forum/#!topic/eunet.micro.acorn/w6Icb__amCw

[60] Email comments from Chris Shore of ARM to Daniel Nenni, August 2015.

Chapter 4

[61] "Oral History of Sir Robin Saxby", Elliot and Fairbairn.
[62] "From One ARM to the next! ARM Processors and Architectures", University of Maryland Computer Science Department, ARM6 entry, https://www.cs.umd.edu/~meesh/cmsc411/website/proj01/arm/armchip.html#Arm6
[63] ARM6 entry on Everything2 by alisdair, http://everything2.com/title/ARM6
[64] ARM610 Data Sheet, Advanced RISC Machines Ltd, August 1993.
[65] Larry Tesler's website, "The Fallen Apple Corrections".
[66] "The Story Behind Apple's Newton", Tom Hornby, Gizmodo, January 19, 2010, http://gizmodo.com/5452193/the-story-behind-apples-newton
[67] "Newton, Reconsidered", Harry McCracken, Time, June 1, 2012, http://techland.time.com/2012/06/01/newton-reconsidered/
[68] "Apple Confidential 2.0", Linzmayer, pp. 190-191.
[69] "Newton: New and Improved", Lisa Picarille, Computerworld, November 20, 1995, p. 39.
[70] Larry Tesler's website, "The Fallen Apple Corrections".
[71] "1946: First Mobile Telephone Call", AT&T Labs Technology Timeline, http://www.corp.att.com/attlabs/reputation/timeline/46mobile.html
[72] "Advanced Mobile Phone Service: The Cellular Concept", V. H. MacDonald, The Bell System Technical Journal, AT&T, January 1979, http://www3.alcatel-lucent.com/bstj/vol58-1979/articles/bstj58-1-15.pdf
[73] "The Impact of Law and Regulation on Technology: The Case History of Cellular Radio", John W. Berresford, Business Lawyer, American Bar Association, May 1989, http://transition.fcc.gov/Bureaus/OGC/Reports/cellr.txt
[74] "The mobile phone adventure", Telenor Group, January 2012, http://www.telenor.com/media/articles/2012/the-mobile-phone-adventure/
[75] "Mobile Telecommunications Standards: GSM, UMTS, TETRA, and ERMES", Rudi Bekkers, Artech House, January 1, 2001, p. 268.
[76] "Cold Chicago Day Becomes Bright Cellular Future", Wireless Week, October 1, 2008, http://www.wirelessweek.com/articles/2008/10/cold-chicago-day-becomes-bright-cellular-future
[77] "Changing the World: The Story of Lars Magnus Ericsson and his Successors", section "Handheld or Not?", Svenolof Karlsson and Anders Lugn, http://www.ericssonhistory.com/changing-the-world/World-leadership/Handheld-or-not/
[78] "Lead Markets: Country Specific Success Factors of the Global Diffusion of Innovation", edited by Marian Beise, Springer Science & Business Media, October 23, 2001, p. 151.
[79] For general background on the early GSM meetings, read "Inside the Mobile Revolution: A Political History of GSM", Stephen Temple, 2010, http://www.gsmhistory.com/
[80] "Changing the World: The Story of Lars Magnus Ericsson and his Successors", section "Eight Contestants", Karlsson and Lugn, http://www.ericssonhistory.com/changing-the-world/World-leadership/Eight-contestants-/
[81] "Brief History of GSM & the GSMA", GSMA.
[82] "Changing the World: The Story of Lars Magnus Ericsson and his Successors", section "God Send Mobiles", Karlsson and Lugn, http://www.ericssonhistory.com/changing-the-world/World-leadership/God-send-mobiles/
[83] "Oral History of Sir Robin Saxby", Elliot and Fairbairn.
[84] "On a Roll After Apple Newton Deal, Advanced RISC Machines Introduces QuickDesign Service for Embedded Controllers", Computer Business Review, November 26, 1992, http://www.cbronline.com/news/on_a_roll_after_apple_newton_deal_advanced_risc_machines_introduces_quickdesign_service_for_embedded_controllers
[85] "Establishing ARM, by Sir Robin Saxby", Electronics Weekly, June 8, 2007, http://www.electronicsweekly.com/mannerisms/yarns/eastablishing-arm-by-sir-robin-2007-06/
[86] "Vintage Mobiles", http://www.gsmhistory.com/vintage-mobiles/
[87] Email comments from Wally Rhines to Daniel Nenni, March 2015.
[88] "Management Innovation: Essays in the Spirit of Alfred D. Chandler, Jr.", William Lazonick and David Teece, Oxford University Press, March 8, 2012, pp. 188-197
[89] "Software Defined Radio Transceiver Front-ends in the Beginning of the Internet Era", Silvian Spiridon, COCORA 2013: The Third International Conference on Advances in Cognitive Radio, April 21, 2013, http://www.thinkmind.org/index.php?view=article&articleid=cocora_2013_1_40_60037
[90] "Hello, Mr. Chips", S. C. Gwynne, Texas Monthly, January 2001, http://www.texasmonthly.com/content/hello-mr-chips/page/0/1
[91] Email comments from Wally Rhines to Daniel Nenni, March 2015.
[92] ARM7 entry on Everything2 by alisdair, http://everything2.com/title/ARM7
[93] "20 years ago today – the making of ARM", Chris Edwards, Engineering and Technology Magazine, November 8, 2010, http://eandt.theiet.org/magazine/2010/17/the-making-of-arm.cfm

.

[94] ARM7TDMI Technical Reference Manual, The Thumb Instruction Set, ARM, http://infocenter.arm.com/help/index.jsp?topic=/com.arm.doc.ddi0210c/CACBCAAE.html

[95] "ARM has entered a new market by signing a deal with Texas Instruments", Richard Wilson, Electronics Weekly, May 26, 1993, as submitted to usenet group comp.sys.acorn, http://www.poppyfields.net/acorn/docs/armdocs/texas.shtml

Chapter 5

[96] Observation of chips on photo of 3DO motherboard, http://www.the-liberator.net/site-files/retro-games/hardware/Panasonic-3DO/panasonic-real-3do-fz-1.htm

[97] "Gamers at Work: Stories Behind the Games People Play", Morgan Ramsay, Apress, January 30, 2012, pp. 11-12.

[98] "Oral History of Sir Robin Saxby", Elliot and Fairbairn.

[99] "Advanced RISC Machines Announces the ARM7 Technology", ARM press release, October 20, 1993, http://chrisacorns.computinghistory.org.uk/docs/Acorn/PR/ARM_announces_ARM7.txt

[100] posting in comp.sys.arm newsgroup by Torben Mogensen, December 13, 1994, referencing information from Dave Seal of ARM, http://web.mit.edu/cfields/News/ARMcycles

[101] "Advanced RISC Machines Wins Cirrus Logic as Fifth ARM Licensee", Computer Business Review, December 7, 1993, http://www.cbronline.com/news/advanced_risc_machines_wins_cirrus_logic_as_fifth_arm_licensee

[102] "Apple Announces Licensing Strategies and Alliances for Newton", Apple press release, March 25, 1993, http://diswww.mit.edu/zeus.MIT.EDU/bcs-newton/69

[103] "Simon Segars, ARM Holdings Chief", Henry Mance, Financial Times, July 7, 2013, http://www.ft.com/intl/cms/s/0/8a805806-e400-11e2-91a3-00144feabdc0.html

[104] BeBox entry in BeBits wiki, http://wiki.bebits.com/page/BeBox

[105] "AT&T Pulls the Plug on Wireless Communicator", Leslie Helm, Los Angeles Times, July 28, 1994, http://articles.latimes.com/1994-07-28/business/fi-20947_1_personal-communicator

[106] "General Magic shows slick Magic Cap communications", Yvonne Lee, InfoWorld, January 10, 1994, p. 10.

[107] Email comments from Chris Shore of ARM to Daniel Nenni, August 2015.

[108] "Samsung Licenses RISC Technology from ARM", Samsung press release, May 23, 1994, http://www.thefreelibrary.com/SAMSUNG+LICENSES+RISC+TECHNOLOGY+FROM+ARM%3b+TARGETS+CONVERGING+...-a015258869

[109] "Seventh Son for ARM", I.C. Europe newsletter, Dataquest, August 1994, http://archive.computerhistory.org/resources/access/text/2013/04/102723298-05-01-acc.pdf

[110] "Sharp Ships LH74610", Telecompaper, March 3, 1994, http://www.telecompaper.com/news/sharp-ships-lh74610--19504

[111] "VLSI Implements ARM7 Core Onto New ARM 710", Computer Business Review, July 20, 1994, http://www.cbronline.com/news/vlsi_implements_arm7_core_onto_new_arm710

[112] "ARM Announces Single Chip Solution for Multimedia and Portable Applications", ARM press release, October 18, 1994, http://www.poppyfields.net/acorn/news/armpress/arm7500.shtml

[113] "Samsung to license UK chip designs", Susan Watts, The Independent, May 23, 1994, http://www.independent.co.uk/news/business/samsung-to-license-uk-chip-designs-1437982.html

[114] "Oral History of Sir Robin Saxby", Elliot and Fairbairn.

[115] "A Conversation with Dan Dobberpuhl", ACM Queue, December 5, 2003, http://queue.acm.org/detail.cfm?id=957732

[116] "A 160 MHz, 32-b, 0.5W CMOS RISC Microprocessor", James Montanaro and Richard Witek et al, IEEE Journal of Solid State Circuits, November 1996, reprinted in Digital Technical Journal, http://www.hpl.hp.com/hpjournal/dtj/vol9num1/vol9num1art5.pdf

[117] "ARM and DEC developing StrongARM", ARM press release, February 6, 1995, posted in comp.sys.acorn, https://groups.google.com/forum/#!topic/comp.sys.acorn/-mz-XUpNRYU%5B1-25-false%5D

[118] "ARM innovation gives 32-bit RISC performance at 16-bit system cost", ARM press release, March 6, 1995, http://www.cpushack.com/CIC/otherpr/ARM_thumb

[119] "About the ARM7TDMI Core", ARM7TDMI Technical Reference Manual, ARM, http://infocenter.arm.com/help/topic/com.arm.doc.ddi0210c/DDI0210B.pdf

[120] "Simon Segars, ARM Holdings Chief", Mance.

[121] "Atmel to Acquire ES2", Telecompaper, April 19, 1995, http://www.telecompaper.com/news/atmel-to-acquire-es2--53855

[122] "Atmel Licenses ARM Thumb RISC Core", Atmel press release, April 15, 1996, http://www.thefreelibrary.com/ATMEL+LICENSES+ARM+THUMB+RISC+CORE-a018187913

[123] "NEC Signs with ARM for 'Thumb'", Peter Clarke and David Lammers, EE Times, September 18, 1995, http://business.highbeam.com/3094/article-1G1-17587613/nec-signs-arm-thumb

[124] "MIPS and NEC Announce Advanced 64-bit RISC Processor to Power New Class of Interactive Consumer Products", MIPS and NEC joint press release, April 17, 1995, http://www.futuretech.blinkenlights.nl/mips-nec.html

125 "TI Samples First ARM Thumb Core", ARM and TI joint press release, October 9, 1995, http://www.programd.com/24_060cefb83baae02a_1.htm
126 "First StrongARM Processor Core from Digital Semiconductor", The CPU Shack, Octiber 1995, http://www.cpushack.com/CIC/embed/announce/DigitalStrongARM.html
127 "ARM Continues Drive Into New High-Volume Markets through Symbios Logic Agreement", ARM press release, October 31, 1995, http://www.thefreelibrary.com/ARM+Continues+Drive+Into+New+High-Volume+Markets+through+Symbios...-a017501156
128 "LG Semicon Licenses ARM's RISC Technology", LG Semicon press release, November 13, 1995, http://www.thefreelibrary.com/LG+Semicon+Licenses+ARM's+RISC+Technology%3B+Fastest+Growing...-a017588326
129 "ARM8 Architectural Overview", excerpted from ARM press release, November 1995, http://www.poppyfields.net/acorn/news/armpress/arm8view.shtml
130 ARM8 entry on everything2 by alisair, http://everything2.com/title/ARM8
131 "ARM Aims ARM7100 at Personal Electronics", ARM press release, December 4, 1995, http://www.thefreelibrary.com/ARM+aims+ARM7100+at+Personal+Electronics%3B+High+Integration...-a017799200
132 "Oki and ARM Announce License Agreement on 32-bit Embedded RISC Core", ARM press release, January 23, 1996, http://www.poppyfields.net/acorn/news/armpress/oki.shtml
133 "Alcatel selects ARM core as best for ASICs", ARM press release, February 22, 1996, http://www.poppyfields.net/acorn/news/armpress/asics.shtml
134 "Yamaha to Integrate ARM RISC Core in Custom Multimedia Chips", Yamaha press release, March 4, 1996, http://www.thefreelibrary.com/Yamaha+to+Integrate+ARM+RISC+Core+in+Custom+Multimedia+Chips%3B+World...-a018051280
135 "Rohm licenses ARM7TDMI Thumb processor core", Rohm press release, November 19, 1996, http://www.m2.com/m2/web/story.php/1996852568440080DDE88025683C002920E8
136 "A 160 MHz, 32-b, 0.5W CMOS RISC Microprocessor", Montanaro and Witek et al.
137 "Digital Targets Supercharged StrongARM Chip at Consumer Electronics Market", DEC press release, February 5, 1996, http://www.cpushack.com/CIC/embed/announce/DigitalStrongARMIntro.html
138 "Cirrus Announces Smart Phones Chip", Reily Gregson, RCRWireless, July 29, 1996, http://www.rcrwireless.com/19960729/archived-articles/cirrus-announces-smart-phones-chip
139 "Psion Forms New Company to License its World Leading PDA Platform", Psion press release, July 15, 1996, http://tech-insider.org/mobile/research/1996/0715.html
140 Psion Series 3 entry, The Centre for Computing History, http://www.computinghistory.org.uk/det/4020/Psion-Series-3/
141 "VLSI Technology Now Shipping ARM810", EE Times, August 19, 1996, http://www.eetimes.com/document.asp?doc_id=1208831
142 "Texas Instruments to Introduce New DSP Baseband Chip", Telecompaper, November 4, 1996, http://www.telecompaper.com/news/texas-instruments-to-introduce-new-dsp-baseband-chip--93741
143 Email discussion between John Biggs and Bryan Lawrence of ARM, dated January 30, 2014.
144 "Nokia introduces the naturally-shaped phone", Nokia press release, March 13, 1996, http://company.nokia.com/en/news/press-releases/1996/03/13/nokia-introduces-the-naturally-shaped-phone
145 "Apple Launches New Generation of User-Centric Information Appliances with the MessagePad 2000", Apple press release, October 28, 1996, http://tech-insider.org/mobile/research/1996/1028.html
146 "Cirrus Logic Debuts Voyager Chipset in New Apple Newton Based Platforms", Cirrus Logic press release, October 28, 1996, http://myapplenewton.blogspot.com/2012/06/cirrus-introduces-voyager-chipset.html
147 "NEC Electronics Announces VR4101 MIPS RISC CPU", EE Times, August 19, 1996, http://www.eetimes.com/document.asp?doc_id=1208865
148 "Hitachi's 60MIPS SH-3 Series 32-bit RISC Microprocessor Enables Cost-Effective Portable Processing, Consumer, and Wireless Applications", Hitachi press release, September 16, 1996, http://www.cpushack.com/CIC/embed/announce/HitachiSH-3RISC.html
149 "Hitachi Licenses SuperH RISC Engine for Use in VLSI Technology, Inc. ASIC and ASSP Products", Hitachi press release, July 29, 1996, http://www.hitachi.com/New/cnews/E/1996/960729B.html
150 "NEC Electronics Provides Single-Chip Solution for Windows CE Products", NEC press release, September 16, 1996, http://tech-insider.org/mobile/research/1996/0916-b.html
151 "Hitachi and Microsoft Collaborate on Windows CE Platform", Hitachi press release, September 17, 1996, http://www.hitachi.com/New/cnews/E/1996/960917B.html
152 "Microsoft Announces Broad Availability of Handheld PCs With Windows CE", Microsoft press release, November 18, 1996, http://news.microsoft.com/1996/11/19/microsoft-announces-broad-availability-of-handheld-pcs-with-windows-ce/
153 "Microsoft Expands List of Supported CPUs for Windows CE Platform", Microsoft press release, December 4, 1996, http://news.microsoft.com/1996/12/04/microsoft-expands-list-of-supported-cpus-for-windows-ce-platform/
154 "ARM and Microsoft Work Together to Extend Windows CE Platform", ARM press release, December 4, 1996, http://www.thefreelibrary.com/ARM+and+Microsoft+Work+Together+to+Extend+Windows+CE+Platform.-a018905731

[155] "Rockwell Licenses ARM's RISC Technology", Rockwell press release, January 6, 1997,
http://www.thefreelibrary.com/Rockwell+licenses+ARM%27s+RISC+technology%3B+Leading+communications-IC...-a018985993
[156] "Lucent Technologies Licenses Microprocessor Technology from ARM", ARM press release, April 16, 1997,
http://www.poppyfields.net/acorn/news/armpress/lucent.shtml
[157] "ARM targets 8-bit with RISC chip core", Richard Wilson, Electronics Weekly, May 14, 1997,
http://www.poppyfields.net/acorn/news/armdocs/8bit.shtml
[158] "Sony Licenses ARM's Technology", ARM press release, July 14, 1997,
http://www.thefreelibrary.com/Sony+Licenses+ARM'S+Technology%3B+Leading+Consumer+Electronics...-a019578830
[159] "Hyundai Licenses 32-bit RISC CPU from ARM", ARM press release, July 14, 1997,
http://www.thefreelibrary.com/Hyundai+Licenses+32-Bit+RISC+CPU+From+ARM%3B+HEI+to+develop+CDMA-PCS...-a019578831
[160] "Oral History of Sir Robin Saxby", Elliot and Fairbairn.
[161] "LSI Logic Announces Availability of the First Synthesize-able ARM7 Thumb Core For Communications Applications",
LSI press release, September 8, 1997, http://phx.corporate-ir.net/phoenix.zhtml?c=98123&p=irol-newsArticle&ID=592813
[162] "ARM and Sun Team Up to Offer Direct JavaOS Support for ARM RISC Architecture", ARM press release, February 11,
1997, http://www.thefreelibrary.com/ARM+and+Sun+Team+Up+to+Offer+Direct+JavaOS+Support+for+ARM+RISC...-a019109299
[163] "Psion Announces New Generation of Handheld Computing Power", Psion press release, June 16, 1997,
http://www.prnewswire.co.uk/news-releases/psion-announces-new-generation-of-handheld-computing-power-156581085.html
[164] Psion Series 5 entry, The Centre for Computing History, http://www.computinghistory.org.uk/det/5300/Psion-Series-5/
[165] "Psion Boosted by Network Product Sales in 1998", Telecompaper, March 4, 1999,
http://www.telecompaper.com/news/psion-boosted-by-network-product-sales-in-1998--165950
[166] "Leading mobile communications products manufacturers partner with Psion to create major engine of growth for
wireless information devices", Symbian press release, June 24, 1998, http://company.nokia.com/en/news/press-releases/1998/06/24/leading-mobile-communications-products-manufacturers-partner-with-psion-to-create-major-engine-of-growth-for-wireless-information-devices
[167] "Nokia Introduces Next Generation Product Family for GSM", Nokia press release, November 10, 1997,
http://company.nokia.com/en/news/press-releases/1997/11/10/nokia-introduces-next-generation-product-family-for-gsm
[168] "Wireless technology show opens: Nokia 6110 announced in Beijing", Jiang Shaodi, China Daily, November 12, 1997,
http://www.chinadaily.com.cn/epaper/html/cd/1997/199711/19971112/19971112006_6.html
[169] "The Best Wireless Phone on the Market", Stephen Baker, Business Week, August 10, 1998,
http://www.businessweek.com/1998/32/b3590010.htm
[170] "GartnerGroup's Dataquest Says Nokia Became No. 1 Mobile Phone Vendor in 1998", GartnerGroup press release,
February 8, 1999, http://tech-insider.org/mobile/research/1999/0208.html
[171] "ARM announces new higher performance, lower power ARM9 processor architecture", ARM press release, October
16, 1997, http://www.cpushack.com/CIC/announce/1997/ARM9Architecture.html
[172] "Dataquest Reports Top 3 Semiconductor Vendors Maintain Market Position in 1997", Electronics Web,
http://www.electronicsweb.com/doc/dataquest-reports-top-3-semiconductor-vendors-0001
[173] "DEC Becomes Fabless as Intel Buys Alpha Plant for $700M", Computer Business Review, October 27, 1997,
http://www.cbronline.com/news/dec_becomes_fabless_as_intel_buys_alpha_plant_for_700m
[174] "FTC Ensures that Digital's Alpha Chip – a Key Rival to Intel's Chips – Remains Competitive", United States Federal
Trade Commission, April 23, 1998, http://www.ftc.gov/news-events/press-releases/1998/04/ftc-ensures-digitals-alpha-chip-key-rival-intels-chips-remains
[175] "How Motorola Lost its Way", Roger Crockett and Peter Elstrom, BusinessWeek, May 3, 1998,
http://www.bloomberg.com/bw/stories/1998-05-03/how-motorola-lost-its-way
[176] Comments by Tim O'Donnell of ARM, "Oral History of Sir Robin Saxby", Elliot and Fairbairn.
[177] "Motorola expands offerings in microprocessor cores", Andy Santoni, InfoWorld, September 22, 1997, p. 29.
[178] "MIPS16: High-density MIPS for the Embedded Market", Kevin Kissell, Silicon Graphics MIPS Group,
http://www.iuma.ulpgc.es/~nunez/procesadoresILP/MIPS16_whitepaper.pdf
[179] New Advances in Motorola's M-Core Architecture Deliver Decreased Power Consumption, Added Cache and MMU
for Quick Deployment", Motorola press release, October 15, 1998,
http://www.thefreelibrary.com/New+Advances+In+Motorola's+M.CORE+Architecture+Deliver+Decreased...-a053085340
[180] Advanced RISC Machines Holdings Limited annual report for the year ended 31 December 1997,
http://media.corporate-ir.net/media_files/irol/19/197211/ar/ar97.pdf

228

181 "MIPS is now the Leading 32-bit Embedded Architecture", Silicon Graphics press release, March 16, 1998, http://www.prnewswire.com/news-releases/mips-is-now-the-leading-32-bit-embedded-architecture-77113042.html
182 "Embedded RISC market hits high as MIPS share grows", Richard Ball, Electronics Weekly, January 14, 1998, http://www.electronicsweekly.com/news/archived/resources/embedded-risc-market-hits-high-as-mips-share-grows-1998-01/
183 "Inside the New Computer Industry", Andrew Allison, January 1998, http://cordis.europa.eu/esprit/src/omi-risc.htm

Chapter 6

184 "Apple Computer Inc. Agrees to Acquire NeXT Software Inc.", Apple press release, December 20, 1996, http://www.nextcomputers.org/NeXTfiles/Docs/Press_releases/apple_agrees_to_acquire_next.pdf
185 "Apple's CEO Is Ousted as Steve Jobs' Role Expands", Karen Kaplan, Los Angeles Times, July 10, 1997, http://articles.latimes.com/1997/jul/10/news/mn-11353
186 ARM Holdings plc Annual Report and Accounts 1998, March 5, 1999, http://media.corporate-ir.net/media_files/irol/19/197211/ar/ar98.pdf
187 Apple Computer, Inc. Form 10-K, for the fiscal year ended December 31, 1998, http://investor.apple.com/secfiling.cfm?filingid=1047469-98-44981&cik=320193
188 "IBM Licenses ARM7TDMI Microprocessor Core", IBM press release, March 18, 1998, https://www-03.ibm.com/press/us/en/pressrelease/2748.wss
189 STMicro ARM7TDMI license in 1998 is referenced in several subsequent ARM press releases for follow-on ST licenses, such as http://www.arm.com/about/newsroom/2673.php
190 "ARM Introduces Three New ARM7 Microprocessor Cores", ARM press release, March 9, 1998, http://www.cpushack.com/CIC/embed/announce/arm7tcores.html
191 "National Semiconductor First to License New Synthesizable Processor Core from ARM", National Semiconductor press release, July 13, 1998, http://newscenter.ti.com/index.php?s=32851&item=125607
192 ARM Holdings plc Annual Report and Accounts 1998.
193 "Saxby justifies price tag of ARM9 license", David Manners, Electronics Weekly, July 1, 1998, http://www.electronicsweekly.com/news/archived/resources/saxby-justifies-price-tag-of-arm9-licence-1998-07/
194 "VLSI Technology Announces The First Customizable Single-Chip GSM Platform", VLSI press release, November 24, 1997, http://www.thefreelibrary.com/VLSI+Technology+Announces+The+First+Customizable+Single-Chip+GSM...-a020007525
195 "LSI Logic Introduces Programmable Single Chip Baseband Processor Architecture for Wireless Handsets", LSI Logic press release, April 6, 1998, http://phx.corporate-ir.net/phoenix.zhtml?c=98123&p=irol-newsArticle&ID=593278
196 "VLSI Enters CDMA Market with the Most Highly Integrated, Single-Chip Solution Available", VLSI press release, June 15, 1998, http://www.cdg.org/news/search/1998/jun98/061598.html
197 "Qualcomm Acquires License for ARM7TDMI and ARM Software Development Tools", Qualcomm press release, July 7, 1998, https://www.qualcomm.com/news/releases/1998/07/07/qualcomm-acquires-license-arm7tdmi-and-arm-software-development-tools
198 "ARM Announces its Next Generation ARM10 Thumb Family Processors", ARM press release, October 15, 1998, http://www.cpushack.com/CIC/announce/1998/arm10.annc.html
199 ARM10 entry on Everything2 by alisdair, http://everything2.com/title/ARM10
200 "Intel lands StrongARM win with HP", Michael Kanellos, CNET, October 7, 1998, http://news.cnet.com/Intel-lands-StrongARM-win-with-HP/2100-1033_3-216437.html
201 ARM Annual Report 99, February 14, 2000, http://media.corporate-ir.net/media_files/irol/19/197211/ar/ar99.pdf
202 "Stock Split Approved at ARM Holdings plc AGM", ARM press release, April 20, 1999, http://ir.arm.com/phoenix.zhtml?c=197211&p=irol-newsArticle&ID=831310
203 "ARM claws back MIPS in embedded RISC market", Richard Ball, Electronics Weekly, January 13, 1999, http://www.electronicsweekly.com/news/archived/resources/arm-claws-back-mips-in-embedded-risc-market-1999-01/
204 Apple Computer, Inc. Form 10-K, for the fiscal year ended September 25, 1999, http://investor.apple.com/secfiling.cfm?filingid=912057-99-10244&cik=320193
205 "Ailing Acorn agrees to pounds 270M US takeover", Nigel Cope, The Independent, April 28, 1999, http://www.independent.co.uk/news/business/ailing-acorn-agrees-to-pounds-270m-us-takeover-1090136.html
206 "VLSI Raises $35M with Sale of ARM Shares", Computer Business Review, February 11, 1999, http://www.cbronline.com/news/vlsi_raises_35m_with_sale_of_arm_shares
207 "Royal Philips to acquire VLSI in $1 billion deal", CBS Marketwatch.com, May 3, 1999, http://www.marketwatch.com/story/royal-philips-to-acquire-vlsi-in-1-billion-deal-19995303100
208 "Fast Facts: Welcome to Bluetooth Technology 101", Bluetooth SIG website, http://www.bluetooth.com/Pages/Fast-Facts.aspx
209 "VLSI Announces Bluetooth Market Entry", EE Times, March 8, 1999, http://www.eetimes.com/document.asp?doc_id=1213026

[210] VWS26001 Bluetooth Baseband Processor data sheet, VLSI Technology, 1999.
[211] "Texas Instruments Announces an Open Multimedia Application Platform to be Used in Next Generation Wireless Products", Texas Instruments press release, May 27, 1999, http://www.prnewswire.co.uk/news-releases/texas-instruments-announces-an-open-multimedia-application-platform-to-be-used-in-next-generation-wireless-products-156767965.html
[212] "Show report – ARM hands DSP extensions to ARM9 processor core", Richard Ball, Electronics Weekly, May 5, 1999, http://www.electronicsweekly.com/news/archived/resources/show-report-arm-hands-dsp-extensions-to-arm9-processor-1999-05
[213] "Lucent Technologies licenses ARM9E processor core for mass storage applications", Lucent press release, June 14, 1999, archived URL.
[214] "ARM Promotes SoC Design Reuse with New PrimeCell Peripherals and AMBA 2.0 On-Chip Bus Specification", EE Times, May 17, 1999, http://www.eetimes.com/document.asp?doc_id=1213209
[215] "ARM Introduces Synthesizable ARM9E Processor Family", ARM press release, August 16, 1999, http://www.thefreelibrary.com/ARM+Introduces+Synthesizable+ARM9E+Processor+Family%3B+LSI+Logic+First...-a055453400
[216] "ARM Buys Micrologic for Instant Development Team", Computer Business Review, October 31, 1999, http://www.cbronline.com/news/arm_buys_micrologic_for_instant_development_team
[217] "ARM buys software developer", Richard Ball, Electronics Weekly, November 3, 1999, http://www.electronicsweekly.com/news/archived/resources/arm-buys-software-developer-1999-11/
[218] ARM Annual Report 99 quoted an estimate of 175M units; final audit showed 182M units.
[219] "ARM and UMC Announce Foundry Program for Advanced SoC Solutions", UMC press release, February 28, 2000, http://www.umc.com/English/news/2000/20000228.asp
[220] "TSMC and ARM Take Next Step to Leading-Edge, Foundry-Specific SoC Solutions", TSMC press release, March 14, 2000, http://www.tsmc.com/tsmcdotcom/PRListingNewsArchivesAction.do?action=detail&newsid=962&language=E
[221] ARM Report and Accounts 2000, February 8, 2001, http://media.corporate-ir.net/media_files/irol/19/197211/ar/ar00.pdf
[222] "CSR to select ARM architecture", CSR press release, October 30, 2000, http://www.csr.com/news/pr/release/411/en
[223] "DoJa in NTT DoCoMo Phones", Zev Blut, Java Developers Journal, September 1, 2001, http://java.sys-con.com/node/36692
[224] "ARM Adds Java Extensions to ARM9 core", Peter Clarke, EE Times, October 11, 2000, http://www.eetimes.com/document.asp?doc_id=1142439
[225] "ARM Lends a Java Hand to Wireless Devices", Ashlee Vance, Computerworld, October 12, 2000, http://www.computerworld.com.au/article/77375/arm_lends_java_hand_wireless_devices/
[226] DSP & SIMD, ARM web site, http://www.arm.com/products/processors/technologies/dsp-simd.php
[227] "ARM Launches SecurCore for Smart Cards", ARM press release, October 24, 2000, http://www.design-reuse.com/news/1129/arm-securcore-smart-cards.html
[228] "Intel readies scalable StrongARM processors for handheld systems", Mark LaPedus, EE Times, August 23, 2000, http://www.eetimes.com/document.asp?doc_id=1185694
[229] "Intel and Analog Devices Ring in New DSP", John Spooner, ZDNet, December 6, 2000, http://www.zdnet.com/article/intel-and-analog-devices-ring-in-new-dsp/
[230] "Intel announces new architecture for next-gen wireless application", ZDNet, September 22, 2000, http://www.zdnet.com/article/intel-announces-new-architecture-for-next-gen-wireless-application/
[231] "Texas Instruments and Ericsson Cooperate on a DSP-based Open Multimedia Applications Platform for Next Generation Wireless Handsets", Texas Instruments press release, January 10, 2000, http://www.prnewswire.com/news-releases/texas-instruments-and-ericsson-cooperate-on-a-dsp-based-open-multimedia-applications-platform-for-next-generation-wireless-handsets-71998427.html
[232] "Sony Selects Texas Instruments' DSP-based OMAP(TM) and Symbian for Its Next-Generation Wireless Phones", Sony press release, April 26, 2000, http://www.sony.net/SonyInfo/News/Press_Archive/200004/00-0427/
[233] "Analog Devices Unveils RAM-based SoftFone Baseband Chipset for GSM Handsets", Analog Devices press release, January 25, 2000, http://www.sourcewire.com/news/5600/analog-devices-unveils-ram-based-softfone-baseband-chipset-for-gsm-handsets#.VPE37_nF9-A
[234] "Lucent fabricates ARM10 processor core ICs for wireless applications", EE Times, April 12, 2000, http://www.eetimes.com/document.asp?doc_id=1184351
[235] "Lucent rolls out its first StarCore-based DSP, promises to double Internet chip capacity", June 12, 2000, http://www.eetimes.com/document.asp?doc_id=1185116
[236] "ZTEIC Licenses ARM Technology for Mobile Applications", ZTEIC and ARM press release, October 30, 2000, http://www.thefreelibrary.com/ZTEIC+Licenses+ARM+Technology+for+Mobile+Applications%3B+ARM+Expands...-a066470667
[237] "BellSouth, IBM unveil personal communicator phone", Mobile Phone News, November 8, 1993, http://research.microsoft.com/en-us/um/people/bibuxton/buxtoncollection/a/pdf/press%20release%201993.pdf

[238] "Simonizing the PDA", Chris O'Malley, BYTE Magazine, December 1994,
http://web.archive.org/web/19990221174856/byte.com/art/9412/sec11/art3.htm
[239] "Nokia Starts Sales of the Nokia 9000 Communicator", Nokia press release, August 15, 1996,
http://company.nokia.com/en/news/press-releases/1996/08/15/first-gsm-based-communicator-product-hits-the-market-nokia-starts-sales-of-the-nokia-9000-communicator
[240] Nokia 9000 Communicator and 9100i Communicator entries, GSMArena,
http://www.gsmarena.com/compare.php3?idPhone1=16&idPhone2=18
[241] "Qualcomm Unveils "pdQ" CDMA Digital Smartphone", Qualcomm press release, September 21, 1998,
https://www.qualcomm.com/news/releases/1998/09/21/qualcomm-unveils-pdq-cdma-digital-smartphone
[242] "Ericsson unveils mobile phone equipped for communication and organization", Ericsson press release, March 18, 1999, http://www.wapforum.org/new/990318_ericsson.htm
[243] Ericsson R380 entry, GSMArena, http://www.gsmarena.com/ericsson_r380-195.php
[244] "The R380s – The first smartphone from the Ericsson-Symbian partnership", Steve Bridges, Ericsson Review No. 1, 2001, pp. 44-48, http://www.ericsson.com/ericsson/corpinfo/publications/review/2001_01/files/2001015.pdf
[245] "Ruiz quits Motorola for AMD", Brian Fuller, EE Times, January 25, 2000,
http://www.eetimes.com/document.asp?doc_id=1140994
[246] "TriMedia Technologies, Inc. Announces Appointment of Jim Thomas to Vice President, VLSI Design", TriMedia Technologies press release, August 1, 2000, http://www.design-reuse.com/news/1385/trimedia-appointment-jim-thomas-vice-president-vlsi-design.html
[247] "ARM license for Motorola hints at lost faith in M-Core", Anthony Clark and John Walko, EE Times, December 5, 2000, http://www.eetimes.com/document.asp?doc_id=1142793
[248] "PDA sales soar in 2000", CNNfn, January 26, 2001, http://cnnfn.cnn.com/2001/01/26/technology/handheld/
[249] "Palm arms handhelds for 'wireless revolution'", Stephanie Miles, CNET, April 24, 2000, http://news.cnet.com/Palm-arms-handhelds-for-wireless-revolution/2100-1040_3-239638.html
[250] "Ruiz quits Motorola for AMD", Fuller.
[251] ARM Report and Accounts 2000.
[252] "TI Delivers First DSP-based OMAP Application Processor Revolutionizing Performance and Power Efficiency for 2.5 and 3G Wireless", TI press release, February 19, 2001, http://www.ti.com/sc/docs/news/2001/01040.htm
[253] "ARM Expands Java Technology Support With New Jazelle Solutions", ARM press release, April 10, 2001,
http://www.thefreelibrary.com/ARM+Expands+Java+Technology+Support+With+New+Jazelle+Solutions.-a073027052
[254] ARM Holdings plc Preliminary Results for the Year Ended 31 December 2001,
http://ir.arm.com/phoenix.zhtml?c=197211&p=irol-newsArticle_print&ID=831305
[255] ARM9 processor family, ARM website, http://www.arm.com/products/processors/classic/arm9/
[256] "ARM Announces Technical Details of Next-Generation Architecture", ARM press release, October 17, 2001,
http://www.thefreelibrary.com/ARM+Announces+Technical+Details+of+Next-Generation+Architecture.-a079198526
[257] Game Boy Advance, Nintendo UK corporate site, https://www.nintendo.co.uk/Corporate/Nintendo-History/Game-Boy-Advance/Game-Boy-Advance-627139.html
[258] "The Nokia 9210 Communicator is now shipping", Nokia press release, June 19, 2001,
http://company.nokia.com/en/news/press-releases/2001/06/19/the-nokia-9210-communicator-is-now-shipping
[259] Nokia 9210 Communicator entry, GSMArena, http://www.gsmarena.com/nokia_9210_communicator-210.php
[260] "Ericsson and Sony Discussing Mobile Phone Joint Venture", Suzanne Kapner, The New York Times, April 29, 2001,
http://www.nytimes.com/2001/04/20/business/ericsson-and-sony-discussing-mobile-phone-joint-venture.html
[261] "Sony and Ericsson complete joint venture agreement", Ericsson and Sony press release, August 28, 2001,
http://www.sony.net/SonyInfo/News/Press_Archive/200108/01-0828/
[262] "Oral History of Sir Robin Saxby", Elliot and Fairbairn.
[263] ARM Holdings plc Preliminary Results for the Year Ended 31 December 2001.
[264] "iSuppli: Top 30 ranking of semiconductor suppliers shows devastating effects of 2001", Adam Connors,
DigiTimes.com, March 29, 2002, http://adamconnors.net/network/digitimes/mar29_isupplitop30.shtml
[265] "Intel Advances Power and Performance for Wireless Devices", Intel press release, February 12, 2002,
http://www.intel.com/pressroom/archive/releases/2002/20020212net.htm
[266] "ARM Announces Next-Generation ARM11 Microarchitecture", ARM press release, April 29, 2002,
http://www.arm.com/about/newsroom/2230.php
[267] "ARM Sets Performance Standard With Two New ARM11 Cores", ARM press release, October 14, 2002,
http://www.arm.com/about/newsroom/2201.php
[268] "Qualcomm Licenses Next-Generation ARM Core", ARM press release, October 15, 2002,
http://www.arm.com/about/newsroom/2195.php
[269] "TI Licenses ARM11 Cores for Future OMAP Processors and Wireless Chipsets", ARM press release, October 15, 2002,
http://www.arm.com/about/newsroom/2197.php
[270] "Symbian integrates latest 3G technologies in Symbian OS v7.0 to drive 2.5G and 3G mobile phones and services",
Symbian press release, February 19, 2002, http://tech-insider.org/mobile/research/2002/0219.html

[271] "PalmSource Ships Faster, More Powerful Palm OS 5", Palm press release, June 10, 2002, http://gl.access-company.com/news_event/palmsource/061002_1/
[272] "Microsoft Launches Windows Powered Smartphone Software", Microsoft press release, October 22, 2002, http://news.microsoft.com/2002/10/22/microsoft-launches-windows-powered-smartphone-software/
[273] "Linux coming to cell phones", Ben Charny, CNET, January 10, 2003, http://news.cnet.com/Linux-coming-to-cell-phones/2100-1037_3-980214.html
[274] "RIM Introduces Java-Based BlackBerry Handheld With Integrated Phone for GSM/GPRS Networks in North America", Research In Motion press release, March 4, 2002, http://press.blackberry.com/press/2002/pressrelease-640.html
[275] ARM Holdings PLC Preliminary Results For The Year Ended 31 December 2002, http://ir.arm.com/phoenix.zhtml?c=197211&p=irol-newsArticle_print&ID=831268
[276] "ARM and Broadcom Announce Strategic Partnership to Develop Next-Generation Communications Products", ARM press release, July 20, 2004, http://www.arm.com/about/newsroom/5736.php
[277] "ARM And Mediatek Partner To Bring RISC Technology To Taiwan", ARM press release, July 24, 2002, http://www.arm.com/about/newsroom/2221.php
[278] "ARM licenses core to Taiwan-based Faraday", Faith Hung, EETimes, January 18, 2002, http://www.eetimes.com/document.asp?doc_id=1131838
[279] "ARM Collaborates With Seagate For Hard Disc Drive Control", ARM press release, June 11, 2002, http://www.design-reuse.com/news/3377/arm-collaborates-seagate-hard-disc-drive-control.html
[280] "Flextronics Semiconductor Becomes First Partner In new ARM licensing program", ARM press release, November 14, 2002, http://www.arm.com/about/newsroom/2183.php
[281] "ARM And Cadence Establish New Five-Year Agreement Targeting Design Chain Optimization", ARM press release, March 4, 2003, http://www.arm.com/about/newsroom/350.php
[282] "ARM And Synopsys Announce Availability Of Reference Methodology For All Synthesizable ARM Cores", ARM press release, March 3, 2003, http://www.arm.com/about/newsroom/351.php
[283] "ARM Announces AMBA SystemC Interface to Enable System-Level Design", ARM press release, March 3, 2003, http://www.arm.com/about/newsroom/352.php
[284] "ARM Extends AMBA Specification With AXI Protocol For High-Performance System-on-chip Design", ARM press release, June 16, 2003, http://www.arm.com/about/newsroom/318.php
[285] "ARM Builds Security Foundation For Future Wireless And Consumer Devices", ARM press release, May 27, 2003, http://www.arm.com/about/newsroom/323.php
[286] "ARM Announces New ARM11 Cores And Platform Support For Trusted Computing", ARM press release, October 13, 2003, http://www.arm.com/about/newsroom/3791.php
[287] "New ARM Thumb-2 Core Technology Provides Industry-Leading Levels Of Code Density And Performance", ARM press release, June 16, 2003, http://www.arm.com/about/newsroom/319.php
[288] "ARM Continues To Drive Performance Of Highly Reliable Applications With New Breed Of ARM11 Cores", ARM press release, October 13, 2003, http://www.arm.com/about/newsroom/3794.php
[289] Email comments from Chris Shore of ARM to Daniel Nenni, August 2015.
[290] "STMicroelectronics and Texas Instruments Joined by ARM and Nokia as Founding Members of MIPI Alliance to Define Open Standards for Mobile Application Processors", MIPI press release, July 29, 2003, http://www.ti.com/corp/docs/mipi/july29.shtml
[291] "New ARM9E Family Core Provides Unrivalled Low-Power Performance", ARM press release, December 3, 2003, http://www.arm.com/about/newsroom/4525.php
[292] "Intel Unveils New Technologies For Future Cell Phone, PDA Processors Based On Intel® XScale® Technology", Intel press release, September 17, 2003, http://www.intel.com/pressroom/archive/releases/2003/20030917net.htm
[293] Palm Treo 600 entry, GSMArena, http://www.gsmarena.com/palm_treo_600-622.php
[294] "Palm Agrees to Acquire Handspring As Hand-Helds Morph Into Phones", Pui-Wing Tam, Wall Street Journal, June 5, 2003, http://www.wsj.com/articles/SB105472474479757100
[295] Nokia 6600 entry, GSMArena, http://www.gsmarena.com/nokia_6600-454.php
[296] "The Nokia 6600 captures mobile business", Nokia press release, June 16, 2003, http://company.nokia.com/en/news/press-releases/2003/06/16/the-nokia-6600-captures-mobile-business
[297] "Motorola Integrates ARM Core", ARM press release, October 1, 2003, http://www.arm.com/about/newsroom/3799.php
[298] Motorola MPx200 entry, GSMArena, http://www.gsmarena.com/motorola_mpx200-514.php
[299] "Google Buys Android for its Mobile Arsenal", Ben Elgin, BusinessWeek, August 16, 2005, http://www.bloomberg.com/bw/stories/2005-08-16/google-buys-android-for-its-mobile-arsenal
[300] "Andy Rubin: After rough start, Android goes viral", Rick Merritt, EETimes, November 27, 2012, http://www.eetimes.com/author.asp?section_id=36&doc_id=1266265
[301] ARM Annual report and accounts 2003, March 10, 2004, http://media.corporate-ir.net/media_files/irol/19/197211/ar/ar03.pdf

[302] "ARM Announces First Integrated Multiprocessor Core", ARM press release, May 17, 2004, http://www.arm.com/about/newsroom/5346.php
[303] "ARM and Imagination Technologies Collaborate To Offer Greater Support For Advanced 3D Graphics", ARM press release, February 23, 2004, http://www.arm.com/about/newsroom/4861.php
[304] "ARM NEON Technology Fuels Consumer Electronics Growth With Next-Generation Mobile Multimedia Acceleration", ARM press release, October 4, 2004, http://www.arm.com/about/newsroom/6540.php
[305] NEON, ARM web site, http://www.arm.com/products/processors/technologies/neon.php
[306] "MobilEye Licenses ARM Technology For On-board Driving Assistance Technologies", ARM press release, January 13, 2004, http://www.arm.com/about/newsroom/4681.php
[307] "Marvell Announces First Family of High Performance Embedded Microprocessors Utilizing the ARM Architecture", Marvell and ARM press release, May 19, 2004, http://www.marvell.com/company/news/pressDetail.do?releaseID=424
[308] "HuaWei Technologies To Launch ARM Powered Wireless Products", ARM press release, July 19, 2004, http://www.arm.com/about/newsroom/5728.php
[309] "ARM And Artisan Combine To Deliver System-On-Chip IP Solutions", ARM press release, August 23, 2004, http://www.arm.com/about/newsroom/6014.php
[310] ARM Annual report and accounts 2004, March 4, 2005, http://media.corporate-ir.net/media_files/irol/19/197211/ar/ar04.pdf
[311] "ARM Introduces The Cortex-M3 Processor To Deliver High Performance In Low-Cost Applications", ARM press release, October 19, 2004, http://www.arm.com/about/newsroom/6750.php
[312] "ARM Discloses Technical Details and Partner Support For ARMv7 Architecture", ARM press release, March 7, 2005, http://www.arm.com/about/newsroom/8513.php
[313] "New ARM Jazelle RCT Technology Provides As Much As Three Times Reduction In Java Memory Footprint", ARM press release, June 27, 2005, http://www.arm.com/about/newsroom/9621.php
[314] "ARM Introduces Industry's Fastest Processor For Low-Power Mobile And Consumer Applications", ARM press release, October 4, 2005, http://www.arm.com/about/newsroom/10548.php
[315] Motorola Q8 entry, GSMArena, http://www.gsmarena.com/motorola_q8-1232.php
[316] "Verizon to ship $300 Motorola Q on 31 May", Tony Smith, The Register, May 22, 2006, http://www.theregister.co.uk/Print/2006/05/22/verizon_launches_moto_q/
[317] Palm Treo 700w entry, PhoneArena, http://www.phonearena.com/phones/Palm-Treo-700w--700wx_id1373
[318] "The Egregious Incompetence of Palm", Daniel Eran, RoughlyDrafted, January 31, 2007, http://www.roughlydrafted.com/RD/RDM.Tech.Q1.07/E1DD097F-EE28-4FBA-A1F2-D831512E423F.html
[319] "ACCESS to Extend Leadership in Mobile Device Software with Acquisition of PalmSource", ACCESS press release, September 8, 2005, http://www.palmsource.com/press/2005/090905_access.html
[320] RIM BlackBerry 8700v entry, PDAdb.net, http://pdadb.net/index.php?m=specs&id=1791&c=rim_blackberry_8700v_rim_electron
[321] Nokia N70 entry, GSMArena, http://www.gsmarena.com/nokia_n70-1153.php
[322] "Dogfight: How Apple and Google Went to War and Started a Revolution", Fred Vogelstein, Macmillan, November 12, 2013, pp. 48-54.
[323] ARM Annual Report and Accounts 2005, March 6, 2006, http://library.corporate-ir.net/library/19/197/197211/items/188715/ar05.pdf
[324] "Actel and ARM Sign Landmark Agreement To Bring ARM7 Processor Family To Burgeoning FPGA Market", ARM press release, March 7, 2005, http://www.arm.com/about/newsroom/8507.php
[325] "NVIDIA And ARM Announce Licensing Agreement Targeted At Next-Generation Consumer Devices And Platforms", ARM press release, May 31, 2005, http://www.arm.com/about/newsroom/9285.php
[326] "Renesas Technology Selects ARM Processors For 3G Mobile Phone and Consumer Devices", ARM press release, July 19, 2005, http://www.arm.com/about/newsroom/9848.php
[327] "Feroceon processor reorganizes ARM's pipeline, says In-Stat", Peter Clarke, EETimes, May 31, 2005, http://www.eetimes.com/document.asp?doc_id=1154385
[328] ARM Annual Report and Accounts 2006, April 2, 2007, http://media.corporate-ir.net/media_files/irol/19/197211/reports/ar06.pdf
[329] "ARM Launches Next-Generation Processor", ARM press release, May 15, 2006, http://www.arm.com/about/newsroom/13213.php
[330] "Marvell To Purchase Intel's Communications And Application Processor Business For $600 Million", Intel press release, June 27, 2006, http://www.intel.com/pressroom/archive/releases/2006/20060627corp.htm

Chapter 7

[331] "16 Brilliant Insights from Steve Jobs Keynote Circa 1997", transcript and video of Steve Jobs Q&A at Apple WWDC 1997, Dharmesh Shah, OnStartups.com, July 1, 2011, http://onstartups.com/tabid/3339/bid/58082/16-Brilliant-Insights-From-Steve-Jobs-Keynote-Circa-1997.aspx

[332] "Steve Jobs at Macworld Boston in 1997", Ben Thompson, Stratechery, June 27, 2013, (video link broken), http://stratechery.com/2013/steve-jobs-at-macworld-boston-in-1997/

[333] "The Complete History of Apple Stock (AAPL)", Michael Flannery, Dividend.com, December 29, 2014, http://www.dividend.com/dividend-education/the-complete-history-of-apple-aapl/

[334] "Apple Stock: from $6.56 to $403 in about 8 years", Tom Petruno, Los Angeles Times, August 24, 2011, http://latimesblogs.latimes.com/money_co/2011/08/apple-stock-steve-jobs-ceo-ipad-iphone-ipod-mac.html

[335] "How Steve Jobs' Love of Simplicity Fueled a Design Revolution", Walter Issacson, Smithsonian Magazine, September 2012, http://www.smithsonianmag.com/arts-culture/how-steve-jobs-love-of-simplicity-fueled-a-design-revolution-23868877/

[336] "How Apple Went from Underdog to Cult in Six Design and Innovation Strategies from the Early Days", Maria Popova, Brain Pickings, http://www.brainpickings.org/2014/02/10/hartmut-esslinger-keep-it-simple-apple-steve-jobs/

[337] "Apple Makes Sweeping Changes Among Execs", Julie Pitta, Los Angeles Times, February 5, 1997, http://articles.latimes.com/1997-02-05/business/fi-25505_1_apple-executives

[338] "Who Is Jonathan Ive?" Peter Burrows, BusinessWeek, September 24, 2006, http://www.bloomberg.com/bw/stories/2006-09-24/who-is-jonathan-ive

[339] "The Shape of Things to Come", Ian Parker, The New Yorker, February 23, 2015, http://www.newyorker.com/magazine/2015/02/23/shape-things-come

[340] "10 Things You Didn't Know about Apple Design Chief Jony Ive", Seth Fiegerman, Mashable, November 6, 2013, http://mashable.com/2013/11/06/jony-ive-biography/

[341] "Hartmut Esslinger Oral History", interview by Barry Katz, Computer History Museum, April 20, 2011, http://archive.computerhistory.org/resources/access/text/2011/10/102743122-05-01-acc.pdf

[342] "Innovation By Design: A Q&A With Frog Design Founder Hartmut Esslinger", Mark Wilson, Fast Company, September 27, 2013, http://live.fastcompany.com/Event/Innovation_By_Design_A_QA_With_Frog_Design_Founder_Hartmut_Esslinger

[343] "Napster: the day the music was set free", Tom Lamont, The Guardian, February 23, 2013, http://www.theguardian.com/music/2013/feb/24/napster-music-free-file-sharing

[344] "Sony Announces Memory Stick Walkman", Sony press release, September 22, 1999, http://www.sony.net/SonyInfo/News/Press_Archive/199909/99-072A/

[345] "Sony Japan's Bitmusic Site to Offer SDMI-Compliant Downloads", HITS Daily Double Rumor Mill, May 3, 2000, http://hitsdailydouble.com/news&id=273303

[346] "The Perfect Thing: How the iPod Shuffles Commerce, Culture, and Coolness", Steven Levy, Simon and Schuster, October 23, 2006, pp. 27-46.

[347] "Apple Introduces iTunes – World's Best and Easiest to Use Jukebox Software", Apple press release, January 9, 2001, http://www.apple.com/pr/library/2001/01/09Apple-Introduces-iTunes-Worlds-Best-and-Easiest-To-Use-Jukebox-Software.html

[348] "An Oral History of Apple Design: 1992-2013", Max Chafkin, Fast Company, September 10, 2013, http://www.fastcodesign.com/3016520/an-oral-history-of-apple-design-1992-2013

[349] "Creative NOMAD Jukebox Digital Audio Player Review", Ilya Gavrichenkov, Xbit Laboratories, November 7, 2000, http://www.xbitlabs.com/articles/multimedia/display/creative-jukebox.html

[350] "The birth of the iPod", Benj Edwards, Macworld, October 23, 2011, http://www.macworld.com/article/1163181/the_birth_of_the_ipod.html

[351] PortalPlayer company profile, Pinestream Consulting Group, July 2000, http://www.pinestream.com/demodetail/1193/Portalplayer

[352] PP5002 datasheet, PortalPlayer, circa 2001, http://web.archive.org/web/20061202104706/http://www.portalplayer.com/products/documents/5002_brief_0108_Public.pdf

[353] "eSilicon: Outsource and Thrive", Gale Morrison, EDN, January 21, 2002, http://www.edn.com/electronics-news/4344372/eSilicon-Outsource-and-Thrive

[354] "High-tech products often outsourced", USA Today, July 18, 2005.

[355] "The world in the iPod", Andrew Leonard, Salon, June 3, 2005, http://www.salon.com/2005/06/03/portalplayer/

[356] "Those OS X iPods? They're Already Here! Pixo, ARM, and the Mac OS", Daniel Eran Dilger, RoughlyDrafted, July 15, 2007, http://www.roughlydrafted.com/RD/RDM.Tech.Q3.07/DD5FFFA5-2CDA-46C7-ADE9-E4AD4BF01602.html

[357] "Apple Presents iPod", Apple press release, October 23, 2001, http://www.apple.com/pr/library/2001/10/23Apple-Presents-iPod.html

[358] "Apple Reports First Quarter Profit of $38M", Apple press release, January 16, 2002, http://www.apple.com/pr/library/2002/01/16Apple-Reports-First-Quarter-Profit-of-38-Million.html

[359] "Apple Launches the iTunes Music Store", Apple press release, April 28, 2003, https://www.apple.com/pr/library/2003/04/28Apple-Launches-the-iTunes-Music-Store.html

[360] "Steve Jobs' Music Vision", Steve Knopper, Rolling Stone, October 7, 2011, http://www.rollingstone.com/music/news/steve-jobs-music-vision-20111007

[361] "Apple Introduces iPod shuffle", Apple press release, January 11, 2005, https://www.apple.com/pr/library/2005/01/11Apple-Introduces-iPod-shuffle.html

[362] "Apple Introduces iPod nano", Apple press release, September 7, 2005, http://www.apple.com/pr/library/2005/09/07Apple-Introduces-iPod-nano.html

[363] "Samsung grabs iPod design win", Mark LaPedus, EETimes, April 26, 2006, http://www.eetimes.com/document.asp?doc_id=1160995

[364] "NVIDIA to Acquire PortalPlayer", NVIDIA press release, November 6, 2006, http://www.nvidia.com/object/IO_37040.html

[365] "Working with Steve Jobs", Peter Burrows, BusinessWeek, October 12, 2011, http://www.bloomberg.com/bw/technology/working-with-steve-jobs-10122011.html#p2

[366] "Gartner Says Strong Fourth Quarter Sales Led Worldwide Mobile Phone Sales to 30 Percent Growth in 2004", Gartner press release, March 2, 2005, http://www.gartner.com/newsroom/id/492110

[367] "Nano Steals the Spotlight from iTunes Phone", John Day, Electronic Design, September 14, 2005, http://electronicdesign.com/boards/nano-steals-spotlight-itunes-phone

[368] Motorola ROKR E1 entry, GSMArena, http://www.gsmarena.com/motorola_rokr_e1-1273.php

[369] "Motorola ROKR E1 (AT&T) review", Kent German and James Kim, CNET, September 16, 2005, http://www.cnet.com/products/motorola-rokr-e1-at-t/2/

[370] "The Ed & Steve Show – Starring Steve", Mark Veverka, Barron's, September 12, 2005, http://online.barrons.com/articles/SB112632840144837139?tesla=y

[371] "Project Vogue: Inside Apple's iPhone Deal with AT&T", Peter Cohan, Forbes, September 10, 2013, http://www.forbes.com/sites/petercohan/2013/09/10/project-vogue-inside-apples-iphone-deal-with-att/

[372] "The Untold Story: How the iPhone Blew Up the Wireless Industry", Fred Vogelstein, Wired, January 9, 2008, http://archive.wired.com/gadgets/wireless/magazine/16-02/ff_iphone?currentPage=all

[373] "Live from SF: Apple and Motorola's iTunes phone announcement", Peter Rojas, Engadget, September 7, 2005, http://www.engadget.com/2005/09/07/live-from-sf-apple-and-motorolas-itunes-phone-announcement/

[374] "Motorola's iTunes Phone Gets Off to Rough Start", Jason Kelly, Bloomberg, October 21, 2005, http://www.bloomberg.com/apps/news?pid=newsarchive&sid=aVAltTesg0vE

[375] "Motorola: Screw the nano!", Clint Ecker, Ars Technica, September 23, 2005, http://arstechnica.com/apple/2005/09/1352/

[376] "Battle for the Soul of the MP3 Phone", Frank Rose, Wired, November 2005, http://archive.wired.com/wired/archive/13.11/phone.html

[377] Motorola ROKR E2 entry, GSMArena, http://www.gsmarena.com/motorola_rokr_e2-1401.php

[378] "Apple Engineer Recalls the iPhone's Birth", Daisuke Wakabayashi, The Wall Street Journal, March 25, 2014, http://www.wsj.com/articles/SB10001424052702303949704579461783150723874

[379] "The Untold Story: How the iPhone Blew Up the Wireless Industry", Vogelstein, Wired.

[380] "Project Vogue: Inside Apple's iPhone Deal with AT&T", Cohan, Forbes.

[381] "Apple's Phone: From 1980s Sketches to iPhone, Part 3", Eldar Murtazin, Mobile-Review.com, http://mobile-review.com/articles/2010/iphone-history3-en.shtml

[382] "Apple says it didn't copy iPhone from Sony, releases Purple prototype to prove it", Nate Ralph, The Verge, July 30, 2012, http://www.theverge.com/2012/7/30/3201162/apple-refutes-claim-they-cribbed-notes-from-sony-reveal-prototype

[383] "And Then Steve Said, Let There Be an iPhone", Fred Vogelstein, The New York Times Magazine, October 4, 2013, http://www.nytimes.com/2013/10/06/magazine/and-then-steve-said-let-there-be-an-iphone.html

[384] "iPhone video teardown reveals Samsung, Intel, Balda design wins", Prince McLean, AppleInsider, July 2, 2007, http://appleinsider.com/articles/07/07/02/iphone_video_teardown_reveals_samsung_intel_balda_design_wins

[385] "The Untold Story: How the iPhone Blew Up the Wireless Industry", Vogelstein, Wired.

[386] "Life After the iPhone: How AT&T's Bet on Apple Mobilized the Company", Connie Guglielmo, Forbes, January 21, 2013, http://www.forbes.com/sites/conniegublielmo/2013/01/02/life-after-the-iphone-how-atts-bet-on-apple-mobilized-the-company/

[387] PMB8876 datasheet, Infineon, 2004.

[388] "Steve Jobs – iPhone Introduction in 2007 (Complete)", https://www.youtube.com/watch?v=9hUIxyE2Ns8

[389] "Apple Reinvents the Phone with iPhone", Apple press release, January 9, 2007, https://www.apple.com/pr/library/2007/01/09Apple-Reinvents-the-Phone-with-iPhone.html

[390] "Apple sold 270,000 iPhones in the first 30 hours", Paul Miller, Engadget, July 25, 2007, http://www.engadget.com/2007/07/25/apple-sold-270-000-iphones-in-the-first-30-hours/

[391] "Apple Sells One Millionth iPhone", Apple press release, September 10, 2007, http://www.apple.com/pr/library/2007/09/10Apple-Sells-One-Millionth-iPhone.html

[392] "Gartner Says Worldwide Mobile Phone Sales Increased 16 Per Cent in 2007", Gartner press release, February 27, 2008, http://www.gartner.com/newsroom/id/612207

[393] "Bad Connection: Inside the iPhone Network Meltdown", Fred Vogelstein, Wired, July 19, 2010, http://www.wired.com/2010/07/ff_att_fail/

235

[394] "AT&T to Deliver 3G Mobile Broadband Speed Boost", AT&T press release, May 27, 2009,
http://www.att.com/gen/press-room?pid=4800&cdvn=news&newsarticleid=26835
[395] "Infineon Wins iPhone with Two-Die Package", Linley on Mobile, July 18, 2008,
http://www.linleygroup.com/newsletters/newsletter_detail.php?num=767
[396] "Apple Introduces the New iPhone 3G", Apple press release, June 9, 2008,
https://www.apple.com/pr/library/2008/06/09Apple-Introduces-the-New-iPhone-3G.html
[397] "Apple Sells One Million iPhone 3Gs in First Weekend", Apple press release, July 14, 2008,
https://www.apple.com/pr/library/2008/07/14Apple-Sells-One-Million-iPhone-3Gs-in-First-Weekend.html
[398] "Apple iPhone 3GS (16GB) Mobile Phone Teardown", HIS Electronics & Media, reposted November 30, 2012,
http://electronics360.globalspec.com/article/2178/apple-iphone-3gs-16gb-mobile-phone-teardown
[399] "Apple Announces the New iPhone 3GS – The Fastest, Most Powerful iPhone Yet", Apple press release, June 8, 2009,
https://www.apple.com/pr/library/2009/06/08Apple-Announces-the-New-iPhone-3GS-The-Fastest-Most-Powerful-iPhone-Yet.html
[400] "P. A. Semi's PA6T-1682M System-on-a-Chip", David Kanter, Real World Technologies, October 24, 2006,
http://www.realworldtech.com/pa-semi/
[401] "Apple buys chip designer PA Semi for $278M: lower power chips?", Charles Arthur, The Guardian, April 23, 2008,
http://www.theguardian.com/technology/blog/2008/apr/23/applebuyschipdesignerpase
[402] "Paul Otellini's Intel: Can the Company That Built the Future Survive It?", Alexis Madrigal, The Atlantic, May 16, 2013,
http://www.theatlantic.com/technology/archive/2013/05/paul-otellinis-intel-can-the-company-that-built-the-future-survive-it/275825/
[403] "ARM.L – Q2 and Interim 2008 ARM Holdings plc Earnings Presentation", Thomson Financial, July 30, 2008,
http://media.corporate-ir.net/media_files/irol/19/197211/Q2_2008_transcript.pdf
[404] "Intrinsity Announces 2 GHz FastMATH Adaptive Signal Processor and FastMIPS Microprocessor for Embedded Systems", Intrinsity press release, April 22, 2002,
http://www.thefreelibrary.com/Intrinsity+Announces+2+GHz+FastMATH+Adaptive+Signal+Processor+and...-a084961065
[405] "SAMSUNG and Intrinsity Jointly Develop the World's Fastest ARM® Cortex™-A8 Processor Based Mobile Core in 45 Nanometer Low Power Process", Intrinsity and Samsung joint press release, July 27, 2009,
http://www.samsung.com/global/business/semiconductor/minisite/Exynos/news_8.html
[406] "Apple Launches iPad", Apple press release, January 27, 2010, https://www.apple.com/pr/library/2010/01/27Apple-Launches-iPad.html
[407] "Apple Sells One Million iPads", Apple press release, May 3, 2010,
https://www.apple.com/pr/library/2010/05/03Apple-Sells-One-Million-iPads.html
[408] "Meet the A4, the iPad's Brain", Jon Stokes, Ars Technica, February 28, 2010,
http://arstechnica.com/apple/2010/02/meet-the-a4-the-ipads-brain/
[409] "Apple's A4 dissected, discussed ... and tantalizing", Paul Boldt, Don Scansen, and Tim Whibley, EETimes, June 17, 2010, http://www.eetimes.com/document.asp?doc_id=1256680
[410] "Apple Buys Intrinsity, a Maker of Fast Chips", Ashlee Vance and Brad Stone, The New York Times, April 27, 2010,
http://www.nytimes.com/2010/04/28/technology/28apple.html?_r=0
[411] Applied Micro Q4 2010 earnings conference call, April 29, 2010,
http://www.sec.gov/Archives/edgar/data/711065/000119312510109166/dex992.htm
[412] "Apple Presents iPhone 4", Apple press release, June 7, 2010, https://www.apple.com/pr/library/2010/06/07Apple-Presents-iPhone-4.html
[413] "iPhone 4 Sales Top 1.7 Million", Apple press release, June 28, 2010,
https://www.apple.com/pr/library/2010/06/28iPhone-4-Sales-Top-1-7-Million.html
[414] "Gartner Says Worldwide Mobile Device Sales to End Users Reached 1.6 Billion Units in 2010; Smartphone Sales Grew 72 Percent in 2010", Gartner press release, February 9, 2011, http://www.gartner.com/newsroom/id/1543014
[415] "Apple Launches iPad 2", Apple press release, March 2, 2011, https://www.apple.com/pr/library/2011/03/02Apple-Launches-iPad-2.html
[416] "Apple's Intrinsity Acquisition: Winners and Losers", Ganesh T S, AnandTech, April 28, 2010,
http://www.anandtech.com/show/3665/apples-intrinsity-acquisition-winners-and-losers
[417] "iPhone 4S Carries BOM of $188, IHS iSuppli Teardown Analysis Reveals", IHS press release, October 20, 2011,
https://technology.ihs.com/389429/iphone-4s-carries-bom-of-188-ihs-isuppli-teardown-analysis-reveals
[418] "Why Apple's A5 is so big--and iPhone 4 won't get Siri", Stephen Shankland, CNET, February 4, 2012,
http://www.cnet.com/news/why-apples-a5-is-so-big-and-iphone-4-wont-get-siri/
[419] "Steve Jobs Resigns as CEO of Apple", Apple press release, August 24, 2011,
https://www.apple.com/pr/library/2011/08/24Steve-Jobs-Resigns-as-CEO-of-Apple.html
[420] "Tegra 3's Fifth 'Companion' Core Enables Ultra-Low Power Consumption, While Advanced Quad-Core Processors Drive Record-Breaking Performance", NVIDIA press release, November 9, 2011,
http://nvidianews.nvidia.com/news/nvidia-quad-core-tegra-3-chip-sets-new-standards-of-mobile-computing-performance-energy-efficiency

[421] "Apple Launches New iPad", Apple press release, March 7, 2012, https://www.apple.com/pr/library/2012/03/07Apple-Launches-New-iPad.html
[422] "The iPhone 5 Review", section on The A6 SoC, Anand Lal Shimpi, AnandTech, October 16, 2012, http://www.anandtech.com/show/6330/the-iphone-5-review/4
[423] "Apple Introduces iPhone 5", Apple press release, September 12, 2012, https://www.apple.com/pr/library/2012/09/12Apple-Introduces-iPhone-5.html
[424] "Many iPhone 5 Components Change, But Most Suppliers Remain the Same, Teardown Reveals", IHS press release, September 25, 2012, https://technology.ihs.com/411502/many-iphone-5-components-change-but-most-suppliers-remain-the-same-teardown-reveals
[425] "iPhone 5 First Weekend Sales Top Five Million", Apple press release, September 24, 2012, https://www.apple.com/pr/library/2012/09/24iPhone-5-First-Weekend-Sales-Top-Five-Million.html
[426] "iPad 4 (Late 2012) Review", section on CPU performance and memory bandwidth, Anand Lal Shimpi, AnandTech, December 6, 2012, http://www.anandtech.com/show/6472/ipad-4-late-2012-review/3
[427] "Apple Sells Three Million iPads in Three Days", Apple press release, November 5, 2012, https://www.apple.com/pr/library/2012/11/05Apple-Sells-Three-Million-iPads-in-Three-Days.html
[428] "ARM Discloses Technical Details Of The Next Version Of The ARM Architecture", ARM press release, October 27, 2011, http://www.arm.com/about/newsroom/arm-discloses-technical-details-of-the-next-version-of-the-arm-architecture.php
[429] "ARM Launches Cortex-A50 Series, the World's Most Energy-Efficient 64-bit Processors", ARM press release, October 30, 2012, http://www.arm.com/about/newsroom/arm-launches-cortex-a50-series-the-worlds-most-energy-efficient-64-bit-processors.php
[430] "Why Apple's 64-bit iPhone chip is a bigger deal than you think", Aaron Souppouris, The Verge, September 12, 2013, http://www.theverge.com/2013/9/12/4722470/iphone-5s-64-bit-processor-is-a-bigger-deal-than-you-think
[431] "Qualcomm gambit: Apple 64-bit A7 is a 'gimmick'", Brooke Crothers, CNET, October 2, 2013, http://www.cnet.com/news/qualcomm-gambit-apple-64-bit-a7-is-a-gimmick/
[432] "The iPhone 5S Review", section on After Swift Comes Cyclone, Anand Lal Shimpi, AnandTech, September 17, 2013, http://anandtech.com/show/7335/the-iphone-5s-review/3
[433] "Apple unveils 64-bit iPhone 5S with fingerprint scanner, $199 for 16GB", Andrew Cunningham, Ars Technica, September 10, 2013, http://arstechnica.com/apple/2013/09/apple-unveils-64-bit-iphone-5s/
[434] "TSMC Apple Rumors Debunked!", Daniel Nenni, SemiWiki.com, January 11, 2013, https://www.semiwiki.com/forum/content/1940-tsmc-apple-rumors-debunked.html
[435] "PowerVR G6230 and G6430: family values gone 'Rogue'", Alexandru Voica, Imagination Technologies, July 9, 2012, http://blog.imgtec.com/powervr/powervr-g6230-and-g6430-family-values-gone-rogue
[436] "Inside the iPhone 5S", Tanner et al, Chipworks September 20, 2013, http://www.chipworks.com/about-chipworks/overview/blog/inside-the-iphone-5s/
[437] "iOS 7.03 fixes iPhone 5S sensor problems, 'sensor-gate' is over", John Koetsier, VentureBeat, October 22, 2013, http://venturebeat.com/2013/10/22/ios-7-03-fixes-iphone-5s-sensor-problems-sensor-gate-is-over/
[438] "Apple Announces iPad Air—Dramatically Thinner, Lighter & More Powerful iPad", Apple press release, October 22, 2013, https://www.apple.com/pr/library/2013/10/23Apple-Announces-iPad-Air-Dramatically-Thinner-Lighter-More-Powerful-iPad.html
[439] "The iPhone 6 Review", section on A8's CPU: What Comes After Cyclone?, Ho et al, AnandTech, September 30, 2014, http://www.anandtech.com/show/8554/the-iphone-6-review/3
[440] "Apple's A8 SoC analyzed: The iPhone 6 chip is a 2-billion-transistor 20nm monster", Sebastian Anthony, ExtremeTech, September 10, 2014, http://www.extremetech.com/computing/189787-apples-a8-soc-analyzed-the-iphone-6-chip-is-a-2-billion-transistor-20nm-monster
[441] "Analyzing Apple's A8 SoC: PowerVR GX6450 & More", Ryan Smith, AnandTech, September 10, 2014, http://www.anandtech.com/show/8514/analyzing-apples-a8-soc-gx6650-more
[442] "Inside the iPhone 6 and iPhone 6 Plus (Part 2)", The A8 Processor, Chipworks, October 1, 2014, http://www.chipworks.com/about-chipworks/overview/blog/inside-iphone-6-and-iphone-6-plus-part-2
[443] "The Apple iPhone 6 & 6 Plus", Teardown.com, http://www.techinsights.com/teardown.com/apple-iphone-6/
[444] "Apple Announces iPhone 6 & iPhone 6 Plus—The Biggest Advancements in iPhone History", Apple press release, September 9, 2014, http://www.apple.com/pr/library/2014/09/09Apple-Announces-iPhone-6-iPhone-6-Plus-The-Biggest-Advancements-in-iPhone-History.html
[445] "First Weekend iPhone Sales Top 10 Million, Set New Record", Apple press release, September 22, 2014, https://www.apple.com/pr/library/2014/09/22First-Weekend-iPhone-Sales-Top-10-Million-Set-New-Record.html
[446] "Apple A8X's GPU – GXA6850, Even Better Than I Thought", Ryan Smith, AnandTech, November 11, 2014, http://www.anandtech.com/show/8716/apple-a8xs-gpu-gxa6850-even-better-than-i-thought
[447] "Apple Introduces iPad Air 2—The Thinnest, Most Powerful iPad Ever", Apple press release, October 16, 2014, https://www.apple.com/pr/library/2014/10/16Apple-Introduces-iPad-Air-2-The-Thinnest-Most-Powerful-iPad-Ever.html

[448] "Gartner Says Smartphone Sales Surpassed One Billion Units in 2014", Gartner press release, March 3, 2015, http://www.gartner.com/newsroom/id/2996817
[449] "The Apple iPhone 6s and iPhone 6s Plus Review", Joshua Ho, AnandTech, November 2, 2015, http://www.anandtech.com/show/9686/the-apple-iphone-6s-and-iphone-6s-plus-review/4
[450] "Apple Announces Record iPhone 6s & iPhone 6s Plus Sales", Apple press release, September 28, 2015, http://www.apple.com/in/pr/library/2015/09/28Apple-Announces-Record-iPhone-6s-iPhone-6s-Plus-Sales.html
[451] "Apple Introduces iPhone 6s & iPhone 6s Plus", Apple press release, September 9, 2015, http://www.apple.com/pr/library/2015/09/09Apple-Introduces-iPhone-6s-iPhone-6s-Plus.html
[452] "Apple Introduces iPad Pro Featuring Epic 12.9-inch Retina Display", Apple press release, September 9, 2015, http://www.apple.com/pr/library/2015/09/09Apple-Introduces-iPad-Pro-Featuring-Epic-12-9-inch-Retina-Display.html
[453] "iPhone 6s Teardown", iFixit, September 25, 2015, https://www.ifixit.com/Teardown/iPhone+6s+Teardown/48170
[454] "Apple: the first $700 billion company", Verne Kopytoff, Fortune, February 10, 2015, http://fortune.com/2015/02/10/apple-the-first-700-billion-company/
[455] "Why does Apple do business with Samsung", Daniel Nenni, SemiWiki.com, May 26, 2015, https://www.semiwiki.com/forum/content/4646-why-does-apple-do-business-samsung.html

Chapter 8

[456] "Samsung's History", Samsung website, http://www.samsung.com/us/aboutsamsung/corporateprofile/history06.html
[457] "Lucky GoldStar Marking 60 Years in Business", The Chosunilbo, January 4, 2007, http://english.chosun.com/site/data/html_dir/2007/01/04/2007010461030.html
[458] "Electronics: a mainstay of Korean economy", Alan Biggs, The Korea Times, August 25, 2010, http://www.koreatimes.co.kr/www/news/biz/2010/09/291_72034.html
[459] "About KIST: History", Korea Institute of Science and Technology website, http://eng.kist.re.kr/kist_eng/?sub_num=628
[460] "Digital Development in Korea: Building an Information Society", Myung Oh and James Larson, Taylor & Francis, March 14, 2011, p. 36.
[461] "What Korea's Electronics Industry Has Done", Chung Myung-Je, Korea IT Times, September 2, 2009, http://www.koreaittimes.com/story/4818/what-korea%E2%80%99s-electronics-industry-has-done
[462] "Samsung Founding Chairman Lee Byung-Chull's Place in Korean Business Management", Chang Jin-Ho, SERI Quarterly, April 2010, pp. 58-69.
[463] "History of Samsung (1): Paving a New Path", SamsungTomorrow, Samsung Electronics Official Global Blog, April 18, 2012, http://global.samsungtomorrow.com/the-history-of-samsung-electronics-1-paving-a-new-path-19681970/
[464] "History of Samsung Electronics (2): Diversification and Expansion", SamsungTomorrow, Samsung Electronics Official Global Blog, April 25, 2012, http://global.samsungtomorrow.com/the-history-of-samsung-electronics-2-diversification-and-expansion-19711974/
[465] "Oral History: Ki-dong Kang", interview conducted by Andrew Goldstein, IEEE History Center, June 13, 1996, http://ethw.org/Oral-History:Ki_Dong_Kang
[466] "Samsung Electronics and the Struggle for Leadership of the Electronics Industry", Anthony Michell, John Wiley & Sons, September 29, 2011.
[467] "History of Samsung (4): Innovation and efficiency combine for record-beating production and export boom", SamsungTomorrow, Samsung Electronics Official Global Blog, May 9, 2012, http://global.samsungtomorrow.com/history-of-samsung-electronics-4-innovation-and-efficiency-combine-for-record-beating-production-and-export-boom-19771978/
[468] "Tiger Technology: The Creation of a Semiconductor Industry in East Asia", John Matthews and Cho Dong-sung, Cambridge University Press, March 5, 2007, p. 256.
[469] "History of Samsung (5): Suwon R&D Center Expands Knowledge Base", SamsungTomorrow, Samsung Electronics Official Global Blog, May 16, 2012, http://global.samsungtomorrow.com/history-of-samsung-electronics-5-suwon-rd-center-expands-knowledge-base-samsung-semiconductor-expands-production-base-19791980/
[470] "Digital Development in Korea: Building an Information Society", Oh and Larson, pp. 25-26.
[471] "History of Samsung (6): Entering the Global Marketplace", SamsungTomorrow, Samsung Electronics Official Global Blog, May 23, 2012, http://global.samsungtomorrow.com/history-of-samsung-6-entering-the-global-marketplace-19811983/
[472] "Imitation to Innovation: The Dynamics of Korea's Technological Learning", Linsu Kim, Harvard Business Press, 1997, pp. 153-155.
[473] "Technology and Productivity: The Korean Way of Learning and Catching Up", Youngil Lim, MIT Press, 1999, pp. 105-106.
[474] "Learning and Innovation in Economic Development", Linsu Kim, Edward Elgar Publishing, January 1, 1999, p. 92.

[475] "History of Samsung (7): Semiconductor Breakthroughs and High-Profile Sponsoring", SamsungTomorrow, Samsung Electronics Official Global Blog, May 30, 2012, http://global.samsungtomorrow.com/history-of-samsung-7-semiconductor-breakthroughs-and-high-profile-sponsoring-1984-1985/

[476] "SK Telecom is 20 Today", Cellular News, March 28, 2004, http://www.cellular-news.com/story/10932.php

[477] "Case Study of Samsung's Mobile Phone Business", Boon-Young Lee and Seung-Joo Lee, KDI School of Public Policy and Management, 2003, http://wenku.baidu.com/view/0f8f82da7c1cfad6195fa796.html

[478] "This was the first Samsung cell phone ever", phoneArena.com, November 23, 2014, http://www.phonearena.com/news/This-was-the-first-Samsung-cell-phone-ever_id63157

[479] "The Seoul of Design", Bill Breen, Fast Company, December 5, 2005, http://www.fastcompany.com/54877/seoul-design

[480] "Fukuda Report author recalls role in reform of a giant", Park Tae-hee and Kim Jung-yoon, Korea JoongAng Daily, December 1, 2012, http://koreajoongangdaily.joins.com/news/article/article.aspx?aid=2963241

[481] "History of Samsung (11): Adoption of new corporate identity and development of world's first 256-mega DRAM semiconductor", SamsungTomorrow, Samsung Electronics Official Global Blog, June 27, 2012, http://global.samsungtomorrow.com/history-of-samsung-11-adoption-of-new-corporate-identity-and-development-of-worlds-first-256-mega-dram-semiconductor-1993-1997/

[482] "Seoul Machine", Frank Rose, Wired, May 2005, http://archive.wired.com/wired/archive/13.05/samsung.html

[483] "Masters of the Clean Room", Laxmi Nakarmi and Neil Gross, BusinessWeek, September 26, 1993, http://www.bloomberg.com/bw/stories/1993-09-26/masters-of-the-clean-room

[484] "Toshiba to Work with Samsung on 'Flash' Chips", Andrew Pollack, The New York Times, December 22, 1992, http://www.nytimes.com/1992/12/22/business/company-news-toshiba-to-work-with-samsung-on-flash-chips.html

[485] "History of Samsung (17): Samsung Electronics ranked No. 1 in NAND Flash", SamsungTomorrow, Samsung Electronics Official Global Blog, August 8, 2012, http://global.samsungtomorrow.com/history-of-samsung-17-samsung-electronics-ranked-no-1-in-nand-flash-2002/

[486] "The Qualcomm Equation: How a Fledgling Telecom Company Forged a New Path to Big Profits and Market Dominance", Dave Mock, AMACOM (American Management Association), January 1, 2005, pp. 82-84.

[487] "Evolution and Standardization of Mobile Communications Technology", Seo Dong-back, IGI Global, May 31, 2013, pp. 101-107.

[488] "Digital Development in Korea: Building an Information Society", Oh and Larson, pp. 96-97.

[489] "SK Telecom's CDMA Mobile Telephone Service Now Serves More Than 1,000,000 Customers", SK Telecom press release, April 23, 1997, http://www.prnewswire.com/news-releases/sk-telecoms-cdma-mobile-telephone-service-now-serves-more-than-1000000-customers-75270587.html

[490] "Samsung Mass Producing CDMA Terminals", Samsung press release, March 14, 1996, http://www.samsung.com/us/news/newsRead.do?news_group=corporatenews=activitynews=&news_seq=16

[491] "Samsung Electronics Begins to Ship CDMA PCS Handsets to Sprint Spectrum", Samsung press release, June 18, 1997, http://www.samsung.com/us/news/newsRead.do?news_group=corporatenews=activitynews=&news_seq=82

[492] 1998 Samsung Electronics Annual Report, http://www.samsung.com/us/aboutsamsung/corporateprofile/download/sec98AR-e-full.pdf

[493] "Samsung Electronics Starts DVD Player Production", Samsung press release, October 5, 1996, http://www.samsung.com/global/business/semiconductor/news-events/press-releases/detail?newsId=4516

[494] "Multimedia Signal Processor Summary", L. T. Nguyen et al, Samsung, HotChips: A Symposium on High Performance Chips, August 20, 1996, http://www.hotchips.org/wp-content/uploads/hc_archives/hc08/3_Tue/HC8.S7/HC8.7.2.pdf

[495] "Conexant Works with Samsung on Next-Generation CDMA Digital Cellular Telephone", Conexant press release, December 7, 1998, http://www.thefreelibrary.com/Conexant+Works+with+Samsung+on+Next-Generation+CDMA+Digital+Cellular...-a053354899

[496] "Samsung Licenses ARM9 Processors and Joins ARM Consortium for Windows CE", Samsung press release, February 22, 1999, http://www.samsung.com/us/news/newsRead.do?news_group=corporatenews=activitynews=&news_seq=283

[497] S3C44B0X RISC Microprocessor product overview, Samsung, circa 2000.

[498] "ARM and Samsung Electronics extend strategic alliance with long-term licensing agreement", ARM press release, July 15, 2002, http://www.arm.com/about/newsroom/2226.php

[499] "Samsung signs "all-you-can-eat" ARM license", Peter Clarke, EETimes, July 15, 2002, http://www.eetimes.com/document.asp?doc_id=1177698

[500] "ARMing for War", Jansen Ng, The Inquirer, October 21, 2002, http://www.theinquirer.net/inquirer/news/1001802/arming-war

[501] "Under the Hood: The MP3 that broke new ground", David Carey, EETimes, March 5, 2007, http://www.eetimes.com/document.asp?doc_id=1281156

[502] "Samsung Electronics Introduces 3 models of MP3 players at the 1999 International CES", Samsung press release, January 7, 1999, http://www.samsung.com/us/news/258

[503] "Samsung Develops Mobile Phone that Doubles as Audio Player", Samsung press release, August 4, 1999, http://www.samsung.com/us/news/newsRead.do?news_seq=349

[504] "Samsung and Sprint PCS Create An Uproar With Innovative Wireless Phone", Samsung press release, November 1, 1999, http://www.prnewswire.com/news-releases/samsung-and-sprint-pcs-create-an-uproar-with-innovative-wireless-phone-75358922.html

[505] "Samsung unveils 8-bit CalmRISC architecture", EETimes, May 14, 1999, http://www.eetimes.com/document.asp?doc_id=1187951

[506] "Samsung Electronics Unveils Single-chip Device with Built-in MCU for Online Players", Samsung press release, August 16, 2001, http://www.samsung.com/global/business/semiconductor/news-events/press-releases/printer?newsId=4415

[507] "The Rise of the Flash Memory Market: Its Impact on Firm Behavior and Global Semiconductor Trade Patterns", Falan Young, US International Trade Commission, July 2007, http://www.usitc.gov/publications/332/journals/rise_flash_memory_market.pdf

[508] "A Memorable Deal for Apple and Samsung?", Arik Hasseldahl, BusinessWeek, August 25, 2005, http://www.bloomberg.com/bw/stories/2005-08-25/a-memorable-deal-for-apple-and-samsung

[509] "Bargains in a Flash", Damon Darlin, The New York Times, September 29, 2005, http://www.nytimes.com/2005/09/29/technology/circuits/bargains-in-a-flash.html

[510] "Samsung Electronics Launches Second-Phase Investment Strategy for Hwaseong Semiconductor Plant", Samsung press release, September 29, 2005, http://www.samsung.com/global/business/semiconductor/news-events/press-releases/detail?newsId=4253

[511] Samsung SPH-i300 entry, PDAdb.net, http://pdadb.net/index.php?m=specs&id=1186&c=samsung_sph-i300

[512] Samsung SPH-i500 entry, PhoneScoop, http://www.phonescoop.com/phones/phone.php?p=187

[513] Samsung SPH-i550 entry, PhoneScoop, http://www.phonescoop.com/phones/phone.php?p=522

[514] "Verizon launches Samsung smart phone", Richard Shim, CNET, November 10, 2003, http://www.cnet.com/news/verizon-launches-samsung-smart-phone/

[515] "Samsung SCH-i730 (Verizon Wireless) review", Denny Atkin, CNET, June 30, 2005, http://www.cnet.com/products/samsung-sch-i730-verizon-wireless/

[516] "Samsung BlackJack SGH-i607 Mobile Phone Teardown", HIS Electronics & Media, May 1, 2007, http://electronics360.globalspec.com/article/3655/samsung-blackjack-sgh-i607-mobile-phone-teardown

[517] "Samsung Omnia SGH-i900", Jamie Lendino, PCMag, September 22, 2008, http://www.pcmag.com/article2/0,2817,2330934,00.asp

[518] "Samsung Redefines Mobile Communication", Samsung press release, September 16, 2003, http://www.samsung.com/us/news/newsRead.do?news_seq=1957

[519] Samsung SGH-D710 entry, PDAdb.net, http://pdadb.net/index.php?m=specs&id=994&c=samsung_sgh-d710

[520] Samsung SGH-Z600 entry, PDAdb.net, http://pdadb.net/index.php?m=specs&id=1032&c=samsung_sgh-z600

[521] Samsung SGH-i520 entry, PDAdb.net, http://pdadb.net/index.php?m=specs&id=991&c=samsung_sgh-i520__sgh-i520v

[522] Samsung SGH-i550 entry, PDAdb.net, http://pdadb.net/index.php?m=specs&id=992&c=samsung_sgh-i550

[523] Samsung GT-i8510 entry, PDAdb.net, http://pdadb.net/index.php?m=specs&id=1375&c=samsung_gt-i8510_innov8_8gb

[524] "[Infographic] History of Samsung Mobile Phones: 10 Million Seller Club", SamsungTomorrow, Samsung Electronics Official Global Blog, December 10, 2013, http://global.samsungtomorrow.com/history-of-samsung-mobile-phones-10-million-seller-club/

[525] "Samsung plant will have Intel inside", Neil Orman, Austin Business Journal, February 16, 1997, http://www.bizjournals.com/austin/stories/1997/02/17/story1.html?page=all

[526] Search of devices using Samsung S3C2410, PDAdb.net, http://pdadb.net/index.php?m=pdamaster&posted=1&cpu=a2410

[527] HP49g+ Emulation Project, http://lebonpoint.chez-alice.fr/hp49g/reverse.htm

[528] Samsung S3C2443 datasheet, circa 2007, http://pdf.datasheetarchive.com/indexerfiles/Datasheet-024/DSA00417367.pdf

[529] "Samsung Electronics Now Mass Producing First 90nm 512Mb Mobile DRAM", Samsung press release, November 10, 2005, http://www.samsung.com/us/news/newsRead.do?news_seq=2917

[530] "The Common Platform Technology: A New Model for Semiconductor Manufacturing", Jim McGregor, In-Stat, January 6, 2007, http://www.commonplatform.com/newsroom/ar/Instat_Common%20Platform%20Report_IN0703405WHT_1Q07.pdf

[531] "Qualcomm Selects Samsung Electronics Co., Ltd. for New Supply Partnership", Qualcomm press release, November 22, 2005, https://www.qualcomm.com/news/releases/2005/11/22/qualcomm-selects-samsung-electronics-co-ltd-new-supply-partnership

[532] "Samsung Expands Foundry Business Management Team with New Vice President", Samsung press release, March 21, 2006, http://www.businesswire.com/news/home/20060321005461/en/Samsung-Expands-Foundry-Business-Management-Team-Vice#.VbO05rNVhBc

[533] "Samsung elbows its way into chip foundry business", Dan Nystedt, Network World, March 28, 2006, http://www.networkworld.com/article/2310139/network-security/samsung-elbows-its-way-into-chip-foundry-business.html

[534] "Samsung gives final approval to new Austin plant", Austin Business Journal, April 13, 2006, http://www.bizjournals.com/austin/stories/2006/04/10/daily36.html

[535] "Samsung grabs iPod design win", LaPedus.

[536] "Tear Down: Inside the Apple 8GB iPod nano", Gregory Quirk, Semiconductor Insights, EETimes, October 8, 2006, http://www.eetimes.com/document.asp?doc_id=1281288

[537] "Nano 2G", freemyipod.org, http://www.freemyipod.org/wiki/Nano_2G

[538] "Linux4Nano's knowledge about the Apple iPod Nano 2G", Jean-Christophe Delaunay and Clement Sudron, Universite de Bordeaux 1, April 2010, http://files.freemyipod.org/reports/Linux4NanoReport.pdf

[539] "Analyst: PortalPlayer nabs Apple iPhone design win", Dylan McGrath, EETimes, November 21, 2006, http://www.eetimes.com/document.asp?doc_id=1164435

[540] "Mobile Leaders Around the World Launch LiMo Foundation", LiMo Foundation press release, January 25, 2007, http://www.prnewswire.com/news-releases/mobile-leaders-around-the-world-launch-limo-foundation-53755757.html

[541] "Industry Leaders Announce Open Platform for Mobile Devices", Open Handset Alliance press release, November 5, 2007, http://www.openhandsetalliance.com/press_110507.html

[542] "Will Motorola Go All-In On Android? It Has No Other Choice", Erick Schonfeld, TechCrunch, October 29, 2008, http://techcrunch.com/2008/10/29/will-motorola-go-all-in-on-android-it-has-no-other-choice/

[543] "Samsung plans Symbian-free future", Bill Ray, The Register, November 11, 2009, http://www.theregister.co.uk/2009/11/11/samsung_symbian/

[544] "Samsung announces its own 'open' mobile platform – bada", Jeremy Kessel, TechCrunch, November 10, 2009, http://techcrunch.com/2009/11/10/samsung-announces-its-own-open-mobile-platform-bada/

[545] Samsung GT-i7500 entry, PDAdb.net, http://pdadb.net/index.php?m=specs&id=1863&c=samsung_gt-i7500_galaxy

[546] Qualcomm MSM7200A Chipset Solution datasheet, Qualcomm, 2007, http://pdf.datasheetarchive.com/indexerfiles/Datasheet-024/DSA00418645.pdf

[547] "It's A Samsung Smartphone World - We Just Live In It", Dan Rowinski, ReadWrite, October 29, 2012, http://readwrite.com/2012/10/29/its-a-samsung-smartphone-world-we-just-live-in-it

[548] Samsung S3C6410 Mobile Processor datasheet, Samsung, 2007, http://www.samsung.com/global/business/semiconductor/file/media/s3c6410_datasheet_200804-0.pdf

[549] "OpenFIMG ARM Graphics Driver Is Still Active", Michael Larabel, Phoronix, January 12, 2012, http://www.phoronix.com/scan.php?page=news_item&px=MTA0MTc

[550] Samsung GT-i5700 entry, PDAdb.net, http://pdadb.net/index.php?m=specs&id=2033&c=samsung_gt-i5700_galaxy_spica

[551] Samsung GT-i8000 entry, PDAdb.net, http://pdadb.net/index.php?m=specs&id=1939&c=samsung_gt-i8000_omnia_ii_m16_16gb

[552] Samsung GT-i9000M Galaxy S Vibrant entry, PDAdb.net, http://pdadb.net/index.php?m=specs&id=2702&c=samsung_gt-i9000m_galaxy_s_vibrant

[553] "Samsung Meets Target on Galaxy as It Takes on Apple", Jun Yang, Bloomberg, January 3, 2011, http://www.bloomberg.com/news/articles/2011-01-03/samsung-says-it-sold-10-million-galaxy-s-smartphones-since-debut-in-june

[554] Exynos 3 Single webpage, Samsung, http://www.samsung.com/global/business/semiconductor/product/application/detail?productId=7645&iaId=834

[555] "Samsung GALAXY Tab Opens a New Chapter in Mobile Industry", Samsung press release, September 2, 2010, http://www.samsung.com/nl/galaxy-tab/press/pressrelease.html

[556] Exynos 4 Dual 45nm webpage, Samsung, http://www.samsung.com/global/business/semiconductor/product/application/detail?productId=7644&iaId=844

[557] "Samsung Galaxy S 2 (International) Review", Brian Klug and Anand Lal Shimpi, AnandTech, September 11, 2011, http://www.anandtech.com/show/4686/samsung-galaxy-s-2-international-review-the-best-redefined

[558] Samsung GT-i9100 entry, PDAdb.net, http://pdadb.net/index.php?m=specs&id=2779&c=samsung_gt-i9100_galaxy_s_ii_16gb

[559] Samsung GT-i9220 entry, PDAdb.net, http://pdadb.net/index.php?m=specs&id=3693&c=samsung_gt-i9220_galaxy_note_16gb

[560] Samsung GT-P7560 entry, PDAdb.net, http://pdadb.net/index.php?m=specs&id=3142&c=samsung_gt-p7560_galaxy_tab_7.0_plus_16gb

[561] "Samsung Unveils its Next High-Performance Application Processor for Smartphone and Tablet Devices", Samsung press release, September 29, 2011, http://www.samsung.com/global/business/semiconductor/minisite/Exynos/w/mediacenter.html#?v=news_Samsung_Unveils_its_Next_High_Performance_Application_Processor_for_Smartphone_and_Tablet_Devices

[562] "Galaxy S III processor made deep in the heart of Texas?", Taylor Wimberly, Android and Me, January 23, 2012, http://androidandme.com/2012/01/news/galaxy-s-iii-processor-made-deep-in-the-heart-of-texas/

[563] "Samsung Announces Industry First ARM Cortex-A15 Processor Samples for Tablet Computers", Samsung press release, November 30, 2011, http://www.samsung.com/global/business/semiconductor/minisite/Exynos/news_11.html

[564] "A closer look at Samsung's killer 2GHz Exynos 5250", Taylor Wimberly, Android and Me, March 23, 2012, http://androidandme.com/2012/03/news/a-closer-look-at-samsungs-killer-2-ghz-exynos-5250/

[565] "Samsung Chromebook review: The one we've been waiting for (at least in price)", Stephen Shankland, CNET, October 18, 2012, http://www.cnet.com/products/samsung-chromebook-series-3/

[566] "Google Nexus 10 review: Regular Google updates in a durable body", Eric Franklin, CNET, November 2, 2012, http://www.cnet.com/products/google-nexus-10/

[567] "Samsung Droid Charge Review – Droid Goes LTE", Brian Klug, AnandTech, June 22, 2011, http://www.anandtech.com/show/4465/samsung-droid-charge-review-droid-goes-lte

[568] "Samsung Galaxy Nexus & Ice Cream Sandwich Review", Brian Klug and Anand Lal Shimpi, AnandTech, January 18, 2012, http://www.anandtech.com/show/5310/samsung-galaxy-nexus-ice-cream-sandwich-review

[569] "Samsung's New Quad-core Application Processor Drives Advanced Feature Sets in Smartphones and Tablets", Samsung press release, April 26, 2012, http://www.samsung.com/global/business/semiconductor/minisite/Exynos/news_12.html

[570] "Samsung confirms Exynos 4 Quad to appear in Galaxy S III", Taylor Wimberly, Android and Me, April 25, 2012, http://androidandme.com/2012/04/news/samsung-confirms-exynos-4-quad-to-appear-in-galaxy-s-iii/

[571] Search of devices using Samsung Exynos 4 Quad, PDAdb.net, http://pdadb.net/index.php?m=pdamaster&posted=1&cpu=a4412

[572] "Samsung Introduces the GALAXY S III, the Smartphone Designed for Humans and Inspired by Nature", Samsung press release, May 3, 2012, http://www.samsungmobilepress.com/2012/05/04/Samsung-Introduces-the-GALAXY-S-III,-the-Smartphone--Designed-for-Humans-and-Inspired-by-Nature

[573] "Samsung Electronics would like to clarify issues regarding certain GALAXY S4 GPU benchmark results", SamsungTomorrow, Samsung Electronics Official Global Blog, July 31, 2013, http://global.samsungtomorrow.com/26314/

[574] "Samsung Introduces the GALAXY S4 - A Life Companion for a richer, simpler and fuller life", Samsung press release, March 14, 2013, http://www.samsungmobilepress.com/2013/03/14/Samsung-Introduces-the-GALAXY-S-4----A-Life-Companion-for-a-richer,-simpler-and-fuller-life

[575] "Samsung GALAXY S4 Hits 10 Million Milestone in First Month", Samsung press release, May 23, 2013, http://www.samsung.com/us/aboutsamsung/news/newsIrRead.do?news_ctgry=irnewsrelease&news_seq=20887

[576] "Samsung Updates Exynos 5 Octa (5420), Switches Back to ARM GPU", Anand Lal Shimpi and Brian Klug, AnandTech, July 22, 2013, http://www.anandtech.com/show/7164/samsung-exynos-5-octa-5420-switches-back-to-arm-gpu

[577] "big.LITTLE Software Update", George Grey, Linaro, July 10, 2013, https://www.linaro.org/blog/hardware-update/big-little-software-update/

[578] "Samsung's Exynos 5422 & The Ideal big.LITTLE: Exynos 5 Hexa (5260)", Anand Lal Shimpi, February 25, 2014, http://www.anandtech.com/show/7811/samsungs-exynos-5422-the-ideal-biglittle-exynos-5-hexa-5260

[579] "The chips of Samsung's Galaxy S5 – Exynos and Snapdragon", Shara Tibken, CNET, February 27, 2014, http://www.cnet.com/news/the-chips-of-samsungs-galaxy-s5-exynos-and-snapdragon/

[580] "Samsung unveils Galaxy S5 to focus on what matters most to consumers", Samsung press release, February 24, 2014, http://www.samsung.com/us/news/22549

[581] Search of devices using Samsung Exynos 5433, PDAdb.net, http://pdadb.net/index.php?m=pdamaster&posted=1&cpu=a5433

[582] "Samsung's Exynos 5433 is an A57/A53 ARM SoC", Andrei Frumusanu, AnandTech, September 16, 2014, http://www.anandtech.com/show/8537/samsungs-exynos-5433-is-an-a57a53-arm-soc

[583] "Samsung Announces Mass Production of Industry's First 14nm FinFET Mobile Application Processor", Samsung press release, February 16, 2015, http://www.samsung.com/global/business/semiconductor/minisite/Exynos/w/mediacenter.html#?v=news_Samsung_Announces_Mass_Production_of_Industrys_First_14nm_FinFET_Mobile_Application_Processor

[584] "Exclusive: Qualcomm to Use Samsung's Foundries for Its Next High-End Chip", Ina Fried, Re/code, April 20, 2015, http://recode.net/2015/04/20/exclusive-qualcomm-to-use-samsungs-foundries-for-its-next-high-end-chip/

[585] "Introducing the Samsung Galaxy S6 and Galaxy S6 edge", Samsung news feed, March 3, 2015, http://www.samsung.com/ae/discover/news-feed/introducing-the-samsung-galaxy-s6-and-galaxy-s6-edge/

[586] "The Samsung Exynos 7420 Deep Dive – Inside a Modern 14nm SoC", Andrei Frumusanu, AnandTech, June 29, 2015, http://www.anandtech.com/show/9330/exynos-7420-deep-dive

[587] Samsung Exynos Solution website, http://www.samsung.com/global/business/semiconductor/minisite/Exynos/w/solution.html#?v=modap

[588] "Samsung and GLOBALFOUNDRIES Forge Strategic Collaboration to Deliver Multi-Sourced Offering of 14nm FinFET Semiconductor Technology", GLOBALFOUNDRIES press release, April 17, 2014, http://www.globalfoundries.com/newsroom/press-releases/2014/04/17/samsung-and-globalfoundries-forge-strategic-collaboration-to-deliver-multi-sourced-offering-of-14nm-finfet-semiconductor-technology

[589] "Inside the new Samsung Galaxy S6", Chipworks, April 2, 2015, https://www.chipworks.com/about-chipworks/overview/blog/inside-the-samsung-galaxy-s6

[590] "BATTERYGATE: Is Apple's Samsung-made iPhone 6s core rotten", Robert Maire, SemiWiki, October 8, 2015, https://www.semiwiki.com/forum/content/5079-batterygate-apples-samsung-made-iphone-6s-core-rotten.html#comments

[591] "Global Smartphone Growth Expected to Slow to 11.3% in 2015 as Market Penetration Increases in Top Markets, According to IDC", IDC press release, May 26, 2015, http://www.idc.com/getdoc.jsp?containerId=prUS25641615

[592] "Samsung Unveils the Latest Application Processor, Exynos 8 Octa, Built on 14-Nanometer FinFET Process Technology", Samsung press release, November 10, 2015, http://global.samsungtomorrow.com/samsung-unveils-the-latest-application-processor-exynos-8-octa-built-on-14-nanometer-finfet-process-technology/

[593] "Mongoose: The Making of Samsung's Custom CPU Core", Majeed Ahmad, SemiWiki, September 14, 2015, https://www.semiwiki.com/forum/content/5004-mongoose-making-samsungs-custom-cpu-core.html

[594] "Samsung's own Exynos M1 CPU core already supported by software tools", Anton Shilov, KitGuru, April 23, 2015, http://www.kitguru.net/components/cpu/anton-shilov/samsungs-own-exynos-m1-processor-core-already-supported-by-software-tools/

Chapter 9

[595] "Section 331: From JPL to USC and Beyond", Carl Marziali, USC Viterbi School of Engineering, January 12, 2005, http://viterbi.usc.edu/news/news/2004/2004_11_12_jpl.htm

[596] Vanguard TV3, National Aeronautics and Space Administration, http://nssdc.gsfc.nasa.gov/nmc/spacecraftDisplay.do?id=VAGT3

[597] "Andrew Viterbi: He's got algorithm", Carl Marziali, USC, February 1, 2009, https://news.usc.edu/16163/he-s-got-algorithm/

[598] "The Birth of NASA", NASA, March 28, 2008, http://www.nasa.gov/exploration/whyweexplore/Why_We_29.html

[599] "A Truly Grand Old Man Marks 50 Years at the Viterbi School", Eric Mankin, USC Viterbi School of Engineering, May 29, 2012, http://viterbi.usc.edu/news/news/2012/a-truly-grand.htm

[600] Andrew Viterbi interview, Joel West, UC San Diego, December 15, 2006, http://libraries.ucsd.edu/sdta/transcripts/viterbi-andrew_20061215.html

[601] "The Qualcomm Equation: How a Fledgling Telecom Company Forged a New Path to Big Profits and Market Dominance", Mock, pp. 18-20.

[602] "Oral History: Irwin Jacobs", interview conducted by David Morton, IEEE History Center, October 29, 1999, http://ethw.org/Oral-History:Irwin_Jacobs

[603] "Error bounds for convolutional codes and an asymptotically optimum decoding algorithm", Andrew Viterbi, IEEE Transactions on Information Theory, Volume 13, Issue 2, April 1967, pp. 260-269, http://ieeexplore.ieee.org/xpl/login.jsp?tp=&arnumber=1054010

[604] A good explanation of the Viterbi Algorithm is found in course notes for CSE590, Jie Gao, State University of New York at Stony Brook, Fall 2009, http://www3.cs.stonybrook.edu/~jgao/CSE590-fall09/viterbi.pdf

[605] "The Viterbi Algorithm: A Personal History", G. David Forney, Jr., Massachusetts Institute of Technology, March 8, 2005, http://digitallibrary.usc.edu/cdm/ref/collection/p15799coll117/id/2744

[606] "Birth of a Blueprint: Profile Internet Father, Leonard Kleinrock", Matt Welch, The Zone News, January 2000, http://mattwelch.com/ZoneSave/Kleinrock.htm

[607] "Before Qualcomm: Linkabit and the Origins of San Diego's Telecom Industry", Joel West, The Journal oF San Diego History, San Diego Historical Society, Volume 55, Numbers 1 & 2, Winter/Spring 2009, pp. 1-20, https://www.sandiegohistory.org/journal/v55-1/pdf/v55-1.pdf

[608] "Viterbi Decoding for Satellite and Space Communication", Jerry Heller and Irwin Jacobs, Linkabit Corporation, IEEE Transactions on Communication Technology, October 1971, pp. 835-848, http://ieeexplore.ieee.org/xpl/login.jsp?tp=&arnumber=1090711

[609] "Performance Study of Viterbi Decoding As Related to Space Communications", Irwin Jacobs and Jerry Heller, Linkabit Corporation, Final Technical Report on Contract No. DAAB07-71-C-0148, for US Army Satellite Communications Agency, August 31, 1971, http://www.dtic.mil/dtic/tr/fulltext/u2/738213.pdf

[610] Andrew Viterbi interview, West.

[611] "Oral History: Andrew Viterbi", interview conducted by David Morton, IEEE History Center, October 29, 1999, http://ethw.org/Oral-History:Andrew_Viterbi

[612] "Coding systems study for high data rate telemetry links", Gilhausen et al, Linkabit Corporation, for NASA Ames Research Center, January 1971, http://ntrs.nasa.gov/archive/nasa/casi.ntrs.nasa.gov/19710018310.pdf

[613] "TDRSS Telecommunications Study, Phase 1: Final Report", Cahn et al, Magnavox Company, for Goddard Space Flight Center, September 15, 1974, https://archive.org/details/nasa_techdoc_19750004105

[614] "Before Qualcomm: Linkabit and the Origins of San Diego's Telecom Industry", West.

[615] "A multi-stack microprocessor for satellite modems", Klein Gilhousen, Linkabit Corporation, National Telecommunications Conference, IEEE, December 1974, http://labs.adsabs.harvard.edu/adsabsadsabs/abs/1974ITCom......543G/

[616] "Irwin Mark Jacobs Oral History", David Morrow, Computerworld Honors Program, March 24, 1999, http://www.cwhonors.org/archives/histories/jacobs.pdf

[617] "Oral History: Irwin Jacobs", Morton.

[618] "Air Force Research Laboratory Sensors Directorate Communications Branch History From 1960-2011", Allen Johnson, SelectTech Services, for Air Force Research Laboratory, December 2011, http://www.dtic.mil/dtic/tr/fulltext/u2/a562382.pdf

[619] "Before Qualcomm: Linkabit and the Origins of San Diego's Telecom Industry", West.

[620] "Irwin Mark Jacobs Oral History", Morrow.

[621] "Oral History: Andrew Viterbi", Morton.

[622] "Mobile Communications Handbook", Jerry Gibson, CRC Press, August 21, 2012, pp. 161-166.

[623] "Q1401 K=7 Rate 1/s Single-Chip Viterbi Decoder Technical Data Sheet", Qualcomm, September 1987.

[624] "An Area-Efficient Topology for VLSI Implementation of Viterbi Decoders and Other Shuffle-ExchangeType Structures", Sparsø et al, IEEE Journal of Solid-State Circuits, Vol. 26 No. 2, February 1991, http://orbit.dtu.dk/fedora/objects/orbit:15811/datastreams/file_3800388/content

[625] "Andrew Viterbi", interview conducted by Joel West and Caroline Simard, San Diego Technology Archive, June 15, 2004, http://libraries.ucsd.edu/assets/sdta/transcripts/viterbi-andrew_20040615.pdf

[626] "Technical Characteristics of the OmniTRACS", Antonio, Gilhousen, Jacobs, and Weaver, Qualcomm, http://www.qsl.net/n9zia/omnitracs/19880016325_1988016325.pdf

[627] "Evolution and Standardization of Mobile Communications Technology", Seo Dong-back, pp. 96-98.

[628] "On the Capacity of a Cellular CDMA System", Jacobs et al, Qualcomm, IEEE Transactions on Vehicular Technology, Vol. 40 No. 2, May 1991, http://wsl.stanford.edu/~ee359/CDcap.pdf

[629] "The Qualcomm Equation: How a Fledgling Telecom Company Forged a New Path to Big Profits and Market Dominance", Mock, pp. 61-63.

[630] "Mobile Communications Design Fundamentals", William C. Y. Lee, John Wiley & Sons, July 15, 2010, pp. xv-xvi.

[631] "Irwin Mark Jacobs Oral History", Morrow.

[632] "Commonalities between CDMA2000 and WCDMA Technologies", Qualcomm, October 2006, https://www.qualcomm.com/media/documents/files/commonalities-between-cdma2000-and-wcdma-technologies.pdf

[633] "Anytime, Anywhere: Entrepreneurship and the Creation of a Wireless World", Louis Galambos and Eric Abrahamson, Cambridge University Press, Jun 10, 2002, pp. 176-178.

[634] "NYNEX Plans Pedestrian's Mobile Phone", Keith Bradsher, The New York Times, August 2, 1990, http://www.nytimes.com/1990/08/02/business/nynex-plans-pedestrian-s-mobile-phone.html

[635] "Can Cellular Phone Companies Agree on a New Standard for Transmission", Keith Bradsher, The New York Times, September 16, 1990, http://www.nytimes.com/1990/09/16/business/technology-can-cellular-phone-companies-agree-on-a-new-standard-for-transmission.html

[636] Qualcomm timeline, Guy Klemens, http://guy.klemens.org/QCOM.html

[637] "Anytime, Anywhere: Entrepreneurship and the Creation of a Wireless World", Galambos and Abrahamson, p. 177.

[638] "Nokia to License Qualcomm's CDMA Digital Cellular Technology", Qualcomm press release, April 14, 1992, http://investorshub.advfn.com/boards/read_msg.aspx?message_id=35161175

[639] Qualcomm 3rd Quarter 1993 earnings release, http://www.thefreelibrary.com/QUALCOMM+REPORTS+81+PERCENT+REVENUE+INCREASE+AND+NET+EARNINGS+FOR...-a013189795

[640] "CDMA Mobile Station Modem (MSM) ASIC", Hinderling et al, Qualcomm, HotChips V, August 1993, http://www.hotchips.org/wp-content/uploads/hc_archives/hc05/2_Mon/HC05.S2/HC05.2.2-Hinderling--QUALCOMM-CDMA.pdf

[641] cdmaOne web page, CDG, https://www.cdg.org/technology/cdmaone.asp

[642] "Harvesting the Blackberry: An Insider's Perspective", Graham Tubbs and Terry Gillett, Wheatmark Inc, January 1, 2011, pp. 112-114.

[643] "Qualcomm introduces second generation CDMA ASICs", Qualcomm press release, February 1, 1995, http://www.thefreelibrary.com/QUALCOMM+introduces+second+generation+CDMA+ASICs%3B+New+ASICs+reduce...-a016398101

[644] "Qualcomm unveils its dual-mode QCP-800 portable cellular telephone", Qualcomm press release, February 2, 1995, http://www.thefreelibrary.com/QUALCOMM+unveils+its+dual-mode+QCP-800+portable+cellular+telephone+--...-a016409329

[645] "Qualcomm Announces New Mobile Station Modem with 13 Kilobit PureVoice Speech Coding". Qualcomm press release, June 25, 1996, https://www.qualcomm.com/news/releases/1996/06/25/qualcomm-announces-new-mobile-station-modem-13-kilobit-purevoice-speech

[646] "Qualcomm Announces Next Generation Mobile Station Modem", Qualcomm press release, March 3, 1997, https://www.qualcomm.com/news/releases/1997/03/03/qualcomm-announces-next-generation-mobile-station-modem

[647] "CDMA ASIC Products Data Book", Qualcomm, September 1997.

[648] "Qualcomm Announces Major Milestone with Shipment of Six Million MSM Chips", Qualcomm press release, June 18, 1997, https://www.qualcomm.com/news/releases/1997/06/18/qualcomm-announces-major-milestone-shipment-six-million-msm-chips

[649] "Qualcomm Acquires License for ARM7TDMI and ARM Software Development Tools", Qualcomm press release, July 7, 1998, https://www.qualcomm.com/news/releases/1998/07/07/qualcomm-acquires-license-arm7tdmi-and-arm-software-development-tools

[650] "Qualcomm Announces Next Generation CDMA Single-chip Modem with Support for High Data Rates and Very Low Power Consumption", Qualcomm press release, February 23, 1998, https://www.qualcomm.com/news/releases/1998/02/23/qualcomm-announces-next-generation-cdma-single-chip-modem-support-high-data

[651] Qualcomm Form 10-K, Fiscal Year Ended September 30, 1999, http://investor.qualcomm.com/secfiling.cfm?filingid=936392-99-1354

[652] "Qualcomm Announces Sixth Generation CDMA Single-Chip Modem Solution", Qualcomm press release, February 8, 1999, https://www.qualcomm.com/news/releases/1999/02/08/qualcomm-announces-sixth-generation-cdma-single-chip-modem-solution

[653] "Qualcomm CDMA Technologies Announces World's First Third-Generation Chip for CDMA Handsets", Qualcomm press release, May 24, 1999, https://www.qualcomm.com/news/releases/1999/05/24/qualcomm-cdma-technologies-announces-worlds-first-third-generation-chip

[654] CDMA history, CDG, https://www.cdg.org/resources/cdma_history.asp

[655] "Qualcomm CDMA Technologies Introduces the iMSM Family of Mobile Station Modem Solutions Enabling New Classes of Internet Capable Smart Devices", Qualcomm press release, September 22, 1999, https://www.qualcomm.com/news/releases/1999/09/22/qualcomm-cdma-technologies-introduces-imsm-family-mobile-station-modem

[656] Forum thread in Silicon Investor, http://www.siliconinvestor.com/readmsg.aspx?msgid=12922646

[657] "Qualcomm and Kyocera Close Agreement for Terrestrial CDMA Phone Business", Qualcomm press release, February 22, 2000, https://www.qualcomm.com/news/releases/2000/02/22/qualcomm-and-kyocera-close-agreement-terrestrial-cdma-phone-business

[658] "Qualcomm Co-Founder Dr. Andrew Viterbi to Retire", Qualcomm press release, February 17, 2000, https://www.qualcomm.com/news/releases/2000/02/17/qualcomm-co-founder-dr-andrew-viterbi-retire

[659] "Qualcomm CDMA Technologies Exceeds 100 Million Mark in MSM Chipsets Shipped", Qualcomm press release, May 23, 2000, https://www.qualcomm.com/news/releases/2000/05/23/qualcomm-cdma-technologies-exceeds-100-million-mark-msm-chipsets-shipped

[660] "Qualcomm CDMA Technologies Unveils Details on MSM6xxx Family of Next- Generation Integrated Circuit Solutions", Qualcomm press release, March 20, 2001, https://www.qualcomm.com/news/releases/2001/03/20/qualcomm-cdma-technologies-unveils-details-msm6xxx-family-next-generation

[661] "Qualcomm Announces Sampling of the MSM6500 Multimedia Single-Chip Solution for Multimode High-Speed Wireless Data Devices", Qualcomm press release, July 9, 2003, https://www.qualcomm.com/news/releases/2003/07/09/qualcomm-announces-sampling-msm6500-multimedia-single-chip-solution

[662] MSM6500 Chipset Solution datasheet, Qualcomm, 2004.

[663] "Donald E. Schrock to Retire as Group President of Qualcomm CDMA Technologies", Qualcomm press release, January 22, 2003, https://www.qualcomm.com/news/releases/2003/01/22/donald-e-schrock-retire-group-president-qualcomm-cdma-technologies

[664] "Qualcomm Announces Highly Integrated Dual-CPU Single Chip Solutions for High-Performance Multimedia Wireless Devices", Qualcomm press release, May 22, 2003, https://www.qualcomm.com/news/releases/2003/05/22/qualcomm-announces-highly-integrated-dual-cpu-single-chip-solutions-high

[665] MSM7600 Chipset Solution datasheet, Qualcomm, 2006.

[666] "Qualcomm and ATI Join Forces to Create Wireless 3D Gaming Platform", Qualcomm press release, March 22, 2004, https://www.qualcomm.com/news/releases/2004/03/22/qualcomm-and-ati-join-forces-create-wireless-3d-gaming-platform

[667] "Qualcomm Ships One Billion Chips to the Wireless Industry", Qualcomm press release, September 15, 2003, https://www.qualcomm.com/news/releases/2003/09/15/qualcomm-ships-one-billion-chips-wireless-industry

[668] "Powering the Mobile Computer: CDMA and the 3G wireless revolution", Klein Gilhousen, Qualcomm, Telecosm 2004, http://www.gildertech.com/public/Telecosm2004/Presentations/Tuesday%20PPT/0910=Gilhousen.ppt

[669] "Qualcomm Names Dr. Paul Jacobs as CEO and Steven Altman as President", Qualcomm press release, March 8, 2005, https://www.qualcomm.com/news/releases/2005/03/08/qualcomm-names-dr-paul-jacobs-ceo-and-steven-altman-president

[670] "Qualcomm Introduces the World's Most Advanced Mobile Microprocessor", Qualcomm press release, November 8, 2005, https://www.qualcomm.com/news/releases/2005/11/08/qualcomm-introduces-worlds-most-advanced-mobile-microprocessor

[671] "New chip a smart move", David Ranii, The News and Observer (Raleigh, NC), January 30, 2010, http://www.techzone360.com/news/2010/01/30/4595774.htm

[672] "Qualcomm Reveals Details on Scorpion Core", Jeff Bier, BDTi, November 14, 2007, http://www.bdti.com/InsideDSP/2007/11/14/Qualcomm

[673] "Qualcomm High Performance Processor Core and Platform for Mobile Applications", Lou Mallia, Qualcomm, ARM Developers Conference 2007, http://rtcgroup.com/arm/2007/presentations/253%20-%20ARM_DevCon_2007_Snapdragon_FINAL_20071004.pdf

[674] Hexagon DSP Processor webpage, Qualcomm, https://developer.qualcomm.com/software/hexagon-dsp-sdk/dsp-processor

[675] "Qualcomm Premieres Snapdragon, First Chipset Solutions to Break the Gigahertz Barrier with Multi-mode Broadband and Multimedia Features", Qualcomm press release, November 14, 2007, https://www.qualcomm.com/news/releases/2007/11/14/qualcomm-premieres-snapdragon-first-chipset-solutions-break-gigahertz

[676] "Qualcomm Acquires Handheld Graphics and Multimedia Assets from AMD", Qualcomm press release, January 20, 2009, https://www.qualcomm.com/news/releases/2009/01/20/qualcomm-acquires-handheld-graphics-and-multimedia-assets-amd

[677] "Qualcomm Introduces Gobi Global Mobile Internet & GPS Solution for Notebook Computers", Qualcomm press release, October 23, 2007, https://www.qualcomm.com/news/releases/2007/10/23/qualcomm-introduces-gobi-global-mobile-internet-gps-solution-notebook

[678] "Qualcomm to Ship Industry's First Multi-mode LTE Chipsets in 2009", Qualcomm press release, February 7, 2008, https://www.qualcomm.com/news/releases/2008/02/07/qualcomm-ship-industrys-first-multi-mode-lte-chipsets-2009

[679] "T-Mobile G1 to Run on Qualcomm's Advanced, Dual-Core Chipset", Qualcomm press release, September 23, 2008, https://www.qualcomm.com/news/releases/2008/09/23/t-mobile-g1-run-qualcomms-advanced-dual-core-chipset

[680] "Qualcomm Bringing Flagship Gigahertz Processing to Mainstream Smartphone Tier of Chipsets", Qualcomm press release, November 12, 2009, https://www.qualcomm.com/news/releases/2009/11/12/qualcomm-bringing-flagship-gigahertz-processing-mainstream-smartphone-tier

[681] Snapdragon S3 S2 S1 processor specs, Qualcomm, https://www.qualcomm.com/documents/snapdragon-s3-s2-s1-processor-product-specs

[682] "Qualcomm Ships First Dual-CPU Snapdragon Chipset", Qualcomm press release, June 1, 2010, https://www.qualcomm.com/news/releases/2010/06/01/qualcomm-ships-first-dual-cpu-snapdragon-chipset

[683] Snapdragon MSM8x60 Product Brief, Qualcomm, 2011, https://www.qualcomm.com/documents/snapdragon-msm8x60-apq8060-product-brief

[684] "Two-Headed Snapdragon Takes Flight", Linley Gwennap, The Linley Group, July 22, 2010, http://www.linleygroup.com/newsletters/newsletter_detail.php?num=4027

[685] "Qualcomm Delivers a Faster Mobile Broadband Experience with New, Higher Speed LTE Devices", Qualcomm press release, February 14, 2011, https://www.qualcomm.com/news/releases/2011/02/14/qualcomm-delivers-faster-mobile-broadband-experience-new-higher-speed-lte

[686] "Qualcomm Introduces World's First Complete Multi-mode 3G/LTE Integrated Solution for Smartphones", Qualcomm press release, February 16, 2009, https://www.qualcomm.com/news/releases/2009/02/16/qualcomm-introduces-worlds-first-complete-multi-mode-3glte-integrated

[687] "Qualcomm Reveals Next-Gen Snapdragon MSM8960: 28nm, dual-core, 5x Performance Improvement", Anand Lal Shimpi, AnandTech, November 17, 2010, http://www.anandtech.com/show/4024/qualcomm-reveals-nextgen-snapdragon-msm8960-28nm-dualcore-5x-performance-improvement

[688] "Qualcomm Announces Next-generation Snapdragon Mobile Chipset Family", Qualcomm press release, February 14, 2011, https://www.qualcomm.com/news/releases/2011/02/14/qualcomm-announces-next-generation-snapdragon-mobile-chipset-family

[689] "Qualcomm's New Snapdragon S4: MSM8960 and Krait Architecture Explored", Brian Klug and Anand Lal Shimpi, AnandTech, October 7, 2011, http://www.anandtech.com/show/4940/qualcomm-new-snapdragon-s4-msm8960-krait-architecture

[690] "Qualcomm Unveils New Snapdragon Mobile Processors Across All Tiers of Smartphones and Tablets", Qualcomm press release, November 16, 2011, https://www.qualcomm.com/news/releases/2011/11/16/qualcomm-unveils-new-snapdragon-mobile-processors-across-all-tiers

[691] Processors Comparison webpage, Qualcomm, https://www.qualcomm.com/products/snapdragon/processors/comparison

692 "Qualcomm retracts 'gimmick' comment on Apple 64-bit chip", Brooke Crothers, CNET, October 8, 2013, http://www.cnet.com/news/qualcomm-retracts-gimmick-comment-on-apple-64-bit-chip/
693 "Qualcomm Technologies Announces Fourth-Generation 3G/LTE Multimode Modem and RF Transceiver Chip", Qualcomm press release, November 20, 2013, https://www.qualcomm.com/news/releases/2013/11/20/qualcomm-technologies-announces-fourth-generation-3glte-multimode-modem-and
694 "Qualcomm Technologies Introduces Snapdragon 410 Chipset with Integrated 4G LTE World Mode for High-Volume Smartphones", Qualcomm press release, December 9, 2013, https://www.qualcomm.com/news/releases/2013/12/09/qualcomm-technologies-introduces-snapdragon-410-chipset-integrated-4g-lte
695 "Qualcomm Names Steve Mollenkopf CEO and President", Qualcomm press release, December 13, 2013, https://www.qualcomm.com/news/releases/2013/12/13/qualcomm-names-steve-mollenkopf-ceo-and-president
696 "Qualcomm Announces "The Ultimate Connected Computing" Next- Generation Snapdragon 810 and 808 Processors", Qualcomm press release, April 7, 2014, https://www.qualcomm.com/news/releases/2014/04/07/qualcomm-announces-ultimate-connected-computing-next-generation-snapdragon
697 "Understanding Qualcomm's Snapdragon 810: Performance Preview", Joshua Ho and Andrei Frumusanu, AnandTech, February 12, 2015, http://www.anandtech.com/show/8933/snapdragon-810-performance-preview
698 "Qualcomm Announces Fifth-Generation LTE Multimode Modem for Download Speeds of Up to 450 Mbps", Qualcomm press release, November 19, 2014, https://www.qualcomm.com/news/releases/2014/11/19/qualcomm-announces-fifth-generation-lte-multimode-modem-download-speeds-450
699 "Qualcomm to cut nearly 5,000 jobs", Mike Freeman, The San Diego Union Tribune, July 22, 2015, http://www.sandiegouniontribune.com/news/2015/jul/22/Qualcomm-jana-layoffs-smartphones-samsung/
700 "Qualcomm Finally Speaks Out About Samsung And Snapdragon", Jay McGregor, Forbes, May 6, 2015, http://www.forbes.com/sites/jaymcgregor/2015/05/06/qualcomm-finally-speaks-out-about-samsung-and-snapdragon/
701 "Qualcomm Previews The Next-Generation of Snapdragon Experiences at MWC 2015", Qualcomm press release, March 2, 2015, https://www.qualcomm.com/news/releases/2015/03/02/qualcomm-previews-next-generation-snapdragon-experiences-mwc-2015
702 "Qualcomm Announces Kryo CPU Details: Quad-Core 2.2 GHz, 14nm FinFET", Joshua Ho, AnandTech, September 2, 2015, http://www.anandtech.com/show/9595/qualcomm-announces-kryo-cpu-details-22-ghz-14nm-finfet
703 "Qualcomm Introduces Next-Generation GPU Architecture and Image Signal Processor for the Ultimate Graphics and Mobile Camera Experience", Qualcomm press release, August 12, 2015, https://www.qualcomm.com/news/releases/2015/08/12/qualcomm-introduces-next-generation-gpu-architecture-and-image-signal
704 "How Qualcomm's Snapdragon 820 will improve next year's gadgets", Devindra Hardawar, Engadget, November 10, 2015, http://www.engadget.com/2015/11/10/qualcomm-snapdragon-820-demo/

Chapter 10

705 "Pre to postmortem: the inside story of the death of Palm and webOS", Chris Ziegler, The Verge, June 5, 2012, http://www.theverge.com/2012/6/5/3062611/palm-webos-hp-inside-story-pre-postmortem
706 "HP to Pay $1.2 Billion for Palm", Ashlee Vance and Jenna Wortham, The New York Times, April 28, 2010, http://www.nytimes.com/2010/04/29/technology/29palm.html
707 "OuchPad: Best Buy Sitting on a Pile of Unsold HP Tablets", Arik Hesseldahl, AllThingsD, August 16, 2011, http://allthingsd.com/20110816/ouchpad-best-buy-sitting-on-a-pile-of-unsold-hp-tablets/
708 "HP Slate 7 review: Low price undone by absent features, dull screen", Eric Franklin, May 2, 2013, http://www.cnet.com/products/hp-slate-7/
709 "RIM Unveils the BlackBerry PlayBook", RIM press release, September 27, 2010, http://press.blackberry.com/press/2010/pressrelease-4577.html
710 "Bowing to Critics and Market Forces, RIM's Co-Chiefs Step Aside", Ian Austen, The New York Times, January 22, 2012, http://www.nytimes.com/2012/01/23/technology/rims-jim-balsillie-and-mike-lazaridis-step-aside.html
711 "Research In Motion Changes Its Name to BlackBerry", BlackBerry press release, January 30, 2013, http://press.blackberry.com/press/2013/research-in-motion-changes-its-name-to-blackberry.html
712 "BlackBerry CEO Questions Future of Tablets", Hugo Miller and Nadja Brandt, BloombergBusiness, April 30, 2013, http://www.bloomberg.com/news/articles/2013-04-30/blackberry-ceo-questions-future-of-tablets
713 "Google to Acquire Motorola Mobility", Google press release, August 15, 2011, http://investor.google.com/releases/2011/0815.html
714 "Intel to Acquire Infineon's Wireless Solutions Business", Intel press release, August 30, 2010, http://newsroom.intel.com/docs/DOC-1173
715 "Qualcomm to Acquire Atheros, Leader in Connectivity & Networking Solutions", Qualcomm press release, January 5, 2011, https://www.qualcomm.com/news/releases/2011/01/05/qualcomm-acquire-atheros-leader-connectivity-networking-solutions

[716] "Nokia CEO Stephen Elop rallies troops in brutally honest 'burning platform' memo?", Chris Ziegler, Engadget, February 8, 2011, http://www.engadget.com/2011/02/08/nokia-ceo-stephen-elop-rallies-troops-in-brutally-honest-burnin/

[717] "Nokia and Microsoft Announce Plans for a Broad Strategic Partnership to Build a New Global Mobile Ecosystem", Nokia press release, February 11, 2011, https://news.microsoft.com/2011/02/10/nokia-and-microsoft-announce-plans-for-a-broad-strategic-partnership-to-build-a-new-global-mobile-ecosystem/

[718] "Changing the game: ST-Ericsson Unveils NovaThor(TM) Family of Smartphone Platforms", ST-Ericsson press release, February 15, 2011, http://www.reuters.com/article/2011/02/15/idUS94540+15-Feb-2011+MW20110215

[719] "Qualcomm dominates cellular baseband chip market in 2011", Strategy Analytics press release, April 26, 2012, https://www.strategyanalytics.com/strategy-analytics/news/strategy-analytics-press-releases/strategy-analytics-press-release/2014/05/19/qualcomm-maintains-lead-with-45-percent-share-of-cellular-baseband-market#.VfcT0hFVhBc

[720] "NVIDIA to Acquire Baseband and RF Technology Leader Icera", NVIDIA press release, May 9, 2011, http://nvidianews.nvidia.com/news/nvidia-to-acquire-baseband-and-rf-technology-leader-icera

[721] "TI to sell part of wireless chip unit", Dylan McGrath, EETimes, October 20, 2008, http://www.eetimes.com/document.asp?doc_id=1169557

[722] "TI calls baseband a distraction, but is it?", Sylvie Barak, EETimes, November 10, 2011, http://www.eetimes.com/document.asp?doc_id=1260586

[723] "Renesas Electronics to acquire Nokia's wireless modem business", Renesas press release, July 6, 2010, http://www.renesas.com/press/news/2010/news20100706.jsp

[724] "Texas Instruments demos first OMAP 5, Android 4.0-based reference design, promises it in laptops next year", Darren Murph, Engadget, January 12, 2012, http://www.engadget.com/2012/01/12/ti-omap-5-exclusive-demo-laptops-ultrabooks-ces-2012-video/

[725] "Texas Instruments eyes shift away from wireless", Sinead Carew, Reuters, September 25, 2012, http://www.reuters.com/article/2012/09/25/texasinstruments-wireless-idUSL1E8KP5FN20120925

[726] "Over 100 tablets were unveiled at CES 2011 – here's a list of all of them", Zach Epstein, BGR, January 24, 2011, http://bgr.com/2011/01/24/over-100-tablets-were-unveiled-at-ces-2011-heres-a-list-of-all-of-them/

[727] "Microsoft Agrees to Acquire Danger Inc., Strengthens Mobile Consumer Vision", Microsoft press release, February 1, 2008, https://news.microsoft.com/2008/02/11/microsoft-agrees-to-acquire-danger-inc-strengthens-mobile-consumer-vision/

[728] "Microsoft Ushers in the Next Generation of the Social Phone With KIN, a New Windows Phone", Microsoft press release, April 12, 2010, https://news.microsoft.com/2010/04/12/microsoft-ushers-in-the-next-generation-of-the-social-phone-with-kin-a-new-windows-phone/

[729] "New NVIDIA Tegra Processor Powers The Tablet Revolution", NVIDIA press release, January 7, 2010, http://www.nvidia.com/object/io_1262837617533.html

[730] "Freescale delivers dramatic performance advances for tablet, smartphone, eReader, automotive infotainment and other hot consumer markets", Freescale press release, January 3, 2011, http://ir.freescale.com/investor-relations/press-release-archive/2011/01-03-11.aspx

[731] "Marvell Raises Technology Bar Again with World's First 1.5 GHz Tri-Core Processor Delivering Dual Stream 1080p 3D Video for Smartphones and Tablets", Marvell press release, September 23, 2010, http://investor.marvell.com/phoenix.zhtml?c=120802&p=irol-newsArticle&ID=1474123

[732] Mobylize web site, Marvell, http://www.mobylize.org/tablets.html

[733] "ARM Technologies Power Nufront's First Computer System Chip To Reshape Laptop Market", ARM media alert, September 24, 2010, https://www.arm.com/about/newsroom/arm-technologies-power-nufronts-first-computer-system-chip-to-reshape-laptop-market.php

[734] "Nufront Preps $250 ARM-based 1080p Desktop PC for CES", Jacqueline Emigh, Notebook Review, September 17, 2010, http://www.notebookreview.com/news/nufront-preps-250-arm-based-1080p-desktop-pc-for-ces/

[735] "Allwinner Technology Selects ARM Cortex-A8 CPU and Mali GPU Technologies to Bring Integrated SoC To Android OS-Based, Connected Consumer Devices", Allwinner press release, April 2011, http://www.allwinnertech.com/en/news/compnews/258.html

[736] "Leadcore Technology Addresses High-end Mobile Market with suite of ARM IP including ARM Cortex-A9 MPCore Processor, Mali-400 MP GPU and Artisan Physical IP", ARM media alert, April 19, 2011, http://www.arm.com/about/newsroom/leadcore-technology-addresses-high-end-mobile-market-with-suite-of-arm-ip-including-arm-cortex-a9.php

[737] Leadcore LC1810 webpage, Leadcore Technology, http://www.leadcoretech.com/LC1810-A9.htm

[738] "HiSilicon Licenses ARM Technology for use in Innovative 3G/4G Base Station, Networking Infrastructure and Mobile Computing Applications", ARM press release, August 2, 2011, http://www.arm.com/about/newsroom/hisilicon-licenses-arm-technology-for-use-in-networking-infrastructure-and-mobile-computing-applications.php

[739] "HiSilicon Announces K3V2 Quad-core Application Processor", HiSilicon press release, February 26, 2012, http://www.hisilicon.com/news/news/k3v2_20120226.html

248

[740] "Huawei Introduces the World's Fastest Smartphone: The Ascend D quad", Huawei press release, Feburary 26, 2012, http://pr.huawei.com/en/news/hw-124124-mwcworldsfastestquad-coresmartphonehuaweiascenddqu.htm#.Vf4Jnt9VhBc

[741] "Rockchip RK2818 Tablets Flooding the Low-End Tablet Market", user 'xaueious', AndroidTablets.net, February 14, 2011, http://www.androidtablets.net/threads/rockchip-rk2818-tablets-flooding-the-low-end-tablet-market.8500/

[742] "Rockchip Licenses a Wide Range of ARM IP for Turnkey Solution Targeting Mass Market, Cost-Effective Android Tablets", ARM press release, February 27, 2012, http://www.arm.com/about/newsroom/rockchip-licenses-a-wide-range-of-arm-ip-for-turnkey-solution-targeting-mass-market-cost-effective.php

[743] MT6205B GSM Baseband Processor Datasheet, MediaTek, October 15, 2003, http://www.kit-iphone.ru/images/stories/datasheets/MT6205B.pdf

[744] "Cell phone chip maker MediaTek thrives during downturn", John Boudreau, San Jose Mercury News, October 29, 2009, http://www.mercurynews.com/top-stories/ci_13669529

[745] "Battling For The Brains Of Cellphones", Joyce Huang, Forbes, November 6, 2009, http://www.forbes.com/global/2009/1116/wireless-chip-telephone-mediatek-beyond-bandits.html

[746] "MediaTek Licenses CEVA-X DSP Core and Subsystem from CEVA", CEVA press release, April 15, 2008, http://ceva-dsp.mediaroom.com/index.php?s=29680&item=91133

[747] "MediaTek Launches MT6575 Android Platform", MediaTek press release, February 13, 2012, http://www.mediatek.com/en/news-events/mediatek-news/mediatek-launches-mt6575-android-platform/

[748] "Spreadtrum Communications Licenses ParthusCeva High Performance TeakLite DSP Core", Spreadtrum press release, November 22, 2002, http://www.spreadtrum.com/en/show_news.html?id=fedd6184-6bbf-4ec1-ace8-b4ceb637ad40

[749] "Spreadtrum Licenses ARM Core For Wireless Solutions", Spreadtrum press release, January 21, 2003, http://www.spreadtrum.com/en/show_news.html?id=182fbe8a-2d23-4d91-9511-3f23000d6cbb

[750] Spreadtrum letter to the US Securities and Exchange Commission, November 10, 2010, http://www.sec.gov/Archives/edgar/data/1287950/000119312510256185/filename1.htm

[751] "Spreadtrum Announces the World's First Commercial 40nm Low Power TD-HSPA /TD-SCDMA Multi-mode Communication Baseband Processor", Spreadtrum press release, January 18, 2011, http://www.spreadtrum.com/en/show_news.html?id=9ffe8b35-0bad-40fb-abd1-f5c6e0a8b653

[752] "Samsung Taps Spreadtrum as Baseband Supplier for High Performance TD-SCDMA Smartphone", Spreadtrum press release, September 2, 2011, http://www.spreadtrum.com/en/show_news.html?id=233b48f2-0eac-43f5-a9fe-7ac0db3e10d9

[753] "What Did Amazon's Kindle Fire Just Do To Android?", Dan Rowinski, ReadWrite, September 28, 2011, http://readwrite.com/2011/09/28/what_did_amazons_kindle_fire_just_do_to_android

[754] "Amazon's Kindle Fire UI: it's Android, but not quite", Sean Hollister, The Verge, September 28, 2011, http://www.theverge.com/2011/9/28/2457111/amazons-kindle-fire-ui-its-android-but-not-quite

[755] "Kindle Fire burned up some holiday iPad sales", Brooke Crothers, CNET, January 3, 2012, http://www.cnet.com/news/kindle-fire-burned-up-some-holiday-ipad-sales/

[756] "Kindle Fire sales were on fire last quarter, analyst says", Don Reisinger, CNET, January 9, 2012, http://www.cnet.com/news/kindle-fire-sales-were-on-fire-last-quarter-analyst-says/

[757] "Kindle Fire Grabs Over 50 Percent of the Android Tablet Market", Adrian Kingsley-Hughes, Forbes, April 27, 2012, http://www.forbes.com/sites/adriankingsleyhughes/2012/04/27/kindle-fire-grabs-over-50-percent-of-the-android-tablet-market/

[758] "Microsoft Announces Support of System on a Chip Architectures From Intel, AMD, and ARM for Next Version of Windows", Microsoft press release, January 5, 2011, https://news.microsoft.com/2011/01/05/microsoft-announces-support-of-system-on-a-chip-architectures-from-intel-amd-and-arm-for-next-version-of-windows/

[759] "Microsoft Announces New Surface Details", Microsoft press release, October 16, 2012, https://news.microsoft.com/2012/10/16/microsoft-announces-new-surface-details/

[760] "Microsoft Announces Surface: New Family of PCs for Windows", Microsoft press release, June 18, 2012, http://news.microsoft.com/2012/06/18/microsoft-announces-surface-new-family-of-pcs-for-windows/

[761] "Microsoft Grows Surface Family", Microsoft press release, January 22, 2013, https://news.microsoft.com/2013/01/22/microsoft-grows-surface-family/

[762] "Microsoft Unveils Windows Phone 8", Microsoft press release, October 29, 2012, https://news.microsoft.com/2012/10/29/microsoft-unveils-windows-phone-8/

[763] "Microsoft to acquire Nokia's devices & services business, license Nokia's patents and mapping services", Microsoft press release, September 3, 2013, https://news.microsoft.com/2013/09/03/microsoft-to-acquire-nokias-devices-services-business-license-nokias-patents-and-mapping-services/

[764] "Lenovo to Acquire Motorola Mobility from Google", Lenovo press release, January 29, 2014, http://news.lenovo.com/article_display.cfm?article_id=1768

[765] "Motorola Launches Brand Strategy", China Telecom Newsletter, Information Gatekeepers, June 1998, p. 14.

[766] "Brand New China: Advertising, Media, and Commercial Culture", Jing Wang, Harvard University Press, April 10, 2010, pp. 214-246.

[767] "Ericsson and STMicroelectronics agree on strategic way forward for ST-Ericsson", Ericsson press release, March 18, 2013, http://www.ericsson.com/news/1685852

[768] "Broadcom to Explore Strategic Alternatives for Cellular Baseband Business", Broadcom press release, June 2, 2014, http://www.broadcom.com/press/release.php?id=s851659

[769] "Broadcom CEO: We were losing $2M per day in cellular baseband biz", Phil Goldstein, FierceWireless, January 15, 2015, http://www.fiercewireless.com/story/broadcom-ceo-we-were-losing-2m-day-cellular-baseband-biz/2015-01-15

[770] "NVIDIA to Wind Down Icera Modem Operations", NVIDIA press release, May 5, 2015, http://nvidianews.nvidia.com/news/nvidia-to-wind-down-icera-modem-operations

[771] "What's Inside the Tesla Model S Dashboard", Arik Hesseldahl, Re/code, October 14, 2014, http://recode.net/2014/10/14/whats-inside-the-tesla-model-s-dashboard/

[772] "SHIELD Family Expands as World's Most Advanced Mobile Processor, 192-Core Tegra K1, Serves Up Unmatched Tablet Experience, Amazing Gaming", NVIDIA press release, July 22, 2014, http://nvidianews.nvidia.com/news/nvidia-launches-world-s-most-advanced-tablet-built-for-gamers-2775407

[773] "NVIDIA Recalls Tablet Computers Due to Fire Hazard", US Consumer Product Safety Commission, July 31, 2015, http://www.cpsc.gov/en/Recalls/2015/Nvidia-Recalls-Tablet-Computers/#remedy

[774] "Q&A: Microsoft Unveils Details for Ultra-Mobile Personal Computers", Microsoft press release, March 9, 2006, https://news.microsoft.com/2006/03/09/qa-microsoft-unveils-details-for-ultra-mobile-personal-computers/

[775] "Asus EeePC 701 Review", Craig Simms, CNET, December 13, 2007, http://www.cnet.com/au/products/asus-eeepc-701/

[776] "Intel Announces Intel Atom Brand for New Family of Low-Power Processors", Intel press release, March 2, 2008, http://www.intel.com/pressroom/archive/releases/2008/20080302comp.htm

[777] "New Intel Atom Processor-Based Platform Using Significantly Lower Power Readies Intel for Smartphone, Tablet Push", Intel press release, May 4, 2010, http://www.intel.com/pressroom/archive/releases/2010/20100504comp.htm

[778] "Intel Expands Mobile Computing with New Silicon, Software and Connectivity Capabilities", Intel press release, February 14, 2011, http://newsroom.intel.com/community/intel_newsroom/blog/2011/02/14/intel-expands-mobile-computing-with-new-silicon-software-and-connectivity-capabilities

[779] "Intel and Google to Optimize Android Platform for Intel Architecture", Intel press release, September 13, 2011, http://newsroom.intel.com/community/intel_newsroom/blog/2011/09/13/intel-and-google-to-optimize-android-platform-for-intel-architecture

[780] "New Mobile Processors, LTE-Advanced Platform and Customer Agreements; New Initiatives Aimed to Transform Network Infrastructure for Internet of Things", Intel press release, February 14, 2014, http://newsroom.intel.com/community/intel_newsroom/blog/2014/02/24/intel-gaining-in-mobile-and-accelerating-internet-of-things

[781] "Intel Launches New Multicore, Low-Power SoCs for Tablets, 2 in 1s and Other Computing Devices", Intel press release, September 11, 2013, http://newsroom.intel.com/community/intel_newsroom/blog/2013/09/11/intel-launches-new-multicore-low-power-socs-for-tablets-2-in-1s-and-other-computing-devices

[782] "The State of the Tablet Market", TabTimes, http://tabtimes.com/resources/the-state-of-the-tablet-market/

[783] "Intel to offer US$1 billion marketing subsidies to promote tablet processors in 2014, say Taiwan makers", Aaron Lee and Joseph Tsai, DIGITIMES, November 27, 2013, http://www.digitimes.com/news/a20131127PD207.html

[784] "Is Intel giving away free tablet chips? CEO's comments cause confusion", Benjamin Pimentel, MarketWatch, January 24, 2014, http://blogs.marketwatch.com/thetell/2014/01/24/is-intel-giving-away-free-tablet-chips-ceos-comments-cause-confusion/

[785] "Intel CEO: We're 'Not Ashamed' Of How Far Behind We Are In Mobile", Eugene Kim, Business Insider, November 20, 2014, http://www.businessinsider.com/intel-ceo-were-not-ashamed-of-how-far-behind-we-are-in-mobile-2014-11

[786] "Intel Enters into Strategic Agreement with Rockchip to Accelerate, Expand Portfolio of Intel-Based Solutions for Tablets", Intel press release, May 27, 2014, http://newsroom.intel.com/community/intel_newsroom/blog/2014/05/27/intel-enters-into-strategic-agreement-with-rockchip-to-accelerate-expand-portfolio-of-intel-based-solutions-for-tablets

[787] "Intel Launches New Mobile SoCs, LTE Solution", Intel press release, March 2, 2015, http://newsroom.intel.com/community/intel_newsroom/blog/2015/03/02/intel-launches-new-mobile-socs-lte-solution

[788] "Introducing Intel® Atom™ x3 (Code-Named "SoFIA") SoC Processor Series", Miao Wei, Intel, April 9, 2015, https://software.intel.com/en-us/blogs/2015/04/09/introducing-intel-atom-x3-code-named-sofia-soc-processor-series

[789] "ARM Delivers The Internet Everywhere With Most Power-Efficient and Cost-Effective Multicore Processor", ARM press release, October 21, 2009, http://www.arm.com/about/newsroom/26196.php

[790] "ARM Unveils Cortex-A15 MPCore Processor to Dramatically Accelerate Capabilities of Mobile, Consumer and Infrastructure Applications", ARM press release, September 8, 2010, http://www.arm.com/about/newsroom/arm-unveils-cortex-a15-mpcore-processor-to-dramatically-accelerate-capabilities.php

[791] "Deep Inside ARM's new Intel killer", Rik Myslewski, The Register, October 20, 2011, http://www.theregister.co.uk/2011/10/20/details_on_big_little_processing/

[792] "ARM Unveils its Most Energy Efficient Application Processor Ever; Redefines Traditional Power And Performance Relationship With big.LITTLE Processing", ARM press release, October 19, 2011,

http://www.arm.com/about/newsroom/arm-unveils-its-most-energy-efficient-application-processor-ever-with-biglittle-processing.php

[793] "ARM Launches Cortex-A50 Series, the World's Most Energy-Efficient 64-bit Processors", ARM press release, October 30, 2012, http://www.arm.com/about/newsroom/arm-launches-cortex-a50-series-the-worlds-most-energy-efficient-64-bit-processors.php

[794] "ARM Targets 580 Million Mid-Range Mobile Devices with New Suite of IP", ARM press release, June 3, 2013, https://www.arm.com/about/newsroom/arm-targets-580-million-mid-range-mobile-devices-with-new-suite-of-ip.php

[795] "ARM Enhances IP Suite for 2015 Mid-Range Mobile and Consumer Markets", ARM press release, February 11, 2014, https://www.arm.com/about/newsroom/arm-enhances-ip-suite-for-2015-mid-range-mobile-and-consumer-markets.php

[796] "ARM Cortex-A17: An Evolved Cortex-A12 for the Mainstream in 2015", Anand Lal Shimpi, AnandTech, February 11, 2014, http://www.anandtech.com/show/7739/arm-cortex-a17

[797] "ARM Supercharges MCU Market with High Performance Cortex-M7 Processor", ARM press release, September 24, 2014, https://www.arm.com/about/newsroom/arm-supercharges-mcu-market-with-high-performance-cortex-m7-processor.php

[798] "ARM Sets New Standard for the Premium Mobile Experience", ARM press release, February 3, 2015, https://www.arm.com/about/newsroom/arm-sets-new-standard-for-the-premium-mobile-experience.php

[799] "ARM Reveals Cortex-A72 Architecture Details", Andrei Frumusanu, April 23, 2015, http://www.anandtech.com/show/9184/arm-reveals-cortex-a72-architecture-details

[800] "Samsung Stays Ahead of the Curve with Bold, Big Screen Smartphones", Samsung press release, August 13, 2015, https://www.samsungmobilepress.com/2015/08/13/Samsung-Stays-Ahead-of-the-Curve-with-Bold,-Big-Screen-Smartphones

[801] "BlackBerry Passport Redefines Productivity for Mobile Professionals with Boundary-Breaking Design and Features", BlackBerry press release, September 24, 2014, http://press.blackberry.com/press/2014/blackberry-passport-redefines-productivity-for-mobile-profession.html

[802] "More BlackBerry layoffs: 200 Venice devs binned amid Android shift", Andrew Orlowski, The Register, September 23, 2015, http://www.theregister.co.uk/2015/09/23/blackberry_layoffs_200_let_go_project_venice/

[803] "BlackBerry's PRIV Secure Smartphone Powered by Android Now Available", BlackBerry press release, November 6, 2015, http://press.blackberry.com/press/2015/blackberrys_priv_secure_smartphone_powered_by_android_now_available.html

[804] "Evolution of LG's Curved Smartphone Unveiled at CES 2015", LG press release, January 6, 2015, http://www.lgnewsroom.com/2015/01/evolution-of-lgs-curved-smartphone-unveiled-at-ces-2015/

[805] "Revised Snapdragon 810 Chip May Mean Its Days of Getting Hot and Bothered Are Over", Andy Boxall, Digital Trends, July 16, 2015, http://www.digitaltrends.com/android/an-overhauled-snapdragon-810-chip-may-have-cured-the-originals-overheating-problems/

[806] "Wireless Power Standards Bodies A4WP and PMA Merge to Form Industry-Leading Organization", Alliance for Wireless Power press release, June 1, 2015, http://www.rezence.com/media/news/wireless-power-standards-bodies-a4wp-and-pma-merge-form-industry-leading-organization

[807] "LG G4 is No. 2 in DxOMark's camera benchmarks", JC Torres, Slashgear, September 23, 2015, http://www.slashgear.com/lg-g4-is-no-2-in-dxomarks-camera-benchmarks-23406169/

[808] "Digital, Social & Mobile Worldwide in 2015", Simon Kemp, We are Social, January 21, 2015, http://wearesocial.net/blog/2015/01/digital-social-mobile-worldwide-2015/

[809] "Low-Power Electronics Design", edited by Christian Piguet, CRC Press, November 29, 2004, pp. 1-8 through 1-10.

[810] "Engineering time: inventing the electronic wristwatch", Carlene Stephens and Maggie Dennis, British Journal for the History of Science, Volume 33, pp. 477-497, 2000, http://www.ieee-uffc.org/main/history/step.pdf

[811] "Recollections of Early Chip Development at Intel", Volk et al, 2001, http://lark.tu-sofia.bg/ntt/eusku/readings/art_1.pdf

[812] "Apple Debuts at the Number Two Spot as the Worldwide Wearables Market Grows 223.2% in 2Q15, Says IDC", IDC press release, August 27, 2015, http://www.idc.com/getdoc.jsp?containerId=prUS25872215

[813] "Apple Watch Captures 75 Percent Global Smartwatch Marketshare in Q2 2015", Strategy Analytics press release, July 22, 2015, https://www.strategyanalytics.com/strategy-analytics/news/strategy-analytics-press-releases/strategy-analytics-press-release/2015/07/22/apple-watch-captures-75-percent-global-smartwatch-marketshare-in-q2-2015#.VgSXD8tVhBc

[814] "The Apple Watch Review", Joshua Ho & Brandon Chester, AnandTech, July 20, 2015, http://www.anandtech.com/show/9381/the-apple-watch-review/3

[815] Samsung Gear S2 web page, Samsung, http://www.samsung.com/global/galaxy/gear-s2/

[816] "Motorola Moto 360 Teardown", iFixit, September 2014, https://www.ifixit.com/Teardown/Motorola+Moto+360+Teardown/28891

[817] "3rd Generation Nest Learning Thermostat Introduces High-Resolution Screen, Slimmer Profile", Nest press release, September 1, 2015, https://nest.com/press/3rd-generation-nest-learning-thermostat-introduces-high-resolution-screen-slimmer-profile/

[818] "Nest Learning Thermostat 2nd Generation Teardown", iFixit, April 2013, https://www.ifixit.com/Teardown/Nest+Learning+Thermostat+2nd+Generation+Teardown/13818

[819] "Apple's chip'n'firmware security demands behind HomeKit delays", Kieren McCarthy, The Register, July 13, 2015, http://www.theregister.co.uk/2015/07/13/security_apple_homekit_delays/

[820] "MediaTek Launches LinkIt Platform for Wearables and Internet of Things", MediaTek press release, June 3, 2014, http://www.mediatek.com/en/news-events/mediatek-news/mediatek-launches-linkit-platform-for-wearables-and-internet-of-things/

[821] MT2502A SoC Processor Technical Brief, MediaTek, September 2014.

[822] "Qualcomm Announces Reference Platform with High-end Performance Capabilities to Advance Consumer Drones", Qualcomm press release, September 10, 2015, https://www.qualcomm.com/news/releases/2015/09/10/qualcomm-announces-reference-platform-high-end-performance-capabilities

[823] "Qualcomm's Snapdragon Flight Promises Lighter, Simpler, More Powerful Flying Cameras", Daniel Terdiman, Fast Company, September 10, 2015, http://www.fastcompany.com/3050210/tech-forecast/qualcomms-snapdragon-flight-promises-lighter-simpler-more-powerful-flying-came

[824] "Samsung Announces ARTIK Platform to Accelerate Internet of Things Development", Samsung press release, May 12, 2015, https://www.artik.io/media#press-releases

[825] Samsung ARTIK web page, https://www.artik.io/

[826] "ARM Holdings PLC Announces CEO Succession", ARM press release, March 19, 2013, http://www.arm.com/about/newsroom/arm-holdings-plc-announces-ceo-succession.php

[827] ARM Holdings plc Strategic Report 2014.

About the Authors

Daniel Nenni has worked in Silicon Valley for the past 30 years with computer manufacturers, electronic design automation software, and semiconductor intellectual property companies. He is the founder of SemiWiki.com (an open forum for semiconductor professionals) and the co-author of Fabless: The Transformation of the Semiconductor Industry. Daniel is an internationally recognized business development professional for companies involved with the fabless semiconductor ecosystem.

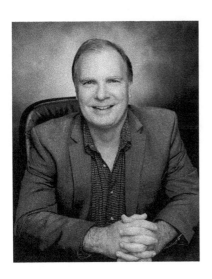

Don Dingee has been in the electronics industry since 1983, with experience spanning engineering, sales, marketing, and web development roles. Currently Don is a product strategy consultant and content marketing freelancer working with firms on embedded, mobile, and IoT applications. Don also blogs on SemiWiki.